CABINET MAKERS and FURNITURE DESIGNERS

GREAT CRAFTSMEN

CABINET MAKERS and FURNITURE DESIGNERS

Hugh Honour

G. P. Putnam's Sons 200 *Madison Avenue, New York*

© 1969 by Hugh Honour
First American edition 1969

All rights reserved. This book, or parts thereof, must
not be reproduced in any form without permission.

Designed by Trevor Vincent
for George Weidenfeld and Nicolson Limited, London
Library of Congress Catalog Card No.: 77–77548
Printed in Italy Arnoldo Mondadori, Verona

Contents

List of Plates

The author and publishers are grateful to the owners and trustees of the various private and public collections listed below for permission to reproduce photographs, and for their co-operation in allowing objects from their collections to be specially photographed for this book. They would also like to thank photographers Derrick Witty and J. R. Freeman & Co, and R. Bonnefoy, who took the photograph on the front of the jacket.

COLOUR ILLUSTRATIONS

Gilt bronze decorations on a cabinet made by Piffetti in the 1730s *(Palazzo Reale, Turin)*

Occasional table made for Vittorio Amadeo III of Sardinia, *c.* 1750 *(Palazzo Reale, Turin)*

Writing-table inlaid with rosewood, violet wood, palisander etc., *c.* 1760 *(Casa di Caccia, Stupinigi, near Turin)*

BERNARD II VAN RISEN BURGH
(between pages 102 and 107)

Lady's work-table *(National Gallery of Art, Washington: Widener Collection)*

Large marquetry writing-table decorated with gilt bronze mounts *(Cleveland Museum of Art: bequest of Mrs Frances F. Prentiss)*

Marquetry corner shelf, with veneers of tulip-wood and king-wood on an oak carcase *(Metropolitan Museum of Art, New York: Collection of Mr and Mrs Charles B. Wrightsman)*

Commode decorated with Japanese lacquer and gilt bronze mounts *(Metropolitan Museum of Art, New York: Collection of Mr and Mrs Charles B. Wrightsman)*

WILLIAM VILE AND JOHN COBB
(between pages 108 and 113)

One of the chairs supplied by Vile and Cobb for the Hon. John Damer of Came House, Dorset, between 1756 and 1762 *(Came House, Dorset: photo copyright Country Life)*

Sofa supplied by Vile and Cobb for Came House, Dorset *(Came House, Dorset: photo copyright Country Life)*

Mahogany secrétaire made by Vile for George III's consort Queen Charlotte in 1761 *(Reproduced by gracious permission of H.M. the Queen: copyright reserved)*

Chest-of-drawers supplied to James West of Alscot Park, Warwickshire in 1766 by Cobb *(Private Collection: photo copyright Country Life)*

Marquetry commode with gilt bronze mounts supplied by Cobb in 1772 to Mr Paul Methuen *(Collection of Lord Methuen, Corsham Court, Wiltshire)*

JOHANN MICHAEL HOPPENHAUPT
(between pages 114 and 119)

Engraved design for the decoration of a room, probably in Berlin, 1751–5 *(Victoria and Albert Museum, London)*

Design for a chest-of-drawers, 1751–5 *(Victoria and Albert Museum, London)*

Design for a pier glass and table, 1751–5 *(Victoria and Albert Museum, London)*

Design for a chest-of-drawers, 1751–5 *(Victoria and Albert Museum, London)*

Design for a side-table, 1751–5 *(Victoria and Albert Museum, London)*

Design for a long-case clock, 1751–5 *(Victoria and Albert Museum, London)*

Design for a console table, 1751–5 *(Victoria and Albert Museum, London)*

THOMAS JOHNSON
(between pages 120 and 127)

Engraved design for a candle-stand, published in 1758 *(Victoria and Albert Museum, London)*

Design for five girandoles, 1758 *(Victoria and Albert Museum, London)*

Design for a side-table, 1758, with figures representing Aesop's fable of the bear and the travellers *(Victoria and Albert Museum, London)*

Design for a looking-glass, 1758, with figures representing the fable of the fox and the grapes *(Victoria and Albert Museum, London)*

Engraved design for a kettle-stand, 1758 *(Victoria and Albert Museum, London)*

Looking-glass in carved wood frame attributed to Johnson, *c.* 1760 *(Collection of Lord Methuen, Corsham Court, Wiltshire: photo copyright Country Life)*

Girandole of mahogany and deal painted and gilt, made for Hagley

15

Revolving armchair of chromium-
plated steel tubing and red leather, 1927
(Museum of Modern Art, New York:
gift of Thonet Industries Inc)

Armchair called the *siège grand
confort*, 1926 (Figli di Amedeo Cassina,
Meda, Milan)

Chaise longue, called the cow-boy
chair, 1927 (Museum of Modern Art,
New York: gift of Thonet Industries Inc)

KAARE KLINT
(between pages 286 and 289)

Design showing Klint's concern with
the adaptation of furniture to the needs
of the human body (Det Kongelige
Akademi for de Skønne Kunster,
Copenhagen)

Ladderback chair showing Klint's use
of traditional patterns (Fritzhansen-
Møbler, Denmark)

Teak deck chair, 1933
(Th. Andresen, Copenhagen)

Sideboard with interior designed to
accommodate tablewares (Rud.
Rasmussens Snedkerier, Copenhagen)

GERRIT THOMAS RIETVELD
(between pages 290 and 295)

Armchair of painted wood, 1917
(Museum of Modern Art, New York:
gift of Philip Johnson)

Chair designed by Rietveld, 1934
(Collection of Mr and Mrs Brian
Housden, London)

Armchair designed by Rietveld, 1942
(Collection of Mr and Mrs Brian
Housden, London)

Sideboard designed and made by
Rietveld, 1919 (Collection of Mr and Mrs
Brian Housden, London)

ALVAR AALTO
(between pages 296 and 299)
Convertible sofa-bed with support of
chromium-plated steel tubing and
upholstery of wool, 1930
(Museum of Modern Art, New York:
Phyllis B. Lambert Fund)

Plywood cantilever chair, 1935
(Collection of Mr John Jesse, London)

Laminated plywood furniture, 1933–54
(Museum of Modern Art, New York:
gift of Edgar Kaufmann, Jr)

MARCEL BREUER
(between pages 300 and 305)
Pear-wood tea-table designed and
made at the Weimar Bauhaus, 1921–2
(photo: Klaus G. Beyer, Weimar)

Cantilever side-chair of chromium-
plated steel tubing, wood and cane,
1928 (Museum of Modern Art, New
York)

Armchair of oak with hand-woven
wool seat and back straps, 1924
(Museum of Modern Art, New York:
Phyllis B. Lambert Fund)

Laminated plywood coffee-tables and
chair, 1935–7 (Isokon Furniture
Company, London: photo John Allan
Designs Ltd)

CHARLES EAMES
(between pages 306 and 310)

Drawing for an armchair by Saarinen
and Eames, 1941 (Museum of Modern
Art, New York)

Lounge chair and footstool of
laminated rosewood and anodyzed
aluminium with down and foam-filled
cushions, 1957 (Atelier Peter
Moeshlin, Basel)

Folding screen of moulded ash
plywood and metal rods, 1946
(Museum of Modern Art, New York:
gift of Herman Miller Furniture Co)

Dining-chair of moulded walnut
plywood and metal rods, 1946
(Museum of Modern Art, New York:
gift of Herman Miller Furniture Co)

Chair of plastic reinforced with
fibreglass designed by Saarinen as part
of his Tulip Suite, 1957 (Museum of
Modern Art, New York: gift of Knoll
Associates, Inc.)

19

Introduction

This book is the result of an enquiry into the role played by individuals in the history of furniture. It was prompted partly by natural curiosity about the personalities of men who have contributed so much to the appearance and comfort of the Western interior. Very few of their names have become household words and fewer still are more than names – even to those versed in the history of the visual arts. None stands out as a vivid personality in his own right – like Benvenuto Cellini or Bernard Palissy. A New England furniture maker, John Alden, provided the subject for a poem by Longfellow, but few others have figured prominently in literature. For some strange reason the furniture maker has always seemed a figure of less interest than the goldsmith or the potter.

I was also anxious to investigate the relationships which existed in different periods and places between craftsmen, designers and workshop or factory owners. For although documents may often reveal that a particular table or chest of drawers was supplied to the original owner by a Chippendale or a Riesener they rarely tell us who was responsible for the design and who for the actual workmanship. Candour obliges me to confess that I have very seldom been able to answer such questions with more than a guess. But I hope that these studies will serve as a reminder that the problem is more complex than it may seem at first sight. Most students of French furniture are aware that the *menuisier* whose name is stamped on a chair – Delanois, for example – was the head of a workshop which was sometimes responsible only for its structure. The carving was often the work of a specialist *sculpteur*, the gilding and upholstery was always applied by a member of the guild of *marchands-tapissiers*. Similarly, in other countries and at other times furniture was probably the product of a like division of labour. As early as the thirteenth century in France furniture made by the *huchier* was painted and gilded by an *imagier* while the iron hinges and locks which contribute so greatly to its decoration were the work of a *serrurier*.

Until very recently most books on the history of furniture came to an abrupt halt at or very shortly after the end of the eighteenth century. Interest in Victoriana and *art nouveau* has protracted the termination by another hundred years. But the belief still persists that the industrial revolution marked a decisive break. This seems to be unwarranted. So far as the development of furniture is concerned, the vital change took place, or began to take place, in the sixteenth century when the designer first appeared on the scene. The subsequent history of furniture is largely the story of the designer's gradual rise to absolute pre-eminence over the other two members of the eternal triangle – artisan and workshop owner. Neither the establishment of larger workshops or factories, in the eighteenth century, nor the gradual adoption of mechanized methods of production in the nineteenth, had as great an influence. Nearly all the major developments in furniture since the Middle Ages can be traced to the intervention of designers, mostly architects, rather than to craftsmen. (The exception to prove the rule is, of course, Rietveld who began work as a furniture maker and later became an architect.) The 'death of craftsmanship' so bitterly bewailed in the nineteenth century is, in fact, of less importance in itself than for its effect on the theorists and designers who sought to compensate for it.

The variety of men who engaged in the design and production of furniture is very wide, ranging from simple craftsmen to architects, sculptors, antiquaries, businessmen, art collectors, reactionaries and revolutionaries, soldiers and a Baptist minister. In making a list of those who promised to reward closer study I soon found myself confronted with an *embarras de richesse*, especially in eighteenth-century France and nineteenth-century England. With regret I was forced to omit as many as I have included. Some readers may be surprised to find that I have not devoted individual studies to several very well known personalities, such as Robert Adam, George Hepplewhite and William Morris. I have, however, touched on the problem presented by Adam's influence on and relationship with furniture makers in my account of Thomas Chippendale. And I trust that the accounts of Thomas Sheraton and Philip Webb will suffice to show why I have devoted studies to them and not to George Hepplewhite and William Morris.

This book is neither a history nor a biographical dictionary. By isolating fifty individuals I have attempted to say more about each of them than will be found in histories of furniture and to relate them more closely to general developments than would be possible in a biographical dictionary. But, in the words of an eighteenth-century anthologist: 'It is impossible to furnish out an entertainment of this nature where every part will be relished by every guest. . . . If the reader should happen to find, what I hope he seldom will, any pieces which he may think unworthy of having been inserted; as it would ill become me to attribute his dislike of them to his own want of Taste, so I am too conscious of my own deficiencies not to allow him to impute the insertion of them to mine.'

A book such as this must inevitably be based to a large extent on the researches and writings of others. I should like to express my gratitude to the authors of books and periodical articles mentioned in the brief and selective bibliographies on pages 311–315. I am especially grateful to Mr F. J. B. Watson both for his own works and for reading and commenting most helpfully on a number of these studies.

Tofori, October, 1968   Hugh Honour

Jacques Androuet du Cerceau

(c. 1520–c. 1584)

Throughout the Middle Ages furniture makers plied their craft without asking or needing much help from designers. Even in a royal castle or baronial keep furniture was sparse and generally very simple. If an air of richness was required it was achieved not by woodwork but by the precious fabrics draped over it. Chairs were rarities. The staple pieces were benches, stools, trestle tables, chests and supports for bedding, all made according to patterns which had remained unchanged from century to century. Robust, yet light-weight, and with few protuberances which might be damaged, they were of a kind that could easily be transported. (The French word *mobilier*, Italian *mobilio* and German *möbel* all record the notion of mobility.) For kings and great landowners led roving lives, constantly on the move from one great stony castle to another, accompanied by their retinues of attendants and the bare essentials of furnishings. Paintings reveal that furniture in lesser houses was equally gaunt and plain, made, no doubt, by ordinary household carpenters. The monumentally bulky and elaborately enriched cupboards and big tables on carved legs, some of which have survived, give a very misleading impression of the medieval interior, for they were hardly to be found outside the larger monastic houses – the only places where conditions of life were both affluent and stable. Such pieces appear to have been made by craftsmen who were otherwise engaged in carving doors, screens and other church furnishings and who would have had little need for pattern books.

This situation changed in the fifteenth century. Kings and great landlords began to settle down to more secure and ordered lives and to demand furniture of a less rudimentary character. If, as the economic historians argue, this was a period of economic depression, they may also have found that carved woodwork was a very much less expensive form of decoration than the silks and damasks and oriental carpets formerly used to enrich the interior. Minor noblemen and the increasingly rich burghers now showed a desire for furniture more comfortable and decorative than that which had satisfied their forbears. But already Gothic decorations had come under attack in Italy, and by the early sixteenth century the influence of the Renaissance had begun to spread throughout Europe. Thus, the increase in demand for furniture was accompanied by a fundamental change in style.

In Italy furniture makers were able to acquire the new style from the buildings that were going up around them, and the paintings and sculptures in churches and other public places. Woodworkers who made

Middle sixteenth-century walnut
cabinet with bizarrely rendered antique
style decorations, probably influenced by
the published designs of du Cerceau.

Engraved design for a table, published in France *c.* 1550. Tables of this type, inspired by antique Roman marble tables, had been made in Italy since the early sixteenth century.

cassoni (coffers or chests) were naturally in close contact with the painters who decorated them. But craftsmen north of the Alps were much less fortunate. When required to satisfy the demands of clients who had been infected by the ideas spreading from Italy, they had to acquire an entirely novel repertory of decorative motifs and develop new types of furniture. For such men, and their patrons as well, the pattern books which began to appear in the middle of the sixteenth century must have come as a boon.

The first seems to have been a set of engravings by a certain Master H.S. of Augsburg or Nuremberg published about 1530. These elegant clean-lined designs for cupboards, beds and panelling, from which all traces of Gothic ornament – crockets, pointed arches and ogee tracery – have been ruthlessly omitted, are notable examples of the Northern Renaissance style. But although they are embellished with the classical orders, not too barbarously misused (at this date a Nuremberg carpenter had to make as his 'masterpiece' for the guild a dowelled window frame and a tall veneered cupboard supported on Doric, Ionic or Corinthian columns), they may well have seemed rather tame to the Italophiles of the day. No such complaint could be made about du Cerceau's furniture designs, published in France in about 1550. With their multitude of antique enrichments, caryatids and such antique beasts as the chimera and sphinx, these are Renaissance with a vengeance.

Jacques Androuet du Cerceau was born probably in Paris in about 1520 (though some authorities suggest 1510). Georges d'Armagnac, Bishop of Rodez (who introduced Serlio to François I and was patron of the agreeably named Guillaume Philander) is said to have enabled him to visit Rome in the 1540s. He was back in France by 1549 when he published his first book at Orléans. His first book of architecture appeared in Paris in 1559, dedicated to Henri II. This made his reputation and he was employed as an architect by several members of the Court until 1584 when his name appears for the last time. None of his buildings survives. And even in his own day he was famed mainly for his books of engraved designs.

Du Cerceau's various books of engraved designs, for architecture, silver and textiles, reveal that he was a bare-faced plagiarist. He helped himself freely to the elegant silver patterns of Hans Brosamer and to the delicately engraved ornaments of such Italian artists as Polidoro, Perino del Vaga and Agostino Veneziano. But even if this had been known at the time, it is doubtful whether it would have had an adverse effect on

Design for a bed, *c.* 1550: a
characteristic example of du Cerceau's
practice of loading a simple structure
with antique-inspired ornament.

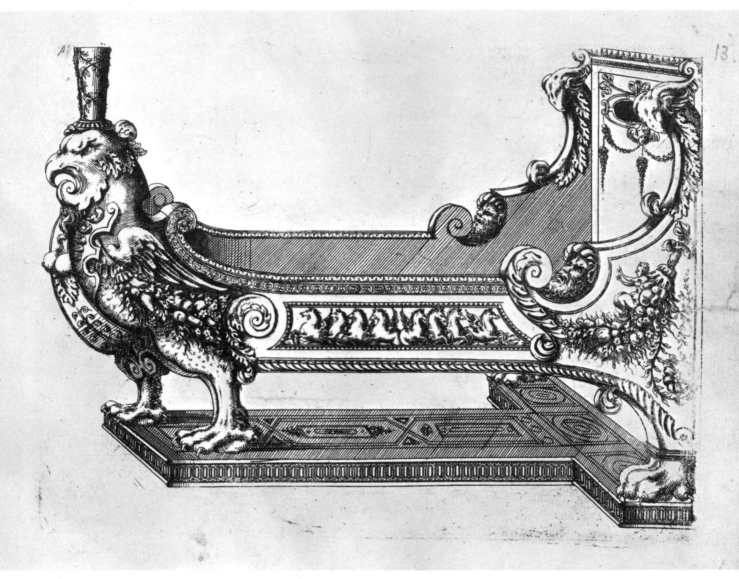

Design for a cradle or bed *c.* 1550.
It is doubtful if any pieces of furniture
as elaborate as this were made in
sixteenth-century France.

Design for a table, *c.* 1550.

his reputation. His achievement was to make Italianate designs fashionable in France. That they were in the 'new style' was all that mattered to those who bought and used his books.

So far as furniture is concerned, du Cerceau is rather more important historically. He was the first, after the Master H.S., to publish a coherent group of designs. And we shall probably never know to what extent they were derived from earlier drawings or engravings (now lost), or from actual pieces of furniture he saw in Italy and the more fashionable houses of France, and to what extent from his own imagination. The tables supported not on legs but on carved upright members at either end – to which he devoted several plates – are of a type first devised in ancient Rome (where they were executed in marble) and revived in Renaissance Italy. Paintings suggest that the grander Italian *palazzi* boasted beds with columns or caryatids supporting the tester, as in du Cerceau's engravings – there is one with correct Corinthian columns in Sodoma's *Marriage of Alexander and Roxana* of 1512 and one with elegantly attenuated caryatids in a painting by Lambert Sustris of about 1550. But for the dressers or buffets to which du Cerceau gave several plates there appear to be no prototypes in Italian furniture. And one can hardly believe that his more fantastic designs – such as the cradle carried by a very cross-faced griffin, or a bed supported at one end on a writhing snake and at the other on an elephant's foot – can have come from any but du Cerceau's imagination.

Like his contemporaries in France, such as Philibert de l'Orme and Philander, du Cerceau acquired a large vocabulary of Renaissance ornament without learning either its grammar or syntax (Philander topped a Gothic gable of Rodez cathedral with a complete Roman church front, its main door some sixty feet above ground level). Corinthian capitals, scrolls of acanthus, terms, grotesque figures derived from Roman paintings by way of Raphael, he used with exuberant abandon. And he made great play with elongated nude figures of the type Primaticcio had incorporated in the stucco-work at Fontainebleau. These designs manifest a *horror vacui* inherited from late Gothic art and architecture. Du Cerceau is generally called a Mannerist, yet when he was not directly imitating Italian designs, he shows no trace of that self-assured stylishness and that fluid grace which mark the work of the Italian artists of the School of Fontainebleau.

A few pieces of sixteenth-century French furniture seem to show du Cerceau's direct influence. But it is difficult to decide whether tables and beds derive from his prints or from the originals on which he relied. Generally, the more bizarre details of decoration have been omitted. There are, however, several sideboards and cupboards fully as fantastic and every bit as free in their use of Renaissance ornament as any in du Cerceau's book. And it seems more than probable that his plates had some influence on their makers.

Design for a cabinet, *c.* 1550. Du Cerceau was the first French architect to publish designs for furniture in the Renaissance style.

Hugues Sambin

(*c.* 1520–*c.* 1601/2)

In histories of furniture Hugues Sambin – 'Mon cher Sambin, la perle de nostre aage' as a contemporary sonneteer apostrophized him – occupies an almost mythological place as the first French cabinet maker, the lineal ancestor, as it were, of eighteenth-century *ébénistes* and *menuisiers*. He is, indeed, the first *menuisier* to emerge out of the heavy mists that hang over the medieval and sixteenth-century guilds of wood-workers. But in his day no very fine distinctions were drawn between one type of carpenter or woodworker and another. And in fact it is not known whether he ever produced a piece of furniture at all. He was certainly a woodcarver and also an architect, but not a single moveable piece of furniture is mentioned in any of the numerous documents which record his life and works.

There is even some doubt about the place of his birth. On the title-page of his only publication he is described as 'living at Dijon', which rather suggests that he had not been born there. It is generally assumed that he was born between 1515 and 1520. He first appears in 1548 when, with two younger brothers named Guillaume and Claude and the *menuisier* Jean Boudrillet, he prepared decorations for Henri II's cere-monial entry into the city of Dijon. In the same year he married the daughter of Jean Boudrillet, a woodcarver from Troyes who settled in Dijon some twenty years earlier to work on the choir stalls of the Cathedral. Sambin was received by the Dijon guild as a *maître menuisier* in 1549. He appears to have worked in partnership with his father-in-law, eventually taking first place in the workshop which was described as belonging to 'master Hugues Sambin and his father-in-law Boudrillet' in 1558. By this time he had already begun, in a modest way, as an 'architecteur', providing a design for the municipal slaughter house. When Charles IX visited Dijon in 1564, Sambin was put in charge of the festal decorations, receiving twenty sous a day (twice as much as he had been paid at the time of Henri II's visit).

Sambin has been credited with a considerable amount of Renaissance architecture in Dijon, including the very handsome main portal to the church of Saint Michel which is like an elongated Roman triumphal arch. He was probably responsible for the façades of the Maison Milsand and the Hôtel Le Compasseur which are richly encrusted with antique motifs, lion heads, grotesque masks, festoons of flowers and leaves and trophies of armour. As M. Lavedan has remarked, 'he treated the façades of private houses as a cabinet-maker would'. In 1581 he drew up

Middle sixteenth-century French cupboard. The architectural ornaments, especially the term figures, suggest the influence of Sambin, and the piece has sometimes been attributed to him.

31

Engraved designs for female term figures, published in Lyon in 1572. As in Sambin's other designs the correctly proportioned frieze and cornice make a striking contrast with the bizarre complexity of the supports, which were, however, similarly inspired by the antique.

opposite Middle or late sixteenth-century Burgundian walnut cupboard, with term figures possibly influenced by Sambin's engraved designs.

plans for the Palais Communal (now Palais de Justice) in Besançon, which was completed in 1585. In 1583 he was paid for work in the interior of the Palais de Parlement (now Palais de Justice) in Dijon, where he was responsible for the wooden screen separating the chapel from what is now the Salle des Pas Perdus. He is also known to have done work in the 1570s in the Château de Pagny which belonged to the 'très haut très puissant seigneur' Léonor de Chabot-Charny, lieutenant-general for the King in Burgundy and *Grand écuyer de France,* to whom he dedicated the volume of engraved designs which was published at Lyon in 1572.

The reputation of Sambin must rest mainly on his work in the Dijon Palais de Justice and on his book – *Œuvre de la diversité des Termes, dont on use en Architecture.* It consists of thirty-seven pages of highly fanciful term figures grouped according to the classical orders of architecture, but of a waywardness to make Vitruvius turn in his sarcophagus. They show the influence of Italian Mannerist ornament, also of the school of Fontainebleau. And those of a male and female figure emerging from heaps of rock work which seethe with insects and lizards, suggest that he had seen pottery by Bernard Palissy. They are all distinctly weird. Despite the title which states that the designs were intended for architects – and in his preface Sambin was at pains to declare that he had been devoted to architecture since his youth – they look as if they would have proved more useful to the painters of temporary triumphal arches and other festal ephemera and to furniture makers and the carvers of panelling. Quite a number of cabinets carved with term figures nearly as strange have thus been attributed to Sambin – and they suggest his influence even if they were not in fact made by him. The Palais de Justice woodwork is tame in comparison, but reveals him to have been a highly talented carver. And there are some similar panels attributed to him in the Museum at Dijon.

In 1588 the peaceful life of Burgundy was shattered by civil war. Sambin allied himself with the Ligueurs, who wanted the French crown to pass to a son of the King of Spain, against the Royalists who favoured Henri de Bourbon of Navarre (later Henri IV). He fled to Franche Comté where as 'maistre architecteur' he was employed in the defence of Salins. At the end of the civil war he returned to Dijon where he died in poverty in 1601 or 1602.

opposite Design for a female term figure, 1572. Figures of this type, though seldom as elaborate, were used for both architecture and furniture.

Designs for term figures, 1572.

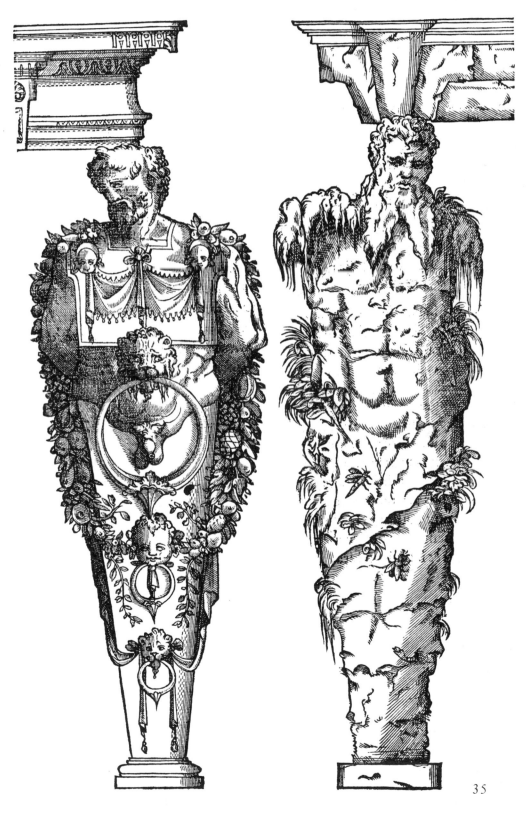

Hans Vredeman de Vries

(1527–c. 1604)

A volume entitled *Differents pourtraicts de la menuiserie a scavoir portaux, bancs, escabelles, tables, buffets licts de camp propres aux menuiziers de l'invention de Jehan Vredeman dict de Vriese, mis en lumière par Philippe Galle* (Antwerp, 1565), contains the widest range of furniture designs published in the sixteenth century. The designs are of particular interest because of their practicability – they could all have been followed without difficulty by any competent woodworker. Their author seems to have wished not so much to show off his skill or originality as to produce a useful manual. Vredeman de Vries also produced various books of architectural designs and these have recently been described as 'popularisations in the worst sense of the word'. But this is more than a little unfair. He may not have been an artist of striking originality, but in codifying a current style he performed a very valuable service for his contemporaries – and for posterity, it may be added.

Born at Leeuwarden in Friesland in 1527, Vredeman was trained as a painter. In 1549 he was involved in the design of triumphal arches for the entry of Charles v into Antwerp. And he remained in Flanders until 1585. In his later years he worked for that inspired patron of Mannerist artists, the Emperor Rudolf II. As a painter he specialized in architectural views – strange Mannerist fantasies in which well-dressed courtiers loiter through marble-cool loggias and down endless colonnades decorated with much intricate carving on every surface. He is not known to have practised as an architect but he began to produce volumes of architectural ornament before 1560. The first appears to have been a series of twenty designs of architectural views surrounded with strapwork borders intended, apparently, as models for intarsia work and illustrating the Italianate architectural style which had recently taken root in the Low Countries. In 1565 he published, as well as the *Differents pourtraicts*, a volume entitled *Architectura* which includes elaborations of the classical orders and also designs for strapwork, probably intended for carvers and painters as much as for architects.

In Flanders the Italian Renaissance repertory of decorative motifs had been accepted early in the sixteenth century. Such cities as Antwerp, Brussels, Bruges and Ghent were closely linked by trade with the Italian states and it is hardly surprising that they should have come under artistic influence from Italy. In 1506, it will be remembered, Michelangelo sent his *Virgin and Child* to Bruges, and between 1516 and 1519 tapestries after Raphael's cartoons of the *Acts of the Apostles* were woven in Brussels. There can be no doubt that Italian works on architecture –

Composita.   Corinthia

·19·

opposite Designs for three tables, Antwerp, 1565. De Vries was not an inventive designer but a codifier of the types of furniture popular in the middle sixteenth century.

Designs for strapwork, a type of ornamentation much used for the decoration of buildings, furniture, metalwork, etc. in the second half of the sixteenth century, 1565.

such as Serlio's *L'Architettura* of 1537–51 – would have reached Flanders soon after publication. Yet Renaissance architecture in the Low Countries was mainly an affair of triumphal arches and other temporary structures (the Renaissance additions to the palace at Malines are exceptional). A certain conservatism encouraged the retention of the Gothic style, and the influence of the Renaissance is apparent mainly in carved work. This attitude combined with a love of rich decorations and, perhaps, an association of Italianate with festal architecture, predisposed the Flemish to welcome the ingenious elaboration of Mannerist ornament. They certainly seem to have responded less to Serlio's painstaking attempts to establish the pure forms of the classical orders than to the fantastic designs he published in the later parts of his book. And in the 1540s the Flemish artist Cornelis Bos began publishing ornamental designs of a wonderful nightmarish complexity, outdoing the Italians. Somewhat similar designs were produced by Cornelius Floris in the following decade.

It should not be supposed that these strange designs manifested a reaction against the classicism of the Italian Renaissance. Rather the reverse: they seem to have been regarded as improvements. And Hans Vredeman de Vries's *Architectura* reveals how he thought classical ornaments might be 'improved' – by a *simpliste* process of multiplying ornamental motifs. For him, even the Corinthian order was insufficiently rich, so he devised a new type of capital and a series of grotesque interlaced decorations to muffle every square inch of the entablature, while retaining respect for the sacrosanct classical proportions which he indicated alongside. In his designs for caryatids and relief work he allowed himself a freer hand, making use of one of Bos's favourite motifs – a human or more usually sub-human figure imprisoned, as it were, in a boldly curving scroll from which his head, legs and arms project.

Woodcarvers may, perhaps, have taken motifs from these engravings. But craftsmen needed rather simpler patterns demonstrating how household objects could be embellished with up-to-date ornaments. These Vredeman de Vries provided in his *Differents pourtraicts* which illustrated everyday objects like stools and tables, beds and cupboards, sparsely decorated with Mannerist ornament. It is now difficult to assess to what an extent these designs were original. Some of the stools are of types which appear to have been in use since early in the sixteenth century. He seems, indeed, to have taken over a large number of stock patterns

Designs for tables by Paulus, son of
Hans Vredeman de Vries, from his
volume *Verscheyden Schrynwerck*,
published in 1630.

Designs for three chairs by Paulus
Vredeman de Vries, 1630.

and modified them only slightly. And it would therefore be wrong to suggest that all the many surviving pieces of late sixteenth-century furniture which can be matched with plates in his book were necessarily executed after his designs.

The date of Hans Vredeman de Vries's death is unknown – it has been placed as early as 1604 and as improbably late as 1623. His son, Paul, who was born in 1567, issued two volumes of furniture designs entitled *Verscheyden Schrynwerck* in 1630. The fact that he took over many of his father's designs testifies to their continuing popularity. His own were in a somewhat richer style with a greater use of figurative carving. Some, indeed, have an elegance which is entirely lacking in the work of Hans. But they are distinctly conservative, showing no awareness of the work of Baroque architects which had already begun to influence furniture in Italy and was soon to extend to northern Europe.

Designs for two cabinets by Paulus Vredeman de Vries published in 1630.

Domenico Cucci

(c. 1635–1704/5)

In the Gobelins tapestry panel woven to commemorate the visit of Louis XIV to the *Manufacture royale des meubles de la Couronne,* there is the figure of a man somewhat darker-skinned than the rest who points with evident pride to a large cabinet. This is probably Domenico Cucci, and the piece of furniture may well be one of the two 'large ebony cabinets inlaid with pewter' with 'four large twisted columns in imitation of lapis and vine scrolls of copper gilt supported by ten lions' paws' which he had made for the King. He was one of the finest craftsmen employed at the Gobelins under Louis XIV and occupies a position of great import-ance in the history of European furniture.

Domenico Cucci was born at Todi in the Papal States. Nothing is known of his background or training but, like so many of the more notable Italian furniture makers, he was also a sculptor. It seems probable that he learned his craft in Rome where the vogue for very rich palace furniture, incorporating much figure sculpture, delicate relief work and incrustations of precious and semi-precious stones, was well established by the middle of the seventeenth century. A connection with the Florentine *Opificio delle Pietre Dure,* which was at this time the most noable workshop producing mosaic panels of hard stone for the decora-tion of tables and cabinets (of a type Cucci was later to use), is less probable but cannot be ruled out. It is, however, clear that he derived both his taste for opulence and his style from Baroque Italy.

He went to France in about 1660, perhaps attracted by the generous patronage of the Italian art-loving Cardinal Mazarin. But Mazarin died in 1661 and it was not until 1664 that Cucci became a naturalized French subject. By this time the young Louis XIV had already begun to surround himself with a magnificence which would outshine even that of Mazarin. Cucci was employed to work for him at the Gobelins where he was provided with accommodation. As head of the *atelier* in which the showiest cabinets were made, he contributed greatly to the luxurious grandeur of Versailles and the other royal palaces. Though fully employed by the Crown until 1683, when Le Brun was disgraced and work at the Gobelins began to decline, he seems later to have been ready to execute occasional private commissions. In 1693 Daniel Cronström, the Swedish Minister in Paris, told Nicodème Tessin that for work in gilded copper 'Le sieur Cussi, at the Gobelins, who has worked almost exclusively for Versailles, is the ablest, and has much good will for me'. He remarked in another letter that Cucci had promised him some designs. According to him, Cucci also made ironwork for the windows

opposite One of a pair of cabinets inlaid with *pietre dure*, made by Cucci at the Gobelins Factory, 1681–3.

The pair to the cabinet on page 42, made in 1681–3 for Louis XIV.

Detail of marble, gilt copper and *pietre dure* on the cabinet on page 42.

and door-furniture for Versailles – the metalwork on a single door costing the considerable figure of 350 livres.

The French royal accounts record in detail the many works produced by Cucci and his assistants. There were the cabinets of War and Peace, one decorated with Louis XIV as Mars, the other with Marie-Thérèse as Pallas Athene, both having columns of aventurine marble and jasper. He carved cases for an organ, a harpsichord and a spinet. For the great casket made to contain the king's jewels he fashioned the bronze decorations. He was also employed on an elaborate marquetry floor made to the design of Le Brun in the Château de Saint-Germain. And in the early 1680s he was at work on the Petite Galerie at Versailles, using quantities of gilded bronze, tortoise-shell and lapis lazuli in its decoration. But before this was completed the War of the League of Augsburg broke out in 1686 and Louis soon found himself financially embarrassed for the first time. Work on the Petite Galerie was called to a halt, the craftsmen at the Gobelins were given less to do and in 1693 the factory was almost closed down. Next year Cronström reported that among the Gobelins employees poverty and lack of work was general; the weavers were almost asking for charity. It was possible, he said, to obtain furniture or tapestries at half their normal prices. No more is heard of Cucci, though he appears to have remained in Paris and died there in 1704 or 1705, just

Gobelins tapestry from the series
L'Histoire du Roi designed by Charles
Le Brun. It shows Louis XIV visiting
the Gobelins factory and inspecting
examples of the furniture,
metalwork and tapestries made there
for his palaces.

after the first emergence of the rococo style which was to drive his pompously magnificent furniture literally out of court.

Cabinets by Cucci remained at Versailles throughout the Régence and the early years of the reign of Louis XV. But in 1741 a sale of out-moded pieces of royal furniture was held at the Tuileries. Seven years later the King gave twelve cabinets (including those of War and Peace) to Buffon for the natural history museum – and as M. Verlet has suggested they were probably broken up so that the pieces of semi-precious stones could be displayed as mineralogical specimens. Despite the nostalgia for the glories of the *grand siècle* which began to manifest itself at this moment, these works must have seemed impossibly vulgar and showy, exemplifying what were thought to be the excesses of the Italian Baroque. In 1751 there was another sale of royal furniture including the two cabinets by Cucci which are now at Alnwick Castle. Similar pieces were broken up and their more valuable parts re-used. In the royal collections of both England and Sweden there are fine Louis XVI style cabinets (the former by Weisweiler) incorporating relief panels of *pietre dure* which are near relations to those on Cucci's cabinets at Alnwick, and must have come from pieces that had been broken up.

Even though most of his cabinets were destroyed, the mark made by Cucci on the history of furniture and decoration was not to be effaced. He, more than anyone else, was responsible for introducing a note of Italianate richness into the splendid rooms at Versailles, thus establishing a new concept of regal magnificence which was to be imitated with varying degrees of success, by German princelings, the rulers of Italian states and even a few English noblemen. He was among those who set the superb standard of craftsmanship which was to be maintained by French furniture makers throughout the eighteenth century. And he was largely responsible for establishing a standard of costliness for furniture, which was also to be kept up until the Revolution. Suffice it to say that the cabinets now at Alnwick cost Louis XIV 16,000 livres (about £800 in the English money of the day). With Boulle he helped to estab-lish the status of the *ébéniste* as a very superior type of craftsman, on a par with painters and sculptors. Two of his daughters married sculptors, one René Chauveau who quarrelled with Cucci and went to work in Sweden, another the 'sculpteur ordinaire des bâtiments du roi', Sébastien Slodtz, whose sons were to attain eminence as sculptors and also to be involved occasionally in furniture design.

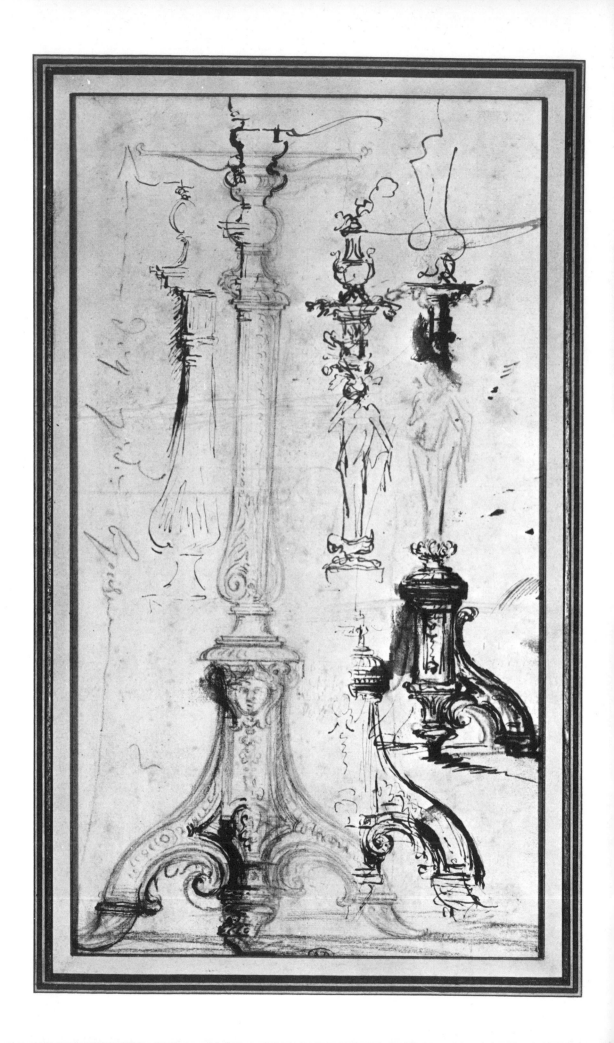

André-Charles Boulle

(1642–1732)

In 1672 a set of apartments in the Galerie du Louvre, hitherto used by a royal cabinet maker Jean Macé, fell vacant. There were two candidates for the privilege of occupying them: Macé's son 'who is not skilful in his craft', and André-Charles Boulle, 'the most skilful in Paris'. Informed of this, Louis XIV briskly replied: 'The apartment in the Galleries to the most skilful'. During the next thirty and more years Boulle was to demonstrate how well founded the choice had been. His fame resounded through Europe. He was the only cabinet maker to be distinguished by a biography in the 1719 edition of Orlandi's *Abecedario Pittorico* published in Florence. And his name is still a household word, even to many who have never seen a single example of his work. There are, indeed, very few pieces of furniture that can with any certainty be attributed to him. And of the vast number commonly ascribed to Boulle, many were made long after his death, some in the nineteenth century and even later.

He was the first great French *ébéniste*. Before his advent the best furniture made for the French Crown had been the work of foreigners like the Dutchman Pierre Golle and the Italian Domenico Cucci. And Boulle himself appears to have been of Swiss extraction, a relation (perhaps grandson) of a certain Pierre Boulle who had been employed as a furniture maker by Louis XIII but of whose work nothing is known. André-Charles Boulle was born in Paris in 1642, the son of a carpenter, sometimes referred to as a cabinet maker, who trained him in his craft. But he was also schooled as a painter, and as such elected to the Parisian Académie de Saint Luc (significantly enough, the first works he executed for the Crown were two paintings for which he was paid in 1669). By 1664 he was, however, established as a maker of marquetry as well as a painter in a studio attached to the Collège de Reims. In the following year Bernini made his famous visit to Paris and is said to have struck up a friendship with Boulle, advising him on his designs. In 1672 Boulle was appointed *ébéniste du roi*. Contemporary documents describe him also as painter, architect, mosaicist, bronze worker and designer of monograms.

As royal *ébéniste* Boulle supplied much furniture for Versailles where he also decorated the Dauphin's *grand cabinet* (1681–3) – now destroyed but recognized at the time as his masterpiece. But he was free to accept private commissions and his clients included the Duke and Duchess of Orléans, the Duke of Bourbon, the Grand Condé, rich commoners like the financier and art collector Pierre Crozat, and some foreign royalty including Philip V of Spain and the Electors of Bavaria and Cologne. To

Engraved designs for an inkstand and dressing-table from *Nouveaux Desseins de Meubles*. . . . by Boulle, published in Paris early in the eighteenth century.

opposite One of a pair of commodes veneered with ebony, inlaid with brass and with gilt bronze mounts, made in 1708–09 for the Trianon.

cope with his numerous commissions, he employed some twenty assistants. He was, nevertheless, seldom free from financial difficulties and was occasionally obliged to seek royal protection from his creditors until, in 1704, the King expressed severe displeasure.

Only two fully documented works by Boulle have so far been traced – a pair of commodes made in 1708–09 for the King's bedroom at the Trianon and now at Versailles. The commode was a new type of furniture, destined to replace the tall cabinets like those made by Cucci. Though hardly less rich in design it was not encrusted with intrinsically precious materials. And, of course, as its height corresponded with the dado, it did not interfere with the decoration of tapestries or mirrored walls above. If he did not invent the commode (as either he or Guillemard, who also made such furniture for the crown, may well have done), Boulle clearly played a role of some importance in its development. Several other pieces of furniture have very reasonably been ascribed to Boulle, notably the Electoral bureau now in the Louvre, a pair of wardrobes, the upper part of a cabinet, a pair of pedestals and some other pieces in the Wallace Collection, London; a clock-case in the Metropolitan Museum, New York; a wardrobe in the Louvre; and two cabinets in the Hermitage Museum, Leningrad.

All these pieces are adorned with the brass and tortoise-shell marquetry to which Boulle gave his name. This type of decoration had in fact been used, especially by Italian craftsmen, since the sixteenth century. And Mazarin had encouraged the production of furniture inlaid with metal, mother-of-pearl, horn and shell as well as semi-precious stones. But Boulle developed it in a highly individual way. The decorative panels were prepared by gluing together sheets of brass and tortoise-shell which were then cut according to the pattern desired by a kind of fret-work technique. When cut the layers were combined to provide one panel of tortoise-shell ground inlaid with brass, and one of brass inlaid with shell, known as 'first part' and 'counter part'. Pairs of wardrobes or commodes might thus be decorated the one with first part, the other with counter part marquetry. Alternatively, first part and counter part panels might be used for the outside and inside of a door, as on a medal cabinet (not by Boulle himself) in the Wallace Collection. Sometimes the brass was engraved. The parts of the furniture not covered with marquetry were veneered with ebony or covered by elaborate gilt bronze mounts which were not only decorative but served to protect corners from damage. These pieces of furniture have an unmistakably

50

Late seventeenth- or early eighteenth-century cupboard in the style of Boulle. He was the most famous practitioner of this type of brass and tortoise-shell marquetry.

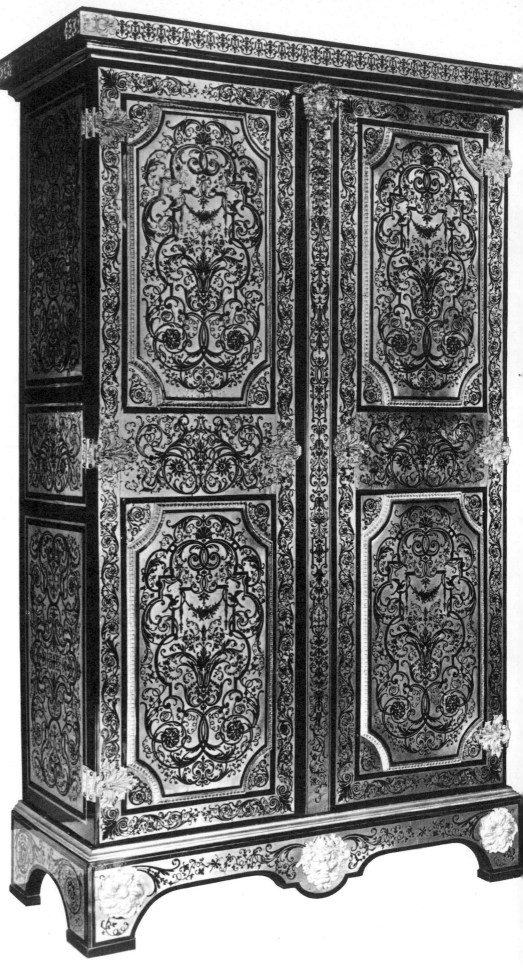

Pendule propre pour une chambre

left Engraved design for a clock-case.

right Desk made for
Maximilian-Emanuel,
Elector of Bavaria, one of the few
extant pieces of furniture that may
be attributed to Boulle, *c.* 1723–5.
The Elector possibly ordered
this piece when he visited Boulle's
workshop in 1723.

opulent air, yet they owe more to the craftsmanship of the men who
made them than to the costliness of the materials employed. Those
made for Louis XIV must have helped to console him for the loss of the
furniture covered with plates of embossed silver and even a few solid
silver pieces which he had sent to the melting pot in an attempt to
replenish a treasury sadly depleted by the extravagance of abortive
European wars. (Boulle's two commodes now in the Louvre cost 3,000
livres, a fraction of the price of Cucci's cabinets.)

Though famed mainly for brass and tortoise-shell marquetry, Boulle
is known to have worked also in rare woods. The biography in the
Abecedario to which I have already referred and which was almost
certainly written by Pierre Crozat in about 1718, refers to his work in

Clock on pedestal attributed to Boulle, c. 1700–20. Boulle is known to have made many clock-cases though none can with certainty be ascribed to him.

variously coloured woods from India and Brazil and states that he represented different 'species of flowers, of fruit, and of animals, composing pictures of hunting scenes, battles and fashions accompanied with ornaments in the most refined taste, enriched with bronze, to form tables, writing desks, caskets, *armi* [probably *armadi* – wardrobes], monograms, clocks, friezes'. This rather confused passage seems to suggest that he had not, as is usually stated, abandoned such ordinary work in marquetry early in his career, even if he no longer produced it for the Crown.

The *Abecedario* biography also refers to Boulle's large collection of old master and modern drawings and prints, which he found 'always most useful' and called his 'sorgente deliziosa' (delightful spring). It is known from other sources to have been very extensive, including forty-eight drawings of scenes from Ovid's Metamorphoses by Raphael, a sketchbook by Rubens, a large number of drawings by Stefano della Bella, as well as prints by him and by Callot. From such works Boulle presumably derived inspiration for the design of his marquetry panels and bronze mounts. He also owned a number of paintings, one ascribed to Correggio (which he valued highly), others by Le Brun, Mignard and Berchem. Expenditure on this collection was the cause of his financial difficulties.

At the time when this biography was written Boulle had retired from work, leaving his four sons to manage his studio. But on the night of 19 August 1720 his premises caught fire and most of his precious possessions were burnt. He estimated the total damage at 383,780 livres. The minute account he compiled of his losses mentions, in addition to the works of art, personal furniture (which appears to have been as grand as that he made for Versailles) and materials, a number of completed pieces of furniture executed on commission and including fifteen clock-cases, five bureaux and eight commodes. This is alone enough to reveal the considerable output of his workshop. After the disaster Boulle, though well advanced in years, is said to have returned to work and to have directed the *atelier* until his death in 1732.

The workshops were carried on by Boulle's sons André-Charles, who died in 1745, and Charles-Joseph, who died in 1754 shortly after taking on the German immigrant J.-F. Oeben through whom the Boulle tradition of superlative craftsmanship was passed on to Riesener. Surprisingly enough, none of these *ébénistes* is known to have used Boulle marquetry – though furniture decorated with it was produced in Paris fairly consistently throughout the eighteenth century.

The back of a toilet mirror made in early eighteenth-century France in the style of Boulle.

Gerreit Jensen

(*fl.* 1680–1715)

Candle-stand decorated with marquetry. Though not documented, these and a few other pieces of late seventeenth- or early eighteenth-century English marquetry furniture of very high quality may confidently be ascribed to Jensen.

opposite Writing-desk inlaid with silver and brass made for William III and Mary II, 1695.

In the inventory 'of what goods is now in hir Laite Ma. ties Lodgeings of blessed Memory at Kensington March ye 24th 1696/7', only one cabinet maker is mentioned by name – 'Mr Johnson' who had made 'two tables looking glasses & stands the frames all inlade with mettle' and 'two foulding writing tables inlade with white and covered with green velvett'. Gerreit Jensen, whose name was spelt in fourteen different ways in the royal accounts, often anglicized as Johnson, might almost be called the English Boulle. For he was not only the most fashionable and prominent cabinet maker in London during the reigns of William and Mary and of Anne, but also specialized in furniture decorated with metal inlays. He appears to have been the first cabinet maker in England to achieve individual distinction. And several of his works survive (ironically enough, more can with certainty be attributed to him than to Boulle), though he was forgotten for over two centuries after his death.

Nothing is known of Jensen's origin. He was presumably Flemish or Dutch by birth. He settled in London before 1680, when the accounts of the Royal Household record a payment to him for furniture which Charles II presented to the Emperor of Morocco. He may perhaps be identical with a 'Garrett Johnson' who purchased his freedom of the City in 1667 or with a 'Gerrard Johnson' who became a liveryman of the Joiners' Company in 1685. After the 1688 Revolution he was much employed by the Crown. In 1693 he took premises in St Martin's Lane, where many of the leading London cabinet makers were later to settle. As his will reveals, he became fairly prosperous, owning a country house with more than an acre of land at Brook Green, Hammersmith. He retired in 1715.

The furniture Jensen made for Charles II has vanished – it included 'a table, stands and looking glass and covers for the table and stands, for Ma.s Bedchamber at Whitehall' for which he was paid £18 in 1685. But several of the pieces made for William and Mary survive. There is at Windsor a handsome writing-table which corresponds with the 'folding writing table fine markatre with a crowne and cypher' for which he received £22.10s. in 1690. The 'glass case of fine markatre upon a cabinett with doors' which cost £34 in 1693 is also at Windsor. And so is the 'fine writing desk table inlaid with mettal' for which he received £70 in 1695. He continued to work for the Crown during the reign of Queen Anne, supplying in 1707 'two tables and four stands, and two

Marquetry writing-table on turned legs (which have been renewed) made *c.* 1690 for William III and now at Windsor Castle.

glasses and each forty-five inches inlayed with mettal, with carved and gilded frames', for £200. But most of the furniture he made for the royal palaces in these years was decorated with lacquer rather than marquetry and was consequently still less expensive.

In a document, probably of 1689, confirming his patent as royal cabinet maker, Jensen is said to have been employed by the Crown 'makeing and selling of all Sorts of Cabbinets, Boxes, Looking Glasses Tables and Stands Ebony Frames and for the Furnishing of all Sorts of Glasse plates of well plained and pollished as not plained or pollished and all things relating to the Cabbinet makers Trade'. He seems to have had the monopoly of providing looking-glasses to go over chimney-pieces and on the piers between windows of the royal palaces (the vogue for this extensive use of looking glass derived, of course, from Versailles). Between 1688 and 1698 he similarly supplied both window glass and looking glass for Chatsworth which was then in the process of trans-formation into one of the greatest houses in England by that singularly unpuritan supporter of Nonconformists and pillar of the Protestant Succession, William Cavendish, first Duke of Devonshire. It is hardly surprising to find that Jensen also worked for other noblemen who had benefited from the Revolution. At Boughton there is a writing-desk inlaid with metal, similar to that at Windsor, made for the first Duke of Montagu who was master of the Great Wardrobe from 1689 to 1695; and another at Wilton probably made for the eighth Earl of Pembroke who held high office under William and Mary and Anne. But it would be a mistake to suppose that he was patronized only by Whigs. At Dray-ton House there is a table and pair of torchères which are said to have belonged to the Jacobite second Earl of Peterborough, and a similar set

Table decorated with marquetry.

at Deene presumably made for the second Earl of Cardigan who played no part in politics.

The inspiration for the design, as well as the technique, of Jensen's metal marquetry derived from France. He is, in fact, known to have had direct contact with Paris and to have supplied a type of glue to the Dutch-born cabinet maker Pierre Golle who worked for Louis XIV. It seems at first sight strange that English decorative arts should have been influenced mainly by Holland under the Francophile Charles II, and by France under Dutch William. The paradox may partly be explained by the fact that the cavaliers spent much of their exile in the Low Countries, and that the influx of Huguenots driven from France by the revocation of the Edict of Nantes introduced a number of highly skilled French refugee craftsmen. But that is not all. Though William III was the fiercest of the opponents of Louis XIV, he spoke French in preference to Dutch or English. And, as much as other European monarchs, he felt that it was necessary to keep up with the Capets. As letters of the period reveal, every detail of decoration and every twist and turn of ceremony at Versailles was closely scrutinized and imitated in the courts of the enemies no less than the allies of Louis XIV. At Windsor Castle Celia Fiennes remarked of the lavish decorations in the State Drawing Room, in about 1701: 'It looked very glorious and was newly made to give audience to the French Embassadour to show the grandeur and magnificence of the British Monarch – some of these foolerys are requisite sometymes to create admiration and regard to keep up the state of a kingdom and nation.' Yet one may question whether Frenchmen familiar with the work of Cucci and Boulle would have been much impressed by Jensen's attractive but modest furnishings.

Gerhard Dagly

(fl. 1687–1714)

Before the end of the sixteenth century pieces of lacquer work began to reach Europe from the Orient. Such objects were, of course, rated below the silks and the spices – pepper, cloves, mace, nutmegs, cinnamon, green ginger – that were the staple items in the Eastern trade. But a market was soon found for them and by the early seventeenth century a fashion for lacquer was well established. An English ship, the *Clove*, which returned from a voyage to Japan in 1614, included in its cargo 'Japanese wares, scritoires, Trunkes, Beoubes [screens], Cupps and dishes of all sorts, and of a most excellent varnish'. The East India Company sold these wares slowly and with such good effect that 'small trunkes or chests of Japan stuff gilded and inlaid with mother of pearl having sundry drawers and boxes' which were first priced at £4. 5s. and £5 could command as much as £17 apiece a few years later when the demand had begun to exceed the supply. Larger quantities of lacquer were imported by the Portuguese and it was 'chez les Portugais' that Paul Scarron noted fine vernis or lacquer at the Foire de Saint-Germain in 1640. Though, by this date, the Portuguese had been expelled from Japan and the Dutch had obtained a monopoly in the finest quality Oriental lacquer.

European cabinet makers may well have regarded the prices paid for Oriental lacquer furniture with some envy. And they were soon trying to imitate it, just as potters were attempting to produce wares comparable with Oriental porcelain. The essential material – the lac – was not available in Europe. But if European craftsmen were unable to reproduce either the waterproof property or the exquisite texture of the best Japanese lacquer, they found that they could make passable imitations of the coarser Chinese type by applying numerous coats of varnish to wood. A number of recipes were published: many more were probably kept secret. And in 1688 John Stalker and George Parker issued in London their *Treatise of Japanning and Varnishing*, which in addition to describing the technical process provided engravings of decorations which they thought suitable. They claimed that these designs were based on imported specimens of lacquer but, they confessed, 'perhaps we have helped them a little in their proportions where they were lame or defective, and made them more pleasant, yet altogether as Antick'.

'English varnished cabinets might vie with the oriental', William Whitewood boldly declared in 1683. But the Dutch, who were the main importers of Oriental lacquer, had already established themselves as the best imitators (it has been suggested that Japanese lacquer workers were,

Cembalo case decorated with japanned chinoiseries, *c.* 1710.

in fact, brought to Holland to impart the secrets of their craft). Excellent work was done in France and Italy. And shortly after the mid-century the little watering place, Spa – just to the south of the Dutch border, near Liège – had begun to emerge as one of the main centres for the production of European lacquer – or 'japan' as it should properly be called to distinguish it from true lacquer. Here Gerhard Dagly, who was to become one of the most notable craftsmen to work in the medium, was born in the early 1650s.

Dagly is first heard of in Berlin in 1687 when he was appointed Kammerkünstler to Friedrich Wilhelm, the 'Great Elector' of Brandenburg. Next year his appointment was confirmed by Friedrich III who succeeded to the Electorate. The main aim of this prince's life was to obtain the title of King of Prussia – which he finally achieved in 1700. But while he was intriguing and negotiating, he lost no time in transforming what had hitherto been an unmistakably provincial Electoral court into one with a semblance of royalty. With what Carlyle calls a 'turn for ostentation', he set about the creation of a truly regal court ceremonial and an appropriate background for it. Inevitably he looked for inspiration to Versailles where Louis XIV had surrounded himself with a décor of unparalleled richness. Friedrich did not, of course, have the benefit of a Le Brun or of furniture makers comparable with Boulle and the various craftsmen employed at the Gobelins. But he did his best to encourage the decorative arts (a tapestry factory and a pottery were founded in Berlin during his reign). And in Dagly, whom he nominated 'Directeur des Ornements', he had perhaps the most gifted japanner in Europe.

For nearly a quarter of a century Dagly worked in Berlin, decorating both furniture and panelling. Sometimes he was obliged to measure his talents against genuine Oriental work, making a dado for a room panelled with leaves from Coromandel screens, and providing appropriate stands for Chinese cabinets. But generally he was employed in decorating pieces of furniture of types not made in China – *guéridons*,

European lacquer cabinet on stand of carved and gilt wood, attributed to Dagly, who was the most famous lacquer painter of his day in Germany.

piano-cases, tables and long-case clocks. He not only worked in the traditional black and gold colour scheme but also painted figures in bright reds, greens and blues on a creamy white ground, giving the appearance of porcelain. For his designs of little Chinamen sauntering in gardens of gigantic flowers he seems to have drawn inspiration from Oriental lacquer and porcelain, but not without 'improvements' – both to correct Oriental perspective and to give buildings an air of more fragile fantasy and to endow animals, birds and human figures with a quainter grotesqueness.

When the Electress of Hanover sent an English japanned clock-case to her Prussian son-in-law, she felt bound to apologize for it, remarking 'Dagly makes much better ones'. But the recipient of the gift, who succeeded to the Prussian Crown as Friedrich Wilhelm in 1713, seems to have been less impressed by Dagly's talents. Immediately after his father's death he made a clean sweep of court officials. 'He reduced his Household', Carlyle tells us with some glee, 'to the lowest footing of the indispensable; and discharged a whole regiment of superfluous official persons, court-flunkies, inferior, superior and supreme, in the most ruthless manner.' And with the Kammerjunker, Kammerherrn, Goldsticks, Silversticks, went the Kammerkünstler Gerhard Dagly. He retired to the Rhineland where he was last heard of in 1714 writing to the philosopher Leibnitz and saying that his future was so uncertain that he could give no precise news. His younger brother Jacques, who had worked with him in Berlin since 1689, went off to Paris where, together with Pierre de Neufmaison and Claude Audran, he obtained a patent to establish a factory for the production of a varnish that could be applied 'to all sorts of linen or wool stuffs, to silk to leather and any other pliable substance of whatever colour to be used to make furniture'. Gerhard's most notable pupil, Martin Schnell, settled in Dresden where he found an appreciative patron in that great lover of chinoiserie – as well as women – Augustus the Strong.

Late seventeenth- or early
eighteenth-century European lacquer
cabinet decorated with chinoiseries,
probably the work of Dagly.

Andrea Brustolon

(1662–1732)

The spectacle of tables supported by sturdy figures of Hercules, or of chairs writhing with wriggling *putti* and giggling mermaids, or of vase- and candle-stands in the form of lithe naked blackamoor slaves with chains dangling from their necks, is not one that appeals immediately to all connoisseurs of furniture. Englishmen, for instance, prefer their chairs and tables to look like pieces of furniture rather than sculptural fantasies which may – or may not – have a practical purpose. Not so the Italians who, from the seventeenth to the mid-nineteenth century, thought more of the grand effect, *la bella figura,* made by very showy furniture than of its mundane utility. In Italy a very wide gulf separated the furniture made for daily use in the ordinary rooms of a palazzo or villa from that which served mainly for display in the state apartments. The genre pictures of Pietro Longhi remind us how very simply – by the standards of London or Paris – the bedrooms and small sitting-rooms of a Venetian house were furnished, while the great state portraits by his son, Alessandro, reveal the sumptuous grandeur of the thrones and tables which were, and some of which still are, disposed beneath the beautifully frescoed ceilings of marbled and stuccoed *saloni.*

It is hardly surprising to find that the makers of this opulent palace furniture were by training and vocation sculptors rather than cabinet makers. The most famous, and perhaps the most expert, was Andrea Brustolon, creator of a set of furniture now in the Ca' Rezzonico, Venice, which seems to epitomize the highly sophisticated decadence of the city at the end of the seventeenth century. The chairs are exquisitely carved of box-wood with legs, stretchers and arms simulating gnarled creeper-encrusted branches of trees supported by little Negro boys with black lacquered heads and arms and feet and patches of lacquered flesh glinting through the slashes in their breeches. Athletically muscular Negro slaves gracefully pose as supports for candelabra or *guéridons* – the French word derives, incidentally, from the name of a famous Moorish galley slave. The largest piece, on which Brustolon carved his signature, can hardly be regarded as furniture at all – it is an elaborate side-table with Hercules, flanked by Cerberus and the Hydra, supporting a platform on which two classical river gods recline, clutching Chinese porcelain vases, and between them three chained nude Negroes, like dusky male Graces, hold aloft a stand for yet another vase.

It might well be supposed that the designer and maker of this exotic furniture was a sophisticated exquisite – a Bakst born before his time realizing in solid wood the entire cast of some fantastic ballet. But this

opposite Chair of carved box-wood partly lacquered, part of a suite made for Pietro Venier in Venice in the 1690s.

Candle-stand or *guéridon*, of box-wood partly lacquered, *c.* 1690–9.

opposite Vase-stand carved by Brustolon, the most elaborate of the pieces of furniture he made for the Venetian nobleman Pietro Venier in the 1690s.

can hardly have been the case. So far as one can judge from the scanty evidence, Andrea Brustolon was a simple, pious craftsman who devoted most of his life to carving crucifixes and altar-pieces for the churches in and around his native city of Belluno, some sixty miles to the north of Venice.

He was born in 1662, received his early training as a sculptor in Belluno and was sent at the age of fifteen to work in Venice. Here he was employed as an assistant by the Genoese sculptor Filippo Parodi, author of the finest Baroque monument in Venice (to the Patriarch Francesco Morosini, in the church of S. Nicolò da Tolentino) and of the strangely sinister figures with wild eyes, tangled hair and puffy flesh in the church of the Santo in Padua. From Parodi he must have learned much of the technique of carving while picking up the hot-house luxuriance of his late Baroque style. He must also have seen, and was perhaps influenced by, the weird allegorical wood carvings which Francesco Pianta executed for the Sala Grande of the Scuola di San Rocco at about this time. The document (unfortunately undated) which records that Brustolon worked under Parodi, states that he was planning a visit to Rome – that visit which was *de rigueur* for every aspiring Italian artist. But we do not know whether in fact he went there. His earliest recorded work is a pair of angels for the sacristy altar in the Frari, Venice, of about 1683. He is known to have gone back to Belluno at least once in the 1680s, and in 1699 he settled there permanently, dying in 1732. The various religious carvings he executed in Belluno are well documented: not so, alas, his furniture.

The Negro suite of furniture is the only one that can securely be attributed to Brustolon. It was made for Pietro Venier, a member of a great Venetian family which had provided the Serenissima with three Doges. No date is recorded and although it is generally assumed that the furniture was made before Brustolon returned to Belluno in 1699, it could equally well have been made later. Two other suites of furniture have been ascribed to Brustolon on stylistic grounds – and the similarities are so strong that the attribution can hardly be doubted (even though very little is known of other Venetian furniture makers at this period). One was made for the Correr family and is to be seen with the Venier set in the Ca' Rezzonico: the other was made for the Pisani, was in their palatial villa at Stra in the early nineteenth century and is now in the Quirinal, Rome. Four armchairs very similar to the Venier suite are in the collection of Lord Burnham at Beaconsfield. Eight box-wood chairs

Drawing for the canopy of a statue of
the Madonna. Brustolon was
primarily a sculptor working for the
churches in and around Belluno, and
was only incidentally engaged in
making furniture.

right Design for a looking-glass frame:
the inscriptions reveal the
symbolism of the various figures, those
on the right representing valour,
those on the left *virtù*, with love in the
centre triumphing over both.

opposite Sketch for a chair and for
carved ornaments.

– six at Belvoir Castle and two at Abbotsford – which were bought in
Rome in the early nineteenth century have also been attributed to
Brustolon, but their similarities with the Venier suite are less close.

Drawings by Brustolon enlarge our knowledge of his work as a
furniture maker. One shows the lower part of the 'side-table' in the
Venier suite. There is a sheet of designs for side-tables supported by
marine monsters and foliage. Another drawing is for an elaborately
allegorical looking-glass frame, not unlike a carved frame in the Ca'
Rezzonico – or the 'frame by the famous Brustolone, the Michelangelo
of wood-carving' owned by Balzac's Cousin Pons.

Daniel Marot

(1663–1752)

In the history of the decorative arts no political event can have had so profound and far-reaching an influence as the revocation of the Edict of Nantes in 1685. Although attempts were made to prevent Huguenots from leaving France, many thousands contrived to flee and find refuge in the Protestant states of Germany, in Switzerland, Holland and England. Among them there were numerous craftsmen – tapestry weavers from Aubusson, silversmiths and cabinet makers – who belonged to the section of the population hardest hit by the wave of persecution. Although they had to leave behind most of their belongings, they were, however, able to take with them an asset which was to prove invaluable – proficiency in what had already become the most fashionable decorative style in Europe.

Of these refugees, Daniel Marot is one of the most notable, though he can hardly be regarded as typical. Born in Paris in 1663, he was the son of an architect, Jean Marot, who is remembered mainly for two volumes of engravings entitled *L'Architecture française,* generally known as *le grand Marot* and *le petit Marot.* He was nephew to Pierre Golle, an important Dutch cabinet maker who had been brought to Paris by Cardinal Mazarin and was later established in the Gobelins, specializing in the production of very costly furniture decorated with marquetry, metal inlays and carving. Daniel was thus brought up in close contact with at least one of the originators of the Louis XIV style. And his later work reveals that he must have been well acquainted with the ornamental designs of Bérain and Lepautre. It is sometimes said that he studied under Le Pautre and worked in Boulle's *atelier.* But very little is known of him before 1685 when he fled to Holland. Adriaan Golle, Pierre Golle's younger brother, also a cabinet maker, took refuge in Holland at the same time and soon began to work for Princess Mary, the wife of William of Orange. He may well have introduced Daniel Marot into the Stadtholder's service.

William and Mary employed Marot as a kind of 'designer general'. He seems to have been capable of turning his hand to practically anything from plans for formal gardens to designs for Delft earthenware *tulipières.* But he was engaged mainly on the decoration of interiors. He was largely responsible for those in the palace at Het Loo. In 1694 he went to England where he stayed for four years, designing rooms and furniture for Hampton Court Palace. His engraved designs, which were issued originally in small groups, were collected in a volume published in Amsterdam in 1702: an enlarged and revised edition was published ten

Engraved designs for metalwork and a bracket clock. The influence of the Louis XIV style and especially the work of Boulle is felt in most of Marot's designs.

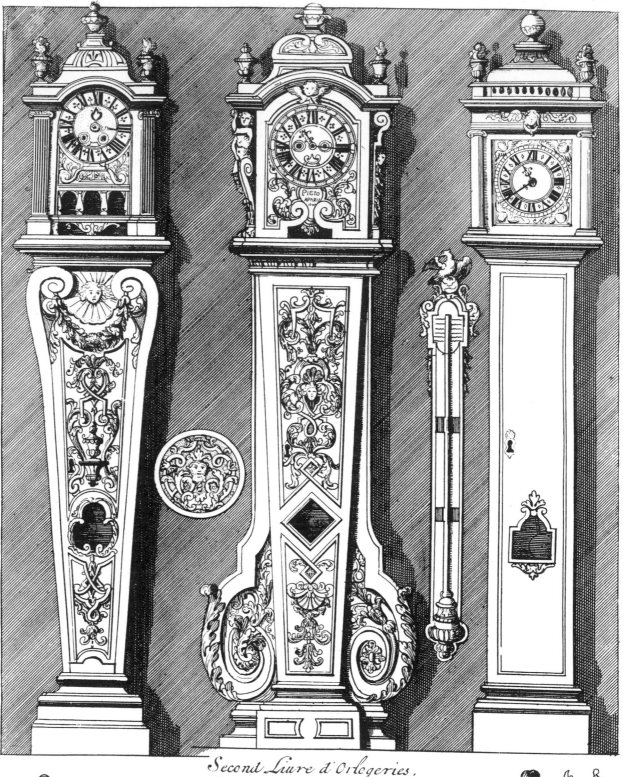

Second Liure d'Orlogeries.
Inventé par D. Marot Architecte.

DANIEL MAROT

Designs for a stool and chair,
c. 1690–1702.

Designs for three long-case clocks,
a barometer and various ornaments,
c. 1690–1702.

years later. The inscriptions on the plates describe him as *Marot Architecte* and sometimes *Architecte du Roi*. But he does not appear to have worked as an all-round architect until about 1715 when he built the Schuylenberg House at the Hague. His other notable buildings include the Hôtels van Wassenar and Huguetan and the Portuguese Synagogue at the Hague. He continued to practise until he was more than seventy years old and died in his ninetieth year in 1752.

By the time that the second edition of Marot's *Œuvres* appeared in 1712 his designs must have seemed woefully antiquated in a France which had already seen the first delicate manifestations of the early Rococo style. Even in Holland and England, which lagged behind the fashionable developments of Paris, they must have looked a little out of date. Through nearly thirty years in which the notion of novelty as one of the most desirable qualities in interior design had become firmly established, he had clung doggedly to the style that was new in his youth, and in the diffusion of which he had played a part of capital importance.

Marot had acquired in the Paris of the early 1680s a taste for Baroque magnificence as expressed in the grand dramatic stage set which Louis XIV created for the long performance of his life. His monumental clocks seem to have been designed to count the hours spent by courtiers kicking their heels in ante-chambers; his chairs are chairs of state from which audience might graciously be granted; his *tabourets* are of a type on which only the very highly born and privileged might be allowed to sit. And his beds, perhaps the most notable of his creations, with their carved decorations at head and foot, their generous flounces of drapery crowned by nodding bunches of ostrich feathers, are quite obviously intended mainly for the complicated ceremonies of the *levée* and the *couchée* and the histrionic scenes that marked the death of a monarch – so different from the luxuriously and voluptuously intimate beds which were to be devised by rococo designers. In Marot's great beds only state secrets could be learned or given away. This decorative style, designed to hedge the divinity of the Sun King, was, however, imitated not only by his main political opponent William of Orange and other lesser rulers but also by numerous noblemen with aspirations to grandeur, especially in England where Marot's interpretation of the Louis XIV style had considerable influence on furniture makers.

Some pieces of Dutch furniture probably executed after Marot's designs are very close indeed to French prototypes. In the Castle of Twickel, for example, there is a centre table supported by carved and

DANIEL MAROT

Design for a pelmet, *c.* 1690–1702. Designs such as these had much influence in England.

Bed made for the first Earl of Melville, *c.* 1692–1707, with draperies showing the influence of Marot's designs.

gilt caryatids that is quite remarkably similar to a table in the Hôtel Lauzun, Paris. It would, however, be a mistake to suppose that Marot was no more than a plagiarist who based his designs precisely on those that were fashionable in France. His published designs generally show a desire to modify and 'improve' on French patterns, with reference, no doubt, to Dutch taste. Generally he was inclined to overdo what had been done richly enough in France. At Versailles there was a vogue for exoticism and many rooms were adorned with Chinese vases and lacquer cabinets. Marot, perhaps responding to Queen Mary's notorious passion for porcelain, devised interiors in which vases were displayed in still greater profusion, sometimes clustered around the chimney-piece, occasionally ranked tier on tier from floor to ceiling. If French chairs had high backs, those designed by Marot had backs that were still higher, to tower above the topmost curl of the amplest *perruque*. Where French *menuisiers* had gone in for rich carving, Marot demanded effects even

Design for a pelmet, *c.* 1690–1702.

Design for a bed included in Marot's 1702 collection.

more deeply and richly sculptural. And where the French had used abundant drapery, Marot used still more, gathering up silks into great billowing swags. He was indeed a master of the pelmet and the flounce, the tassel and the fringe.

The importance he placed on upholstery is perhaps significant. In Holland and England there were relatively few craftsmen capable of producing grandiose furniture comparable with that made for even the less important rooms at Versailles – and there were none with the highly developed talents of a Cucci or a Boulle. Moreover the vast sums needed for making the grandest types of furniture were seldom available either in royal or private houses. But, like many later interior designers, Marot seems to have appreciated that effects of the greatest opulence could be achieved quite easily by the sumptuous use of hangings. It is perhaps significant that in both Holland and England his influence was strongest on the design of beds.

John Gumley & James Moore

(*fl.* 1694–1729 and 1708–1726)

Side-table decorated in gilt gesso by Moore, made for George I, *c.* 1715.

'Though we are at this day beholden to the late witty and inventive duke of Buckingham for the whole trade and manufacture of glass, yet I suppose there is no one will aver, that, were his grace yet living, they would not rather deal with my diligent friend and neighbour, Mr Gumley, for any goods to be prepared and delivered on such a day, than he would with that illustrious mechanic above-mentioned'. So wrote Richard Steele, under the pseudonym of Hezekiah Thrift, in *The Spectator*, 14 October 1712. A couple of years later Steele gave Gumley another puff in *The Lover* where he described his gallery over the Royal Exchange as 'a place where people may go and be very well entertained, whether they have or have not a good taste'. Here the visitor could see 'a long row of tables, on many of which lie cabinets, inlaid or wholly made of corals, ambers, in the like parts'. But it was to the looking-glasses that his attention was particularly directed: 'we have arrived at such perfection in this ware . . . that it is not in the power of any Potentate in Europe to have so beautiful a mirror as he may purchase here for a trifle'.

It is clear that Gumley lived on the fringe, if not quite at the centre of the Kit-Cat club and Will's coffee-house world. Indeed, in 1714 his daughter Maria married the ambitious and well-to-do Whig politician William Pulteney who was later created Earl of Bath (she was then nick-named the Wife of Bath). And we may wonder whether he was not an entrepreneur and dealer rather than a craftsman. He is first heard of in 1694 when he advertised a sale of 'all sorts of cabinet work, as Japan Cabinets, India and English, with Looking Glasses, Tables, Stands, Chests of drawers, Screutores, writing Tables, and dressing suits of all sorts'. In 1701 the Earl of Bristol bought a 'bureau and chinaware' from him. Two years later he supplied for Chatsworth – at a price of £200 – a pair of magnificent twelve foot tall looking-glasses with engraved heraldic devices and applied ornaments of sapphire blue glass – they are still *in situ*. Evidently he prospered, and in 1705 set up a glasshouse at Lambeth. But this provoked trouble from a rival firm of looking-glass makers who petitioned Parliament in an attempt to have Gumley's factory suppressed. Gumley, they declared, was 'no true inventor' but 'still sells glass in his shop in the Strand and the rest of his partners are merchants and tradesmen in the city, and none of them ever bred up in the Art or Mystery of making glass'. Free enterprise triumphed over restrictive practices and in 1712 Gumley was shipping £100 worth of looking-glasses to the Orient through the East India Company. In 1714 he opened a gallery in the New Exchange in the Strand. And in the same

One of a pair of looking-glasses
supplied by Gumley for Chatsworth
House in 1703: they cost the
considerable sum of £200.

Looking-glass in carved and gilt wood
frame supplied by Gumley for
Hampton Court Palace, *c.* 1715.

year, or 1715, the royal accounts reveal that Gerreit Jensen had been
succeeded by John Gumley and James Moore. This is the first indication
of Gumley and Moore working in partnership.

Much less is known about James Moore. The earliest reference to him
is of 1708 when he supplied a 'walnut-tree chest' to the Duke of Montagu
for the modest price of £8. 10s. In 1710 the Earl of Bristol, who had also
been a client of Gumley, bought pier glasses and sconces from him. By
1714 he had become engaged in the furnishing of Blenheim and thus
involved with the formidable Duchess of Marlborough – that 'B★ old
B★ the Dss. of Marlb.' as Vanbrugh styled her – who called Moore her
'oracle', saying that he 'certainly has very good sense and I think him
very honest and understanding in many trades besides his own'. She
even appointed him to take over from Vanbrugh and Hawksmoor as
clerk of the works at Blenheim in 1716.

Even after Gumley and Moore appeared as partners in the Royal
accounts, Moore seems to have continued to work independently. It
is perhaps significant that a table and candle-stand made for George I
and now at Buckingham Palace are inscribed only with the name of
Moore. Accounts for furniture supplied for John Meller's house,
Erthig, in Denbighshire, between 1722 and 1726, are receipted by Moore
alone. This suggests that the partnership was a fairly loose one, linking
an able businessman with an excellent craftsman. The distinction is
borne out by the wills of the two men, Moore, who died in 1726 'of a
wound in his head, which he received by a fall as he was walking in the
street', left to his son James: 'my materialls of Trade, namely Wood and
Tools at ye election of my wife Elizabeth, if she follows the trade to pay
him one Hundred pounds and she keeps the Materialls'. Gumley's will
(he died in 1729), on the other hand, is that of a prosperous and can-
tankerous city man. To the daughter who had married so well he left
£1,000; to his eldest son who, he said, was 'very profligate and diso-
bedient' and 'not fitt to be trusted with an Ample fortune' he left only
£150 on condition that 'he doth not obtrude himself upon or molest
my wife'. His various properties he left to his widow in trust for his
other two sons, one of whom was to receive his share in a Vauxhall
glasshouse and the handsome house he had built for himself at Isleworth.
The contents of his warehouse at the New Exchange went to his mother,
Mrs Elizabeth Gumley. But before the year was out Mrs Gumley was in
trouble with the Comptroller of the Great Wardrobe for overcharging.

Candle-stand decorated in gilt gesso
made by Moore for Queen Anne,
c. 1710.

She was, indeed, struck off the list of 'tradesmen for the Wardrobe' on account of her 'notorious impositions'. Moore's business was carried on after his death by his son, also called James, who supplied furniture for Canons, the palatial country house of the Duke of Chandos. He fared better than Mrs Gumley and in 1732 was appointed chair and cabinet maker to Frederick Prince of Wales, but died two years later.

The pieces of furniture signed by Moore, and a few others that have convincingly been attributed to him, are all of high quality. They are of wood covered with gesso moulded in low relief and gilded. The delicately interlaced patterns of leaf and band work with which he decorated table-tops are clearly inspired by French ornamental designs of which numerous engravings were issued in the first two decades of the eighteenth century, just at the moment when Baroque boldness was beginning to give way to rococo fantasy. On a table-top at Hampton court the main lines of the pattern have the formal rigidity of wrought iron, but the sprays of leaves which spread out from the corners have a very discreetly erring grace which suggests that the rococo sap is beginning to rise. One is reminded of the later designs of Jean Bérain and the early work of Nicolas Pineau. But the base of this table owes little if anything to France: it is distinctly stiff-limbed and English. Other tables reveal a fondness for curiously tapering legs which bulge out suddenly towards the top and are crowned with volutes like those of an Ionic capital.

The relations between Gumley, Moore and contemporary architects are of some interest. Although Moore took over as Clerk of the Works from Vanbrugh at Blenheim, there was not necessarily any connection between them. Indeed, Vanbrugh wrote of him contemptuously to the Duchess as 'your Glassmaker Moor'. Moore is, however, known to have executed furniture to the design of William Kent for Kensington Palace – side-tables supported on sphinxes. The connection with James Gibbs is stronger. Both Moore and his son supplied furniture for Canons which was built mainly to the design of Gibbs. John Gumley employed Gibbs at his own country house at Isleworth and, in 1728, subscribed to his *Book of Architecture*. But only in occasional decorative details does the furniture of Gumley and Moore suggest Gibbs's in-fluence. It must be assumed that they were themselves responsible for their furniture designs.

Side-table decorated in gilt gesso made
for George I by Moore, *c*. 1715.

Charles Cressent

(1685–1768)

It is at first sight somewhat surprising to find that whereas eighteenth-century English furniture makers sometimes amassed considerable fortunes, their much abler *confrères* in Paris, who charged far higher prices for their works, seem often to have died in poverty. The reasons for this unhappy state of affairs in France are not difficult to establish. The luxury-loving members of the French royal family and court had a greater disdain for paying bills than the more bourgeois and mercantile English. To make matters worse, French craftsmen seem to have had a greater taste for expensive living than the frugal English. One may question whether they could have satisfied so brilliantly their patrons' tastes and love of visual luxury had they not shared it to some extent. But it led more than one of them to bankruptcy. Furthermore, the *ébéniste* or *menuisier* was hampered by innumerable guild regulations which prevented him from engaging in any craft but his own, while the English furniture maker was free to engage in a very wide range of activities. (It is significant that among the few *ébénistes* to acquire fortunes, Pierre I Migeon, his son and grandson, and J.-B. Fromageau were also furniture dealers.) The rules of the Paris *corporations* undoubtedly helped to maintain the highest standards ever achieved in opulent furniture. But the craftsmen themselves must sometimes have been reminded of the grains rammed down the necks of Strasbourg geese to produce *foie gras*.

The life of Charles Cressent, one of the finest of all French *ébénistes* – who died in 1768 owing his butcher 1,145 livres – demonstrates both the merits and the disadvantages of the French guild system. He was born at Amiens in 1685, the grandson of a *maître ébéniste*-cum-sculptor, and the son of a sculptor, François Cressent. He appears to have been trained in both arts, but it was as a sculptor that he was elected to the Académie de Saint Luc in Paris in 1714. After a modest beginning, finishing bronzes by Girardon and Robert Le Lorraine, he worked for Joseph Poitou, *ébéniste* to the duc d'Orléans, Régent of France. Poitou died in 1718 and next year Cressent married his widow, thus acquiring a good furniture-making workshop and, shortly afterwards, the title of *ébéniste* to the Régent.

Trained as a sculptor, Cressent not unnaturally wished to make the bronze mounts for the furniture produced in his workshop. But here he ran into trouble with the guild of bronze founders and chasers who restricted such work to members of the guild. Furthermore, the regula-

Medal cabinet made for Louis duc
d'Orléans, the son of the Regent,
c. 1725. Cressent succeeded Boulle as
the most distinguished French
furniture maker: in 1749 the Abbé
Raynal said that he had a place among
the great French artists.

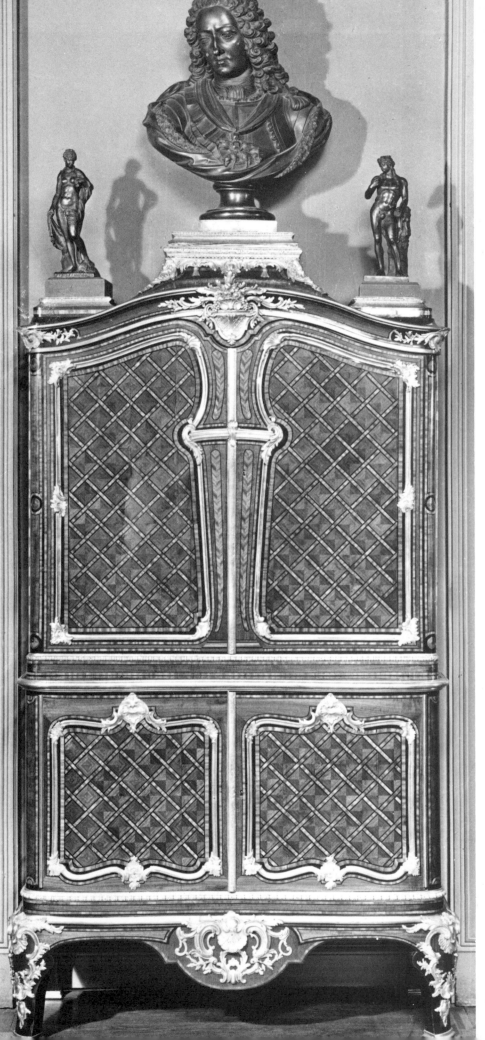

opposite top Commode, *c.* 1730. The magnificent gilt bronze figures at the corners reveal Cressent's abilities as a sculptor.

bottom Commode veneered with king-wood and decorated with gilt bronze mounts, *c.* 1730–5.

tions prescribed that a bronze mount made by one of the *maîtres* of the *Corporation des fondeurs-ciseleurs* could not be gilded by him but had to be taken to the workshop of a qualified *ciseleur-doreur* before it could be passed on to the furniture maker. Nor was the *ébéniste* even allowed to fetch it from the gilder's workshop – it could be carried through the streets only by a member of the *Corporation des ciseleurs-doreurs*. Rules as stringent as these seem almost to have been made to be broken, and Cressent was not the only *ébéniste* to break them.

In 1722 the *fondeurs-ciseleurs* began to take action against Cressent for infringing the rules in several ways – by employing four *maîtres fondeurs* on his premises and producing bronzes that were not even intended for use on furniture. He was protected from the full force of the penalties which might have been imposed (a heavy fine and confiscation of his works) by the intervention of the Régent. And he seems to have been unrepentant. In 1735 he was prosecuted again, when a couple of master gilders were found lurking at the back of his shop, and yet again in 1743 for employing a *fondeur* on his premises. But on both occasions he was protected by the duc d'Orléans, the son of the Régent who had died in 1723.

Documents connected with these processes reveal the extent of Cressent's activity. A single *fondeur* claimed to have executed gilding for him to the value of 24,000 livres in a period of four years. His clients included many of the most distinguished amateurs of the arts in Paris – the duc de Richelieu, Mme de Pompadour and her brother the marquis de Marigny (*Directeur des bâtiments*), the financier Crozat, the collector Julienne. He also supplied furniture for John V of Portugal, and Charles Albert, Elector of Bavaria. Basking in such patronage, he became himself an art collector and assembled more than five hundred pictures attributed to, among others, Raphael, Titian, Rubens, Dürer and Holbein, as well as bronzes and carvings in ivory and semi-precious stones. But by 1748 he was nearly bankrupt. He announced the sale of his collection and stock-in-trade and prepared a catalogue. But as new commissions came in, some of them accompanied by advance payments, he was able to withdraw his own collection from the sale and, indeed, to add to it. But in 1757, at the age of 72, failing eyesight and poor health forced him into partial retirement. Two attempts to sell his collection of works of art failed and he finally left it to his housekeeper (his wife had died many years before).

Gilt bronze cartel clock in a
comparatively restrained style and
probably dating from the 1730s.

Cressent was one of the very few *ébénistes* whose name was well enough known to be mentioned in eighteenth-century sale catalogues. But since *ébénistes* were not obliged to sign their furniture with an *estampille* until 1751, not a single piece stamped by him is known. As a result, a fairly considerable body of furniture has been attributed to him, sometimes on very flimsy evidence. And since the discovery that a number of very handsome commodes, traditionally and very plausibly assigned to Cressent on stylistic grounds, were in fact the work of Antoine-Robert Gaudreau, doubt has been cast on many other works which have for long passed under his name. There can, however, be no doubt that he was responsible for some of the very finest pieces of Régence and Louis XV style furniture – commodes in the Gulbenkian Collection, the Wallace Collection, at Waddesdon Manor and the Munich Residenz, and a large number of cartel clocks.

The clocks reveal – or seem to reveal, for none is precisely dated – the development of Cressent's style from a somewhat tight late Louis XIV or early Régence manner to the airy exuberance of the full Rococo. Contemporary descriptions suggest that the earliest were decorated with 'Boulle' marquetry. But before 1741 he had devised a cartel clock with a face set within an elaborate gilt bronze framework of symmetrically placed curves. The clock-case he was making for John V of Portugal in 1735 when the officials of the *Corporation* descended on him was probably of this kind. By the time he announced his sale in 1749 he had devised two other types. One he described, with an absence of false modesty which seems to have been characteristic, as: 'A clock with a bronze front, the case of inlaid wood; the composition represents a flying figure of Time about to cut the thread of the life of a child who is on a rock and who, seeing Time, drops his quiver and bow; the terror on the face of the child makes a most striking effect. The ornaments which frame the face are in a style quite different from those of all other clocks, made by the most expert practitioners of this art, and may be expected to win the approval of all connoisseurs'. At least three such clocks survive; they are boldly sculptural, conceived indeed as wall decorations which incorporate time-pieces almost as a bonus. Scrolls, rock-work, flowers, leaves and figures are beautifully poised in a rhythmically asymmetrical pattern of curves. The other type of clock in the 1749 sale, described as 'a magnificent bronze clock designed in the best taste', also includes figures of Cupid and Time; but their relationship has been reversed,

Gilt bronze cartel clock, *c.* 1747. Clocks
of this type were described in detail in
a catalogue of 1749.

Cupid now triumphs at the top, and the boldness of line has been broken, the soaring Baroque flame fragmented into innumerable particles of light.

A similar development may be traced in Cressent's commodes. That in the Wallace Collection, perhaps the most handsome, with an *espagnolette* head staring out of the centre and scrolls which merge into the tails of flying dragons on either side, probably dates from the early 1730s. The commodes in the Munich Residenz are probably a little later – the sculptural quality of the mounts is just as high, especially the figures of *putti*, but the slightly heavier appearance may perhaps be ascribed to an attempt to satisfy German taste. At Waddesdon there are commodes with gilt bronze *putti* frolicking amongst luxuriant foliage and monkeys balancing on tight-topes, which are as light-hearted as the later clocks and presumably date from the 1740s.

There can be little doubt that Cressent himself designed the furniture he produced. The bronze figures and reliefs on his clocks and commodes rank amongst the masterpieces of small-scale sculpture of the eighteenth century. They reveal a consistent artistic personality and an individual sense of fantasy. He did, of course, also practise as a sculptor, producing busts and medallions (he inherited from his father the title of sculptor to the King). Among works which stand on the borderline between pure sculpture and furniture are a pair of firedogs in the Wrightsman collection, formed of fluid rococo scrolls on each of which a coquettish sphinx reclines voluptuously, one nursing a kitten, the other a monkey. It is clear that if these elegantly coiffed creatures with their well-manicured feline paws, were to pose riddles, they would concern only the secrets of the alcove. It was characteristic of the period that even the dour Egyptian monster could undergo such a delightful metamorphosis. But if they are unlike their namesakes – one can hardly call them ancestors – in the ancient world, they are very closely related to the monkeys who cavort in the designs of Claude Audran and the paintings of Huet. They were made to satisfy the almost insatiable appetite for elegant, sophisticated novelty which marked Régence taste and influenced the work of Cressent no less than Oppenord (also employed by the Régent), Robert de Cotte, the sculptor Robert Le Lorrain, and even Watteau. At a time when all the arts and all the genres were allowed equal merit – save the despised *genre sérieux* – Cressent was among the leading artists of Paris.

One of a pair of commodes with
gilt bronze mounts, *c.* 1740–5.

Pair of gilt bronze fire-dogs,
c. 1740–5. Fire-dogs of this design were
listed in a catalogue of Cressent's
effects drawn up in 1756.

Ein gantz neu inventirter geheim-Tisch vor grosse Herrn, beÿ dessen gebrauch ³
die Speissen unten durch den Tisch auf einer beweglichen mit gegengewicht versehenen
Scheiben in die höhe gehoben werden. Oben auf den Tisch befindet sich eine zum trieb
mit Lufft angefüllte Fontaine zur Erfrischung der Gläser, an der Seiten ist ein nach
Englischer Façon eingerichter Lehn Sessel nebst einem verguldeten Wand-Leuchter.

Johann Jakob Schübler

(1689–1741)

Among German eighteenth-century furniture designers Johann Jakob Schübler occupies an important if somewhat curious place. Although he is usually described as an architect he is not known to have practised as one. Nor does he appear to have had any direct connection with the furnishing trade. Indeed, very little is known about him apart from the date of his death in 1741 and what can be deduced from his fairly numerous publications. In Germany he has been called a 'Mathematiker und Architekturtheoretiker'. But perhaps he would best be described as an 'inventor' – with all the fairy-tale connotations of the word. One imagines him as the Dr Coppelius of furniture designers.

His first dated book seems to have been a folio entitled: *Perspectiva. Pes picturae. Das ist: kurtze und leichte Verfassung der practicabelsten Regul, zur perspectivischen Zeichnungs-Kunst*. Though brief, the text is anything but easy, including references to every writer on perspective from Dürer, Sirigatti and Serlio. And the plates are not so much a practical guide to perspective as ingenious demonstrations of how architectural forms may be foreshortened, elongated or extenuated from the oddest points of view. The preface is dated 1719 (though no edition is recorded until after Schübler's death). By this time, however, he had probably begun to issue the first part of his great *Werck* which was published in Augsburg and included designs for all types of household furniture, not to mention baptismal fonts, organ-cases, confessionals and garden pavilions. More practical interests are revealed in his *Nützliche Anweisung zur unentbehrlichen Zimmermans-Kunst* – useful advice on the indispensable carpenter's art – which was published in Nuremberg in 1731 and is devoted largely to roof construction but also includes sections on staircases and bridges and on pile-driving machines and cranes. This book is dedicated to the great Baroque architect Balthasar Neumann who, Schübler claimed, had approved some of the preliminary drawings. But he plunged deep into the realms of theory in his *Ars inveniendi* of 1734, an extraordinary system for the representation of hidden truths, in the design of columns, vases, mirrors and garden ornaments.

These publications display the range of Schübler's interests: and the plates demonstrate his ability as a draughtsman. But he is perhaps best remembered for his numerous furniture designs, among which there are many which reveal a genius for gadgetry. The most remarkable are illustrated in a volume entitled *Nützliche Vorstellung*... which appeared in Nuremberg in 1730. One is for a merchant's desk, built on a polygonal plan with projecting bookrests and writing platforms and, in the centre,

Engraved design for a dining-table with combined dumb-waiter and fountain, 1720, for those who wished to eat and drink in privacy.

Design for an interior with an
ornamental pedestal table, published in
Augsburg in 1720.

a revolving drum in which ledgers and correspondence might be stored.
As Siegfried Giedion pointed out, this may owe something to Agostino
Ramelli's design for a rotary reading desk of 1588 and appears to be an
ancestor of the modern rotary file (though one may doubt if there is any
direct connection). The same volume includes a design for a 'French
chair', for a writing-table, which has, according to the description, a
'back padded to the hollow of a man's spine and provided with a
resilient spring so as to yield backwards without breaking' – a precursor
of the modern typist's chair.

Other designs are less practical if no less ingenious. Indeed, they
demonstrate a love of ingenuity for its own sake. For 'grosse Herrn' who
wished to eat unaccompanied by servants, he devised a novel form of
table – 'ein gantz neu inventirter geheim-Tisch' – flanked by a rather

Design for a study with writing-table and stove, Augsburg, 1720.

ornate dumb waiter from the top of which a fountain spouts water, for the cleaning and cooling of glasses. He invented a contraption by which the image of a clock dial could be projected, by means of a lamp, onto the wall or floor beside a bed. Another of his inventions was a collapsible bed which could be extended to its full size by means of ropes and pulleys. But the engraving of this design has a curiously eerie atmosphere, lending it the appearance of some fiendishly elaborate instrument of torture.

There is, indeed, something sinister about nearly all Schübler's designs. The furniture is nearly always shown in rooms rendered with such a perfect command of pictorial space and with such heavy shadows thrown either by candles or through the bars of the window panes that they seem uncannily still and empty. They have a curious resonance.

93

JOHANN JAKOB SCHÜBLER

Design for a clock showing months and days as well as hours, 1720.

One feels drawn into them as if prowling furtively through deserted rooms of a strange house and one almost expects to hear mysterious voices issuing from behind the curtains or the panelling.

In point of ornamental design, Schübler was less original. Like most German designers of the period he was heavily indebted to France and worked in a German version of the Louis XIV style. Although he claimed to have abandoned 'fantasy, deceptive taste and insinuating fashion' in favour of 'geometrical measurements', his designs are so heavily muffled in writhing, serpent-like rather than serpentine, scrolls and ponderous pall-like hangings, that it is difficult to appreciate the nice mathematical calculations on which their proportions were based. This furniture is almost overbearing in its weighty solidity. It is not difficult to find similar furniture in many a German Schloss or Residenz, and

Design for a bed, published in
Augsburg in 1720: a Germanic
variant on a French original of the
Louis XIV period.

tempting to suppose that much of it was inspired by Schübler. His set
of designs for beds, cabinets, tables, commodes and so on, first issued at
Augsburg in about 1720, must certainly have been popular for some
twenty editions of it are recorded. They even reached England, where
Batty Langley borrowed one of his designs for a dressing-table.

It is easier to demonstrate the influence of his ornamental furniture
designs than of his more forward-looking inventions. Later in the century two German craftsmen who specialized in 'mechanical' furniture,
Oeben and Roentgen, won considerable renown in Paris. But whether
they derived anything from him or, as seems more likely, from the same
tradition which goes back to the automata makers of sixteenth-century
Augsburg, we shall probably never know.

Pietro Piffetti

(c. 1700–1777)

Marquetry cabinet, with gilt bronze mounts by Francesco Ladatte, made by Piffetti in 1731 for the Queen's dressing-room in Palazzo Reale, Turin.

In 1739 Thomas Gray described the Royal Palace in Turin as 'the very quintessence of gilding and looking glass; inlaid floors, carved panels, and painting wherever they could stick a brush'. A slightly stronger note of Puritan disapproval is audible in the comments of other English travellers who were surprised, if not shocked, to find such luxurious richness in a palace on classic Italian soil. The French were rather less censorious. P.–J. Groseley in 1758 commented on the 'taste, disposition, and magnificence of furniture', adding as a snide afterthought, that it 'might have vied with those for which the royal houses of France were so much admired before the building of Versailles'. Another French visitor, the Abbé Coyer, thought the palace itself was not at all 'royal' but found the rooms 'delightful, richly decorated and in good taste' and doubted if any monarch was as agreeably lodged as the King of Sardinia. In the creation of this general air of opulent magnificence a considerable part had been played by the royal cabinet maker, Pietro Piffetti – one of the few Italian craftsmen to deserve the title of *ébéniste*.

Pietro Piffetti was born in about 1700, probably in Piedmont. Nothing is known of his background or career before 1730 when he was 'discovered' working in Rome by the powerful first minister of the King of Sardinia, the marchese d'Ormea, who ordered a clock-case, a stand for a crucifix and some small tables from him. Early next year he was summoned to Turin. A walking stick of *bois violet*, or purple-wood, inlaid with ivory on the handle, won royal approval and he presented it to the King. On the 13 July the King issued a patent designating him 'ebanista nostro', obliging him to put and keep in order all the royal furniture, providing at his own expense all the materials (ivory, ebony and brass are mentioned) apart from silver, precious stones and rock crystal, in return for an annual salary of 500 livres. He was promptly commissioned to make a quantity of furniture for the various royal palaces that were then being decorated and continued to work for the royal household until his death in 1777. At some date in the 1740s he returned to Rome for a while to make a very rich altar frontal, inlaid with mother-of-pearl, tortoise-shell, various woods and gold which Cardinal Vittorio Amadeo delle Lanze gave to Benedict XIV for the Cappella Paolina in the Quirinal. This has vanished but it was probably similar to another altar frontal he made in 1749 for the church of S. Filippo in Turin and which survives *in situ*.

Little is known of Piffetti's private life. The date of his marriage is unrecorded, though we know that his wife died in 1770. He had at least

Bureau inlaid with ivory and rare woods, made by Piffetti for the Palazzo Reale, Turin, probably in 1733 to a design by the Sicilian architect Filippo Juvarra.

two brothers. Francesco was some nineteen years younger than he and was working in Rome in 1752 when he addressed a letter to the King of Sardinia saying that as Pietro was prematurely aged and ill he wished to have the succession of his appointment. The other brother, Paolo, was something of a scapegrace, seems to have been an embarrassment to Pietro and even made an attempt on his life. A document of 1749 consigning him to prison in the castle of Ceva declared that despite repeated correction he had refused to reform the 'pessima condotta' of his life and was to be detained *ad correctionem* at Pietro's expense, until further notice.

Pietro Piffetti took up the appointment of royal *ebanista* in Turin at a very propitious moment. The city was prospering as never before. By playing off one great power against another in the War of the Grand Alliance and the War of the Spanish Succession, that nimble diplomat Vittorio Amadeo II, Duke of Savoy, enlarged and enriched his state and acquired by the Treaty of Utrecht in 1713 the Kingdom of Sicily, which he swapped seven years later for that of Sardinia. He had, indeed, raised a frontier buffer-state to the level of an important power – and he soon wished to provide himself with town and country residences of appropriately regal magnificence. In 1714 he invited the Sicilian Filippo Juvarra to Turin and made him royal architect. With astonishing rapidity Juvarra built both churches and palaces – notably the Veneria Reale, the Castello di Rivoli and Stupinigi outside the city and the Palazzo Madama within – supervising the details of their decoration and summoning notable artists from all parts of Italy to carry out his designs. Some drawings executed for the King between 1714 and 1720 reveal that he also sketched designs for carved console tables.

It seems likely that Juvarra was at least partly responsible for Piffetti's appointment as royal *ebanista*. In 1730 he had just begun to build a palace for the marchese d'Ormea who found Piffetti in Rome. Since 1722 a certain Luigi Prinotto had been working as cabinet maker for the Court in Turin, specializing in furniture inlaid with ivory and mother-of-pearl. He and Piffetti collaborated on the very elaborate *prie dieu* in the *gabinetto del pregadio della regina*, probably designed by Juvarra, in the Palazzo Reale, Turin. But the quality of Prinotto's work is markedly inferior to Piffetti's – and no more is heard of him after 1733.

Piffetti's first important work for the Crown is a bureau in the Queen's *gabinetto di toeletta* of the Palazzo Reale, delicately inlaid with ivory, mother-of-pearl and ebony and enriched with gilt bronze ornaments by

Steps inlaid with ivory and rare woods by Piffetti, with gilt bronze ornaments by Paolo Venasca, made for the Queen's toilet chamber in the Palazzo Reale, Turin, 1731–3.

Gilt bronze decorations by Francesco Ladatte on a cabinet made by Piffetti in the 1730s.

Occasional table decorated with inlays of ivory and rare woods made for Vittorio Amadeo III of Sardinia, *c.* 1750.

the Paris-trained sculptor Francesco Ladatte and rather simpler gilt bronze mounts by Paolo Venasca. A similarly decorated stool and a little flight of three steps were made *en suite*. It is tempting to attribute the design of this opulent confection to Juvarra, though it is no more Juvarresque than several of the pieces of furniture Piffetti made long after the architect had left Turin and died in Spain. There can, however, be no doubt of Juvarra's influence on Piffetti, whose works so perfectly fit in with the general decorative schemes of the Piedmontese palaces.

A very handsome bureau *à deux corps* is proudly and prominently inscribed on one of its many panels of ivory inlay: *Petrus Piffetti inve. fecit et sculpsit Taurini 1738.* And he must have been similarly responsible for both the design and execution of the many other pieces of furniture credited to him in the royal accounts. The elaborate patterns of band and leaf work with which they are adorned may owe something to the

Writing-table inlaid with rosewood, violet wood, palisander etc., c. 1760.

overleaf
left Side-table by Bernard II van Risen Burgh decorated with gilt bronze mounts, European japanning and Japanese lacquer, c. 1750–60.
right Writing-table by van Risen Burgh veneered with tulip-wood inlaid with mother-of-pearl, horn and various woods, c. 1750.

engraved ornament of Nicolas Pineau, though they are generally much richer and tighter. A delight in his own prodigious ability as a craftsman seems to have combined with a *horror vacui* to load every surface with busy decorations. The forms are hardly less exaggerated – all curves are corpulently *bombé*, legs scroll outwards in bold Ss, superstructures rise perilously high above their bases. It all has a fascinatingly obsessive, overwrought character, the product of a belief in display, whether of rich materials or virtuoso craftsmanship. One cannot help feeling that for Piffetti the art of cabinet making lay not in concealing but in revealing artistry. Several much more restrained pieces of furniture dating from the 1750s have been ascribed to him and suggest that he later began to adopt the easier manners of the Parisian *salon*. Yet these conventionally elegant tables and commodes come as an anti-climax after the strangely original and bizarre products of his earlier years.

Bernard II van Risen Burgh

(c. 1700–c. 1765)

When the statutes of the Parisian *Corporation des menuisiers-ébénistes* were revised between 1743 and 1751 a very old regulation, long out of use, was once again enforced and cabinet makers were obliged to mark their products with their names or initials. There were, of course, exceptions to every rule in *ancien régime* France – royal craftsmen were exempted, and furniture made by others for the Crown was rarely stamped. But the large majority of pieces of *ébénisterie* made in Paris in the second half of the eighteenth century bear in some inconspicuous place the name or initials of the maker, stamped with a metal punch or, on very delicate objects, written in ink. By insisting on the use of the *estampille*, the Corporation hoped to prevent unadmitted craftsmen from selling furniture. It was not regarded as a signature and was in fact applied not only to new pieces but also to those which had been restored by *maîtres-ébénistes*. *Estampilles* have however made it possible to establish the authorship of numerous pieces of furniture. Attention was first drawn to them in the late nineteenth century and most of them were soon associated with names of craftsmen which appeared in documentary records. But one maker, using as a stamp the initials B.V.R.B, found on many of the very finest pieces of Louis xv furniture, proved strangely elusive. He was clearly among the most talented *ébénistes* of his day and it seemed very surprising that the only trace of his name to survive should be these enigmatic letters. Collectors and students referred to him as 'Burb'. In 1957, however, a scholar discovered that the initials stood for Bernard van Risen Burgh – or Risamburgh or Risenburgh. It is not a name that slips easily off the French tongue and he seems usually to have been referred to in his own time as Bernard; nor is it a name that can easily be accommodated on an *estampille* – hence the use of initials.

This remarkable rococo craftsman should properly be called Bernard II van Risen Burgh, to distinguish him from his father, Bernard I, who was presumably of Dutch origin, settled in Paris towards the end of the seventeenth century, became a *maître ébéniste* in 1722 and died in 1738. Bernard II was probably born in about 1700, for he had become a *maître* before 1730. His earliest documented work is a commode made in 1737 for the *Cabinet de la reine* – Marie Lesczynska – at Fontainebleau and now in a French private collection. It is a strikingly handsome piece, decorated with lacquer panels set in frames of delicately twisting and turning gilt bronze rococo scrolls. Although the use of the *estampille* was not obligatory at this date, it is marked with the initials B.V.R.B. Significantly, it was supplied to the Queen through the *marchand-*

Lady's work-table, stamped with the initials 'B.V.R.B.'

mercier Hébert. Throughout his career Bernard II seems to have dealt with such middle-men rather than with individual clients – all his royal furniture was supplied through them.

The *marchands-merciers* appear to have been the *eminences grises* of eighteenth-century French taste – and one has the impression that few could have been grisier. Hébert was *marchand-mercier suivant le Cour* – holding, that is to say, a royal warrant like an English upholder to the King – and was one of the most famous with a shop in the precincts of Versailles, well placed to tempt courtiers with pretensions to taste. One of them wrote: 'I daren't look at Hébert's door, he sells me a thousand things in spite of myself, He has ruined many others with trifles. He does in France what the French do in America, gives gewgaws in exchange for gold ingots'. Bernard II also supplied Lazare Duvaux whose famous *Livre-Journal* or day-book contains numerous references to him. After Duvaux's death in 1758, Bernard II seems to have been extensively employed by Simon-Philippe Poirier, whose shop became one of the most fashionable in Paris, a constant source of temptation to the *élégants* and a magnet for the richer foreign tourists. Horace Walpole, writing to Anne Pitt from Paris in 1766, tells how he 'went to Poirier's and ordered him to bring me designs for commodes'. Such designs would almost certainly have been made by *ébénistes* such as Bernard II.

It is difficult now to disentangle the relationship between designers, furniture makers and *marchands-merciers* in eighteenth-century Paris. A study of Bernard II's work helps to throw some light upon it. There can be little doubt that he was responsible for the design of the pieces

Large marquetry writing-table, decorated with gilt bronze mounts.

Marquetry corner shelf, with veneers of tulip-wood and king-wood on an oak carcase.

he made. But there can be no doubt whatever that at this period, when the individual craftsman's delicacy of handling counted for so much, the final effect of a piece of furniture was due mainly to the *ébéniste* rather than the designer. Or perhaps one should say to the various craftsmen employed on it – for the bronze mounts were the work of *fondeurs,* the lacquer panels either imported from the Orient or painted by *vernisseurs*, and the marquetry panels made by *marqueteurs*, all of whom worked independently. Early in his career Bernard II used bronze mounts very similar to those employed by Jacques Dubois and probably obtained from the same *bronzier*. The art of the *ébéniste* lay in the skilful combination of elements made by different hands as much as in the actual construction of a piece of furniture. And in this Bernard II was unsurpassed if not unequalled. He was able to give to a piece of furniture an appearance of organic unity of form and decoration. A little console table in the Wrightsman collection, for example, looks almost as if it had been modelled by a sculptor in a single moment of inspiration, though it is, in fact, the work of several different craftsmen and the lacquer panel was painted in Japan and modified in Paris.

If the *marchands-merciers* had provided designs for the *ébénistes* we should expect to find two or more craftsmen executing almost identical works (in the same way that, at various periods, different silversmiths produced vessels of the same design). But the *estampilles* serve to emphasize the difference between the styles of the many *ébénistes* in Paris. The fact that so very few pieces of Louis XV case furniture are identical provides an argument against the use of prescribed designs, no less than an example of the taste for freedom of hand and individuality that was to be ruled out of court by neo-classical theorists. Yet, the *marchands-merciers*, acting as intermediaries between craftsmen and rich patrons, probably exerted some influence on design in general. As dealers in Orientalia, they perhaps encouraged the fashion for furniture decorated with Japanese lacquer – they may even have supplied *ébénistes* with lacquer panels. And it is more than likely that they were responsible for the rather less appealing practice of encrusting furniture with porcelain plaques. At any rate, Bernard II is the first *ébéniste* known to have used porcelain in this way. And Poirier, with whom he was so closely connected, enjoyed what Mr Watson has called 'something like a monopoly of purchasing such plaques for the decoration of furniture from the Sèvres factory'.

Bernard II worked within the general framework of the Louis XV style. And pieces of furniture by his contemporaries – notably Lhermite (his cousin), Feilt and Jacques Dubois – are sometimes remarkably close to his. Yet they generally lack not only his superb craftsmanship, but also the delicate sense of poise, effortless grace and an indefinable air of well-bred distinction. It is significant that in a portrait of 1758 Boucher depicted Mme de Pompadour sitting beside an elegant little writing-table which is clearly the work of Bernard II. And Boucher himself owned a *vuide poche* – a small table designed to receive the contents of the owner's pockets when he undressed – of rosewood and amaranth with marquetry flowers and gilt bronze mounts, made as his inventory declares by 'Bernard'. Even such a plain description summons to the mind the whole elegant, carefree, luxury-loving world of Louis XV which found its prince of court painters in Boucher and its *maître ébéniste* in Bernard II van Risen Burgh. It is hardly surprising to find that in Mme de Pompadour's bedroom at Bellevue the elegant gilt-bronze mounted bidet and the bedside table with a Sarrancolin marble shelf to hold the *vase de nuit* were almost certainly made by him. In this society even the humblest functions of the body could be attended with a certain grace.

Bernard II died between 1765 and 1767. For some years he had been assisted by his son, Bernard III, who appears to have carried on the workshop for a while, probably still using the B.V.R.B stamp. It has been suggested that he was responsible for the bronze mounts on Bernard II's later furniture and that he finally worked as a sculptor for *fondeurs-doreurs*. He never became a *maître*. Having survived the Revolution he died in 1799.

Commode decorated with Japanese lacquer and gilt bronze mounts.

William Vile and John Cobb

(*c.* 1700–1767 and *c.* 1710–1778)

Vile and Cobb are among the several excellent mid-Georgian cabinet makers who were for long overshadowed by the fame of Chippendale, partly because they issued no pattern book. Documented pieces of furniture reveal that their workshops maintained a standard of craftsmanship seldom equalled in England, even if they were stylistically unadventurous. The earliest works ascribed to Vile are in a somewhat muted late Baroque manner which fitted them perfectly for the interior of the neo-Palladian country house; those made in collaboration with Cobb in the early 1760s are in a tamed, solidified and strongly anglicized version of the rococo; while Cobb's furniture of the 1770s is in an elegant Adamesque style, with charmingly delicate marquetry decorations.

William Vile, the elder partner, appears to have hailed from the West Country. Nothing is known of his early years though a writing-table of about 1730 now at Chatsworth and commode made for Sir Hugh Smithson in 1739 and now at Alnwick Castle have been attributed to him. He may also have made a very handsome pair of commodes for Goodwood in about 1750. By 1750 he was in partnership with John Cobb and in 1761 he was appointed cabinet maker to the Royal household. He retired in 1765 and died in 1767. In his will, where he described himself as 'Cabinet maker and upholder', he revealed his prosperity, for in addition to making small bequests to kinsmen in Somerset and Dorset, he was able to leave his widow 'two houses now in my possession situate at Battersea Hill' and the household furniture in 'my houses both in town and country'.

Also in his will, Vile remarked that he had been 'engaged with my co-partner John Cobb in very extensive branches of trade'. Some indication of their extent can be gathered from documents recording their work for the Hon. John Damer at Came House, Dorset, between 1756 and 1762. They supplied a fair amount of furniture including a sofa (£8. 8s.), ten mahogany chairs 'with carv'd feet, stuft and cover'd with damask and finished compleat with Burnish Nails' (£24), an armchair, '2 wrot Brass gerendoles neatly lacquered' (£11) and even 'a mahog.y Cheese Board made to Turn Round' (£1. 1s.) and a 'mahogany Tea Board cut out of the solid' (12s. 6d.). But there are also entries for 'making drawings for the Library ceiling and Bookcase', and for 'a gilder's time 26 weeks, 3 days in the country, gilding and painting a room'. And Vile charged for his post-chaise and expenses, presumably for visiting Came. Another set of accounts, of 1758, for Sir Charles Hanbury Williams' London house, amounts to £437. 14s. 6d., covering

One of the chairs supplied by Vile and Cobb for the Hon. John Damer of Came House, Dorset, between 1756 and 1762.

opposite Jewel cabinet of mahogany inlaid with ivory and various woods, made by Vile and Cobb for Queen Charlotte in 1761.

upholstery and the papering of rooms as well as furniture, both elaborate and simple and inexpensive. It is clear that Vile and Cobb were interior decorators as well as furniture makers.

The finest pieces of Vile and Cobb furniture are those made for the Crown. They appear to have worked for George III before he came to the throne, also for his mother. But the most interesting of their royal works were those executed for the young Queen Charlotte, who was married to George III in 1761. They include the outstanding small cabinet described in their invoice as 'a very handsome jewel cabinet, made of many different kinds of fine wood on a mohog.y fframe richly carved, the ffront, ends and top inlaid with ivory in compartments neatly Ingraved, the top to lift up and two drawers, the drawers all lined with black velvet (for the queen's apartment, St. James's) ... £13. 10s.'. Another piece made for the Queen is a secrétaire, rather tall and with a curiously squat bulbous base. The design is somewhat unusual for England but curiously similar to German pieces of the same period – perhaps it was constructed in this form to help to assuage the Queen's home-sickness for Mecklenburg-Strelitz. But most of Vile and Cobb's royal furniture – like the Corinthian break-front bookcase now at Buckingham Palace – is at least as true-born British as George III liked to think he was. In the household accounts the name of Vile appears

Sofa supplied with the chair on page 108 by Messrs Vile and Cobb for Came House, Dorset.

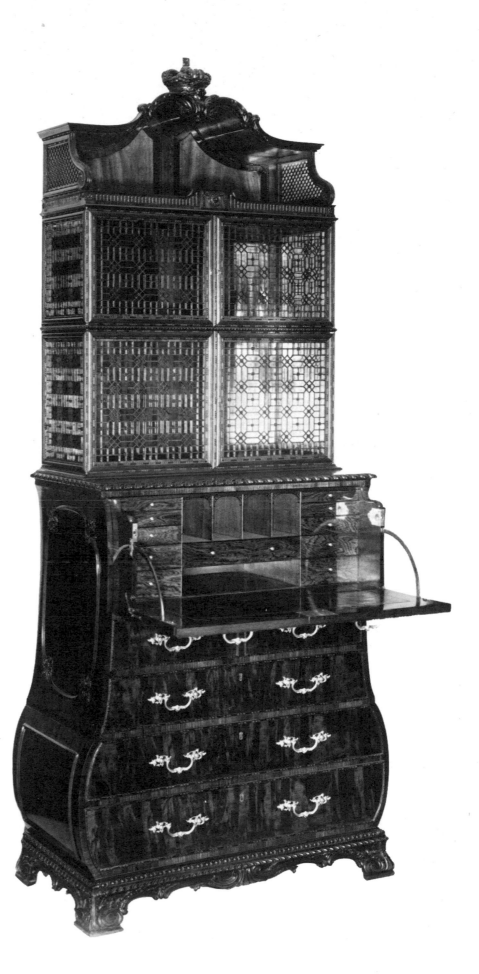

Mahogany secrétaire made by
Vile for George III's consort
Queen Charlotte, in 1761, now at
Buckingham Palace. The crown
on top is a later addition.

alone as a cabinet maker – Cobb as an upholsterer. After Vile's retirement the post of cabinet maker to the royal household went to his former assistant John Bradburn. But it is known, from another source, that Cobb had been employed at the palace.

For John Cobb emerges from the mist surrounding most cabinet makers in a sudden flash of light. There is a vivid sketch of him in *Nollekens and his Times* by J.T. Smith, who records that George III 'frequently employed him, and often smiled at his pomposity. One day, when Mr Cobb was in his Majesty's library at Buckingham-house, giving orders to a workman, whose ladder was placed before a book which the king wanted, his Majesty desired Cobb to hand him the work, which instead of obeying, he called to his man, "Fellow, give me that book!" The King, with his usual condescension arose, and asked Cobb, what his man's name was. "Jenkins," answered the astonished Upholsterer. "Then," observed the King, "Jenkins, you shall hand me the book."' Smith was told this story by a Mr Banks, a cellaret maker occasionally employed by Cobb who, he said, 'was perhaps one of the proudest men in England; and always appeared in full dress of the most superb and costly kind, in which state he would strut through his workshops, giving orders to his men'. He also credited Cobb with bringing into fashion 'that very convenient table...that draws out in front with upper and inward rising desks, so healthy to those who stand to write, read or draw.' Indeed, Nathaniel Dance Holland agreed to paint Cobb's portrait in exchange for one of these tables – and after the portrait 'had remained in Cobb's showroom for some time, purposely

Chest of drawers supplied to James West of Alscot Park, Warwickshire, in 1766, by Cobb who described it as an 'extra fine wood Commode chest of drawers with large Handsome wrought furniture, good brass locks, etc. £16'.

to be serviceable, as he said, to the "*poor painter*", he conveyed [it] in his own carriage, to his seat at Highgate'. One is reminded of fashionable interior decorators of more recent days.

Some confirmation of Smith's stories is provided by Cobb's wills. A will he made in 1774 reveals that he owned a house in the fashionable suburb of Highgate, houses in St Martin's Lane, where his workshop was, and a house at Islington, besides 'a fortune amounting to upwards of £12,000 which I have on the 3 per cent funds'. When he made his second will, in 1776 – two years before his death – that fortune had grown to £22,000 of 3% stock, the greater part of which he left in trust for 'the infant boy William Cobb, grandson of William Cobb of Norfolk' (perhaps a nephew or great-nephew). 'Let it be noticed that the principal twenty thousand pounds stock is never to be broke into,' he added, 'my intent being that there should always be the interest aforesaid to support the name of Cobb as a private gentleman.'

Although the prices charged for furniture by Vile and Cobb were thought to be high, they were far below those of their leading contemporaries in Paris. Nevertheless, they and other English cabinet makers seem often to have accrued much greater fortunes and, when successful, to have acquired rather higher social status. It seems likely that this was mainly because they were unhampered by guild restrictions and were thus enabled to act as dealers and entrepreneurs as well as furniture makers. The work executed by Vile and Cobb for Came House would in France have had to be executed by *maîtres* of five different *Corporations*.

Marquetry commode with gilt bronze mounts supplied by Cobb in 1772 for Mr Paul Methuen of Corsham House, Wiltshire.

Johann Michael Hoppenhaupt

(1709–*c.* 1755)

Engraved design for the decoration of a room, probably in Berlin, 1751–5.

Johann Michael Hoppenhaupt was one of several artists and craftsmen who arrived in Berlin on Frederick the Great's accession to the Prussian throne in 1740. Since the death of Frederick I (Dagly's patron), the arts had been left to languish in Prussia. As Frederick II himself was later to remark about his father's reign, 'The young noblemen who were dedicated to arms, believed themselves misled by studying, regarding ignorance as a title of merit and knowledge as absurd pedantry. For the same reason the liberal arts fell into decadence: the Academy of Painters ceased to function. . . .' The culturally francophile Frederick, with his taste for philosophy, poetry, music and the visual arts, lost little time in transforming his dowdy palaces into models of frenchified elegance to which he could retreat in the intervals between his battles. For the King's curiously fascinating character combined a love of the arts with a genius for warfare. 'Potsdam is Sparta and Athens joined in one; nothing but reviewing and poetry day by day,' wrote Voltaire shortly after his arrival in 1751, 'a Camp of Mars and the Garden of Epicurus; trumpets and violins, War and Philosophy.' But the combination was not always a happy one. Many artists and craftsmen were to discover to their cost that Frederick was no less exigent as a patron than as a general.

In 1740 the *genre pittoresque* – the culminating phase of the rococo – was at the height of its popularity in France; and it was in this style that Frederick wished to have his palaces decorated. Since his youth he had been closely associated with Georg Wenzeslaus von Knobelsdorff, who became his chief architect. But interior decorations were entrusted to a sculptor, Johann August Nahl, who had travelled extensively and picked up the French rococo style (he had, indeed, become a naturalized Frenchman). It was under Nahl that Hoppenhaupt began to work in Prussia as a woodcarver. Hoppenhaupt's background was, however, entirely German. He was born at Merseburg in 1709, trained in Dresden and Vienna and appears to have led a wandering life until he settled in Berlin. In 1746, when Frederick quarrelled with Knobelsdorff and Nahl found it prudent to leave Berlin, Hoppenhaupt was appointed 'Directeur des ornements' in the place of the latter. He thus became responsible for carrying on the interior decorations in the Berlin Schloss (where he had already executed Frederick's writing room), at Sans Souci, where his major achievement was the music room, and in the Potsdam Stadtschloss. But for reasons which are unrecorded – though they may only too easily be guessed – he retired from the royal service in 1750 and returned to Merseburg. His designs, engraved by J. W. Miel, were published in parts between 1751 and 1755. The date of his death is not known. He had a brother who was also a woodcarver and with whom he is often confused, Johann Christian, who continued to work in Prussia, was employed on the interiors of the Neues Palais at Potsdam between 1763 and 1766, and survived into the 1770s.

Hoppenhaupt's are among the most accomplished German rococo furniture designs. Stylistically they derive from the designs of Cuvilliés, which began to appear in 1738, though they are farther removed from French rococo work and still more engagingly fantastic. They include chimney-pieces, sedan chairs of a dashing elegance, even tombs, as well

Design for a chest-of-drawers, 1751–5.

as bombé commodes, clock-cases, chandeliers, console tables with little *putto* heads peeping out of shells, sprays of nodding roses, and little musicians, Chinamen and exotic birds perching insecurely on their tossing waves of scroll work. With their tiny feet these pieces of furniture have a feather-weight buoyancy, a tip-toe sprightliness, as if they were waiting to dance to the tinkle of a *Glockenspiel*.

Such delicate works of fantasy have never enjoyed a good critical press. They are so obviously lacking in seriousness, so very unclassical, so manifestly unpractical. Eighteenth-century comments on the rococo are monotonously abusive. But it is refreshing to find in a book of 1747 by Johann Georg Fünck an appreciation of Nahl which helps us to see

left Design for a pier glass and table, 1751–5.

right Design for a chest-of-drawers, 1751–5.

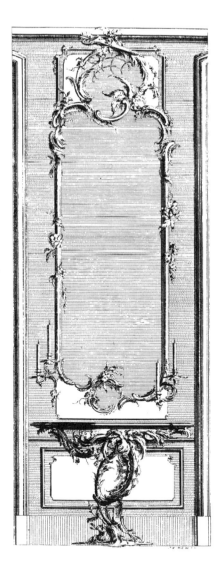

how rococo decorations appealed to sympathetic contemporaries. Nahl's decoration, he writes, 'always retained a natural impetus and inflexion, so that each part seemed to follow the other easily; like the muscles of the human body, one side stretched up when the other was drawn in...' But one may wonder whether Fünck was not striking at Hoppenhaupt, as Nahl's successor, when he goes on to remark that 'instead of wild and shapeless conch shells, Nahl used for his ornament natural foliage and other things wisely selected from nature'. For while Hoppenhaupt had also striven after naturally graceful poise, he had delighted in the use of strangely shaped shells and leaves, breaking delicately out of the surface of his designs.

Design for a side-table, published 1751–5. Designs such as this probably influenced such English designers as Chippendale, Johnson and Matthias Lock.

It may be doubted if any furniture was executed precisely according to Hoppenhaupt's designs. The charm of rococo furniture rests mainly on the spontaneity of its carved decorations and very little appears to have been copied from designs or prints. But console tables and mirror frames and commodes made in mid-eighteenth-century Berlin do often show similarities with his published works. Some of them may, indeed, have been made by him or his brother. And the designs themselves clearly had some influence on other designers, notably Haberman in Augsburg and, perhaps, the most delicately fantastic of English rococo designers, Thomas Johnson.

left Design for a long-case clock published 1751–5.

right Design for a console table published 1751–5.

Thomas Johnson

(1714–c. 1778)

A girandole in the form of a Roman fountain crumbling in pleasing decay with a love-lorn shepherd loitering beside the basin into which the water trickles and, high above, a Chinese phoenix or hoho bird perching on a tree that has rooted itself in the masonry – another like a whimsically asymmetrical, fragilely delicate Chinese fishing pavilion, with a little Chinaman, rod in hand, gazing down from the parapet – a candle-stand apparently made out of a jet of water around which two dolphins entwine themselves – a console table supported on a tree, with a cat sitting on a branch and watching Æsop's fox attacked by a dog on the ground – a mirror frame with another of Æsop's foxes looking up at a group of *putti* harvesting grapes from the vines that have tangled themselves around columns and arches of cobwebby slenderness. Everywhere there are nervous restless curves, sometimes like splashes of water, sometimes like leaves or the branches of gnarled trees – wayward, delicate, insubstantial. Such are the engravings which make up the *Collection of designs* published in London in 1758 by Thomas Johnson. In no other work did the wayward blossoms of the rococo flower with such luxuriance on cold British soil.

Although the rococo was in origin a French style, Johnson was at pains to demonstrate that he was no francophile. He dedicated his work to Lord Blakeney, 'President of the Laudable Association of Antigallicans'. And in the pompous epistle with which he so incongruously prefaced his collection of thistledown fantasies he declared: 'Your Lordships well known Attachment to the Liberty and Welfare of Your Country has been Sufficiently manifested in that Spirit & Vigour with which you have so often distinguish'd yourself in its Favour. It is therefore impossible for anyone to dispute your Patronage especially when what is here addresst to you is the Production of an Englishman one who professes a truly Anti-gallic Spirit & under that Sanction presumes to lay this Work before your Lordship'. Lord Blakeney was the General who in 1756 had gallantly but unsuccessfully attempted to defend Minorca from the French, with whom England was at war. But the Anti-Gallican association of which he was president had been founded in 1745 long before the war, to 'oppose the insidious arts of the French nation' and 'to promote British manufactures, to extend the commerce of England and discourage the introduction of French modes and oppose the importation of French commodities'. Johnson may well have been carrying on a private war with French taste by opposing the use of *papier mâché* instead of carved woodwork in the decoration of

opposite
left Engraved design for a candle-stand published in 1758.

right One of a pair of carved and painted wood candle-stands made for Hagley Hall, Worcestershire and attributed to Thomas Johnson, *c.* 1760.

Plate. 51

T Johnson inv del

Publish'd according to Act of Parliament 1757

B Clowes sculp

furniture (he proudly styled himself 'Carver'). He may even have thought he was fighting against the new anti-rococo *à la grecque* style of furniture which had begun to emerge in France in the 1750s. But there is a certain irony in his anti-gallicism. For in England as, to a still larger extent, in Germany, francophobia was soon to play a part in the nascent neo-classical movement which quickly banished his and other rococo fantasies to the lumber-room, if not to the bonfire.

Thomas Johnson was born in London in 1714 and appears to have established himself as an independent craftsman by the later 1740s. Rating books record his growing prosperity as he moved from small to larger premises. In 1755 he produced his first set of designs, *Twelve Gerandoles*, a modest publication printed on four sheets and sold for 2s. This seems to have met with some success despite the number of books of rococo furniture designs which had appeared in recent years (Delacour's *First Book of Ornament* of 1741; the several publications of Matthias Lock; Copland's *New Book of Ornaments* of 1746; the Copland and Lock, *New Book of Ornaments* of 1752; M. Darly's and Edwards's

Design for a side-table published in 1758. The group of figures representing Aesop's fable of the bear and the travellers is inspired by Francis Barlow's illustrations to a translation of Aesop published in 1687 – a work curiously popular with English rococo designers.

opposite Design for five girandoles published in 1758.

T Johnson inv.ᵗ delᵗ   B Clowes sculp

Publishd by Act of Parliament

above left Engraved design for a kettle-stand published in 1758.

above right Looking-glass in carved wood frame attributed to Johnson, *c.* 1760.

opposite Design for a looking-glass, 1758; the figures represent Aesop's fable of the fox and the grapes.

A New Book of Chinese Designs of 1754 and, most notably, Chippendale's *Director*, also of 1754). Johnson followed up his set of girandoles with the *Collection of Designs* which appeared in monthly instalments from 1756 to 1758 when they were gathered together in book form. In 1760 he issued *A New Book of Ornaments* (from which only one plate survives, though a further seven are known from nineteenth-century reproductions), and in 1762 he re-issued his 1758 collection, which had sold out, as *One Hundred and Fifty New Designs*. Johnson's business must have continued to grow and to have justified his renting additional premises, but in 1768 he gave up one of his workshops. He maintained another until 1778 when his name is mentioned for the last time.

THOMAS JOHNSON

Engraved designs for a bracket
published in 1750.

Girandole of mahogany and deal
painted and gilt, made for Hagley Hall,
c. 1755, and clearly inspired by
Johnson's designs if not in fact
made by him.

All the furnishings for which Johnson published designs are of a type
known at the time as 'carvers' pieces'. They include no case- or seat-
furniture and are limited to such objects as girandoles, mirror frames,
side- or console-tables, candle-stands – all pieces which were decorative
rather than useful and allowed scope for the display of the carver's
fantasy. Stylistically they owe much to France – perhaps more than the
anti-gallican would have cared to admit – yet they could hardly be
mistaken for French work. It is not merely that many designs incorporate
figures of animals lifted bodily from a source as eminently British as
Francis Barlow's illustrations to Æsop (of 1687). But they lack the
elegant and polished fluency, the graceful self-assured poise of the best
French designs of the period. Their jagged outlines are restlessly nervous;
curved forms clash against, rather than run smoothly into, one another;
figures, even Chinamen, comport themselves with a somewhat gauche
rusticity, as if shy of stepping into the world of high fashion.

The intricacy of these designs is such that more than one writer has
doubted if any could be realized in wood. But researchers of recent years
have found quite a number of pieces of furniture which correspond
closely with the engravings in Johnson's publications. It is, however,
difficult to determine whether all, or indeed any, of them were in fact
carved by Johnson or in his workshops. His designs were, after all,
available for anyone to copy. In the preface to his *Collection of Designs*
Johnson himself remarked: 'Tho' these Designs were meant as Assistants
to young Artists, yet I hope I shall not incur the Censure of any superior
Genius, by declaring them of Use to All: And when honoured by the
Hand of the skillful Workman, that shall think proper to put them in
Execution, I flatter myself they will give entire Satisfaction'. And he
concluded the preface with the words: 'The Designs in this Collection,
tho' upwards of 150, may be all performed by a Master of his Art: This
I again assert with greater Confidence, as I am well satisfied they can be
executed by Myself'.

It is interesting to note that, unlike Chippendale's *Director*, which
appears to have been intended mainly to establish his reputation among
rich patrons, Johnson's works seem to have been addressed primarily
to furniture makers. It may also be significant that no bill of his has ever
been found. The most recent writer on Johnson has thus suggested that
he worked – again unlike Chippendale – not for private patrons but for
the firms of upholsterers who supplied them with wallpapers, fabrics
and other things as well as furniture. Although the evidence is mainly
negative, this seems more than probable.

Thomas Chippendale
(1718–1779)

J. T. Smith, writing of St Martin's Lane in 1828, remarked that 'the extensive premises, No. 60... were formerly held by Chippendale, the most famous Upholsterer and Cabinet-maker of his day, to whose folio work on household-furniture the trade formerly made constant reference'. The book contained, he said, specimens of the style 'in vogue in France in the reign of Louis XIV (*sic*) but which for many years past, has been discontinued in England. However, as most fashions come round again, I should not wonder, notwithstanding the beautifully classic change brought in by Thomas Hope Esq. if we were to see the unmeaning scroll and shellwork, with which the furniture of Louis's reign was so profusely incumbered, revive; when Chippendale's book will again be sought after with redoubled avidity, and, as many of the copies must have been sold as waste paper, the few remaining will probably bear rather a high price'. Seldom has a prophecy, spoken perhaps in jest, been so completely fulfilled. Shell and scroll work was well on the way to a return to fashion before Smith died. By the end of the century Chippendale was commonly regarded as the greatest of all English furniture makers and the various editions of his *Director* had become collectors' items.

A hundred years after Smith wrote another reaction set in – not against the style in which he worked but against his claim to pre-eminence. Two American scholars investigated the sources of the Chippendale style and declared him to have been little more than an enterprising gatherer of other men's flowers. And although this sweeping condemnation has since been shown to be unproven, if not wholly incorrect, Chippendale can no longer be regarded as the only important mid-eighteenth-century English furniture designer – a giant towering above pigmies. As a furniture maker his reputation has also suffered and he is now thought to have been no superior in craftsmanship to several contemporaries, notably William Vile, Pierre Langlois or the mysterious John Channon. Thomas Chippendale remains, nonetheless, one of the most interesting, if also most perplexing, figures in the history of English furniture.

He was born at Otley in Yorkshire in 1718, his father being a joiner and his grandfather a carpenter. He was established in London by 1748 when he married. After living in Conduit Street, Long Acre and Somerset Court off the Strand, he settled in 1753 in St Martin's Lane which had become a centre for both artists and members of the furniture trade. Next year he published the first edition of his *Gentleman and Cabinet-*

opposite Japanned bed probably made by Thomas Chippendale for Badminton House, Gloucestershire, *c.* 1750–4.

128

opposite top Engraved design for a sofa, 1760, included in the enlarged third edition of Chippendale's *Gentleman and Cabinet-Maker's Director*, 1762.

opposite bottom Design for a commode and candle-stands, 1761.

Mahogany chest of drawers made for Raynham Hall, Norfolk, probably by Chippendale, *c*. 1755.

maker's Director, prefaced by a list of subscribers who included no fewer than five dukes. Its success must have been immediate for it was reprinted without alteration in the following year. In 1759 he began to bring out the third and considerably enlarged edition in weekly serial parts, completing it in 1762. In the meantime he had gone into partnership with James Rannie, a businessman who appears to have been an upholsterer. Rannie died in 1766 and five years later Chippendale found another partner in Rannie's former clerk, Thomas Haig. During Chippendale's frequent visits to clients at their country seats, Haig seems to have supervised affairs in London. Unfortunately little is known about the craftsmen they employed. In the account of the destruction by fire of a Chippendale workshop in 1755 there is mention of 'the chests of 22 workmen' – but to judge from the quantity of furniture which the firm is known to have produced this can hardly have been the only workshop. Even so, the enterprise seems never to have

A Design for a Commode Table   N.º LXXI.

wᵗʰ two different Designs for Candle Stands.

T. Chippendale inᵗ et delin.   Publish'd according to Act of Parliamᵗ 1761.   Wᵐ Foster Sculp.

been as extensive as that of George Seddon who was employing four hundred journeymen in 1788.

The range of Chippendale's activity was wide. In addition to making the fine pieces of furniture for which he is famous, his workshops turned out considerable quantities of well-made but very simple and correspondingly inexpensive objects. And, like Vile and Cobb, he worked also as an upholsterer and general household furnisher. He is even known to have imported unfinished French furniture in 1769. The bill he rendered in 1774 for furnishings supplied to Ninian Home at Paxton House, refers to '13 pieces of fine blue stripe and sprig paper and one piece of border for a blue bed chamber', '91 yards of fine Wilton carpet', 'a fine bordered bed, tick, bolster, wax and filled with the finest Hudsons Bay feathers', blankets, 'fine chintz paper...the pattern made on purpose to match the cotton', '12 glass soap cups' and even 'four spare close stool pans'. The carved wood furniture he supplied for this house was all fairly simple and modestly priced. For a pair of elegant candlestands he charged £3. 6s., for a mahogany chest of drawers £6. 16s. 4d., for a somewhat austere writing-table £3. 8s. 0d., for a bedside commode £2. 12s. 6d., for a large wardrobe twelve guineas, for a fairly elaborate shaving-table seven guineas, and for a pair of hanging bookshelves with pretty latticed sides only 15s. It seems probable that lavishly decorated pieces of furniture like the magnificent library table he supplied to Nostell in 1767 for £72. 10s., and the commode with marquetry and bronze mounts made for the same house in 1770, costing £40, were somewhat exceptional.

Several of the pieces of furniture he made for Paxton correspond closely with designs published in the *Director* more than a decade earlier. But there are surprisingly few others pieces that both correspond with those designs and can with certainty be traced to Chippendale's workshop. For the *Director* is not so much a record of the furniture he had designed and produced as a catalogue of what he could supply. The two main editions are of permanent interest because they illustrate the types of furniture in use and the styles favoured (rococo, chinoiserie, Gothic revival) in England in 1754 and 1762. Whether Chippendale drew or even sketched the designs himself, or employed other artists, is a matter of merely academic importance – for none is of outstanding originality and many may well have looked rather old-fashioned when the book came out. Furniture of the type now called 'Chinese Chippendale' had certainly been made by other craftsmen, like William Linnell, several years before the *Director* was published. And several designs for carvers'

Design for 'China Shelves' in the Chinese taste, 1761.

pieces are bare-faced plagiarisms of Thomas Johnson.

The main purpose of the *Director* seems to have been to establish Chippendale's reputation, which it undoubtedly did. And it is significant that many of his finest works postdate its publication. Some are in the rococo style of the *Director* – most notably a handsome bookcase at Wilton. But the majority are in the refined antique-revival style introduced into England by Robert Adam and others in the later 1750s and 1760s. And here we encounter another problem that bedevils the study of Chippendale. Who designed these pieces of furniture? Can the artist responsible for the exuberant rococo fantasies published in the 1762 edition of the *Director* be credited also with the elegantly chaste and learnedly correct furniture made by the firm in about 1770?

It used to be assumed that Robert Adam himself supplied Chippendale with designs. But, as recent writers have shown, there is no evidence for this – rather the reverse. Although Chippendale supplied furniture for several houses with interiors by the Adam brothers – Harewood, Mersham le Hatch, Nostell Priory – he dealt directly with the owners. The Nostell accounts provide what is, perhaps, the key to the situation. For here some furniture is known, from drawings, to have been designed by the Adams, while Chippendale's bills reveal that he provided other pieces. The Adam designs are for a picture-frame and side-tables intimately related with the architectural decorations of the rooms; while Chippendale's furniture comprises such movable objects as chairs, tables, commodes and a barometer. Adam may well have seen and commented on Chippendale's designs (this is no more than a hypothesis). But when Adam designed furniture himself he seems invariably to have commissioned its execution and charged the client on his bill. Chippendale was, however, able to produce furniture which harmon-

Writing-table supplied by Chippendale for Paxton House in 1774 for the price of £3. 8s. Though better known for its more elaborate productions, the Chippendale workshop was largely occupied in making simple mahogany furniture of this type.

ized beautifully with Adam's interiors, though individual pieces may usually be distinguished from those actually designed by Adam on stylistic as well as documentary grounds. Chippendale's furniture tends to show off the craftsman's ability in carved work or marquetry: while in Adam's the general architectural design is of paramount importance.

Who then designed Chippendale's Adamesque furniture? He is likely to have employed designers as highly skilled as his *marqueteurs*, carvers and joiners. Yet one may wonder if this designer was not in fact his own son, also called Thomas, who was born in 1749 and was thus twenty years old at about the time when the Chippendale firm began to renounce the ebullient rococo style of the *Director*. He appears to have been trained as an artist rather than a furniture maker, and he exhibited five pictures at the Royal Academy between 1784 and 1801. George Smith (in 1826) referred to his 'very great degree of taste, with great ability as a draughtsman and designer'. This is borne out by a slender series of *Sketches for Ornament* which he published in 1779

Library table supplied by Chippendale for Harewood House, Yorkshire, c. 1770.

proudly declaring: 'T. Chippendale pint. invt. et ex.'.

When the elder Chippendale died in 1779 the firm was carried on by his son in partnership with Thomas Haig. There is a strong sense of continuity in the style of furniture produced and some side-tables made for Harewood House in 1796 could be – and, indeed, have been – mistaken for work of the 1770s. But furniture made for Sir Richard Colt Hoare, at Stourhead, and Charles Hoare, at Luscombe, reflect the growing neo-classical demand for greater simplicity and solidity. Some of the pieces made for Luscombe between 1796 and 1804 – notably some Grecian stools – reveal also the new desire for furniture modelled on antique prototypes.

Thomas Haig retired in 1796 drawing up a will leaving £1,000 to 'his very old friend and late partner, Thomas Chippendale'. But Chippendale was almost immediately faced with embarrassments (perhaps Haig had provided the financial brains of the firm). In 1802 Haig added a codicil to his will, withdrawing the legacy and instructing his executors to recover the money which he had invested in the concern and which Chippendale had not repaid. He died in the following year and in 1804 Chippendale was declared a bankrupt. His entire stock was sold by auction. But he seems to have recovered from this setback and to have continued to work as an 'upholsterer and undertaker' until his death in 1822.

Marquetry dressing commode supplied by Chippendale for Harewood House, Yorkshire, in 1773; it seems probable that the younger Thomas Chippendale was responsible for the design of this and other pieces of furniture in the Adam style.

Jean-François Oeben

(c. 1720–1763)

Chest-of-drawers of a type known as a 'table à la Bourgogne', provided with several mechanical devices, c. 1760.

opposite Secrétaire attributed to Oeben, c. 1760. For much of his career Oeben was not obliged to stamp his products, and as a result the authorship of many pieces attributed to him may be contested.

In the Wernher Collection at Luton Hoo there is a very remarkable piece of furniture known as a *table à la Bourgogne*. At first sight it looks like an elegant small chest of six drawers, decorated on front and sides with parquetry and discreetly mounted in gilt bronze. But when a handle is placed in a hole at one side and turned, a little bookcase slowly rises from the top. At either side of the base of this bookcase there are levers, and when these are pulled its apparently solid flanks revolve to disclose semicircular recesses, each fitted with two shelves, holding a glass tumbler, a porcelain pomade pot, a set of knives and forks. What appears to be the fronts of two upper drawers is in fact a single flap which can be drawn down to serve as a writing platform (the interior of this recess was probably fitted with pigeon-holes, but this part of the piece has been altered). The drawer beneath this is, surprisingly enough, no more than a drawer. But the next one down has a solid top which cannot be opened until the whole drawer has been taken out of the case – the top can then be slid back to reveal compartments for pens, ink and papers; if the handles are then pressed together four little legs spring down to transform it into a writing-table for use in bed. This masterpiece of ingenuity is the work of Jean-François Oeben and corresponds closely with a table described in some detail in the inventory of his possessions drawn up on his death in 1763, when it was valued at 260 livres. Two similar *tables à la Bourgogne* are known, one recently acquired by the Louvre which has a bottom 'drawer' which when pulled out serves as a velvet-padded kneeler and converts the piece into a *prie dieu*.

Mechanical gadgets such as those in *tables à la Bourgogne* had, since the sixteenth century, been a speciality of German craftsmen – it was, of course, in Germany that the making of clocks and automata had been most highly developed. And Oeben was one of several German cabinet makers attracted to eighteenth-century Paris as the capital of taste and patronage. He was born in about 1720, the son of a post-master at Ebern in southern Franconia. He settled in Paris in the 1740s just at the moment when the *Corporation des menuisiers-ébénistes* was revising its statutes, partly with the aim of excluding competition from immigrant craftsmen. In 1749 he married the sister of an *ébéniste* of Flemish extraction, Roger Vandercruse, generally known as Roger Lacroix, who became a *maître* in 1755. Oeben was able to avoid trouble with the *Corporation* by joining the privileged workshop of Charles-Joseph Boulle – the youngest surviving son of André-Charles – from whom he rented rooms in the Galerie du Louvre. The patronage of Mme de Pompadour helped to

The marquetry top of a table with gilt bronze mounts attributed to Oeben, *c.* 1760.

opposite Marquetry secrétaire, *c.* 1760. Oeben's workshop produced some of the finest marquetry made in mid-eighteenth-century France.

establish him, and after C.-J. Boulle's death in 1754 he was appointed *ébéniste du Roi* and granted apartments in the Gobelins where, once again, he was outside the jurisdiction of the *Corporation*. This freedom from guild regulations was most important since it allowed him to work as both an *ébéniste* and a *mécanicien*. In 1761, however, he yielded to pressure from the *Corporation* and became a *maître ébéniste*, though without renouncing the rights of his privileged position as a royal warrant holder. He was much patronized and charged very high prices for his products yet died bankrupt.

In addition to mechanical pieces, Oeben produced furniture decorated with very elaborate marquetry – another speciality of German craftsmen since the sixteenth century. At first he favoured realistically rendered baskets of flowers – jonquils and tulips and carnations of a delightfully wayward naturalism – framed with interlaced ribbons. Sometimes the marquetry is executed with such virtuosity as to give a *trompe l'oeil* effect. By the early 1760s the attacks of high-minded neo-classical theorists were beginning to drive such elegant fantasies out of fashion,

Marquetry secrétaire made for Louis xv, begun by Oeben in 1760 and completed by J.-H. Riesener, 1769.

and although he continued to make use of pictorial marquetry until his death, he slightly modified his style, smoothing out the bolder rococo curves and decorating his furniture with geometrical patterns of inlay.

His marquetry is still more delicately executed than appears at first sight – the outer edges of the panels usually having two or more very slender strings of contrasting ebony and box-wood. Paying meticulous attention to every detail of construction, he was perhaps the first *ébéniste* to attempt to conceal the heads of screws which fasten the bronze mounts to the carcase, hiding them behind foliated motifs. There is reason to suppose that he may also on occasion have had mounts cast with bolts on the inner side, so that they could be fixed through the thickness of the wood with nuts on the inner side.

Oeben is of importance as the master of a workshop no less than as a practitioner. Both Leleu and Riesener were trained under him. He also occupies a notable place in the family network of Parisian *ébénistes*, both by his relationship with Vandercruse and by his sister's marriage to Martin Carlin (another German immigrant). After his death his widow married Riesener who maintained the *atelier* using Oeben's *estampille* for several years. It is worth adding that one of his daughters was the mother of the great Eugène Delacroix (though whether her husband, Charles Delacroix, was the painter's real father remains something of a mystery).

At the time of his death in 1763 Oeben was working on one of the most elaborate of all pieces of eighteenth-century furniture – the *bureau du Roi* (now in the Louvre) which he had been commissioned to make in 1760. It was completed in 1769 by Riesener, whose signature it bears and who began his independent career with some handsome writing-desks which are only slightly less elaborate.

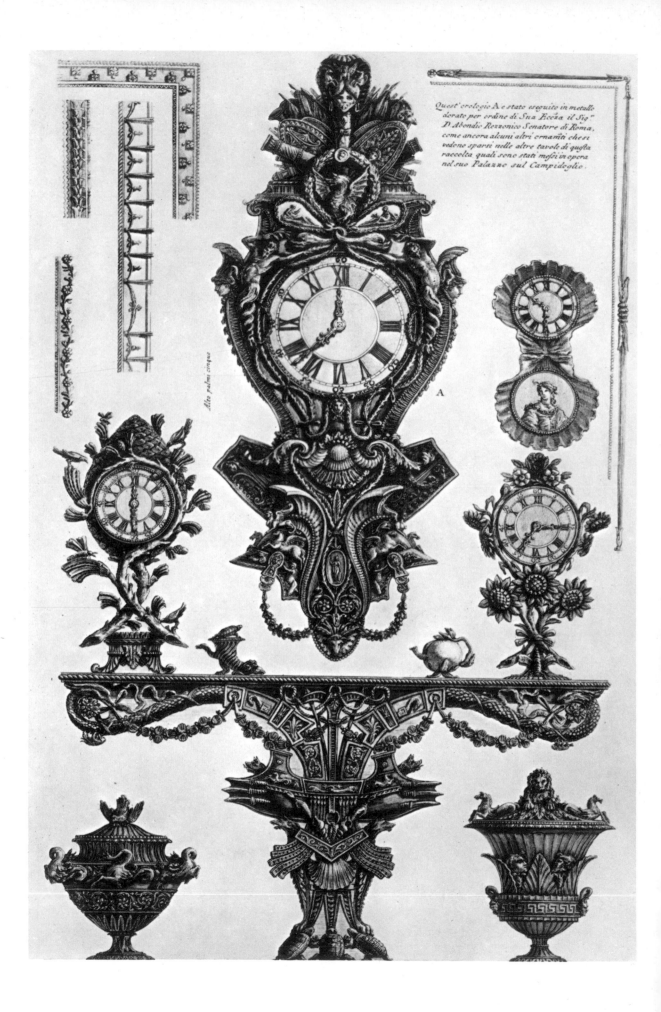

Quest'orologio A. e stato eseguito in metallo dorato per ordine di Sua Eccza il Sigr. D'Abondio Rezzonico Senatore di Roma, come ancora alcuni altri ornamenti che si vedono sparsi nelle altre tavole di questa raccolta quali sono stati messi in opera nel suo Palazzo sul Campidoglio.

Giovanni Battista Piranesi

(1720–1778)

Although Piranesi executed relatively few designs for household furniture, and only one table made exactly according to his design is at present known, he occupies a place of considerable, if generally underrated, importance in the history of the decorative arts. It is difficult to define the nature of his influence on furniture design – as on architecture or, more widely, neo-classicism – for it was oblique rather than direct and was perhaps conveyed less through his writings and etchings than by personal contact. He emerges from the letters of those who met him in Rome almost as a caricature of the 'stage' Italian – a figure from operetta rather than real life. Emotionally generous and financially grasping, as quick to strike up possessive friendship as to take offence, he knew no half-measures in love or hatred. By all reports, the feverish intensity of his drawings provides but a feeble reflection of his dynamically volatile character.

In a letter of 1755 Robert Adam wrote from Rome: 'Piranesi who is I think the most extraordinary fellow I ever saw, is become immensely intimate with me and as he imagined at first that I was like the other English who had a love of antiques without knowledge, upon seeing some of my sketches and drawings was so highly delighted that he almost ran quite distracted and said I have more genius for the true noble architecture than any Englishman ever was in Italy.' A few weeks later he recorded that 'so amazing and ingenious fancies as he has produced in the different plans of the Temples, Baths and Palaces and other buildings I never saw and are the greatest fund for inspiring and instilling invention in any lover of architecture that can be imagined'. And his importance is to be attributed mainly to this ability to inspire and instil invention.

Giovanni Battista Piranesi was born near Treviso in 1720 and trained as an architect in rococo Venice. In 1740 he went to Rome for the first time, began to study the arts of engraving and etching and to draw Roman monuments. In 1743 he published his first book, *Prima parte di architettura, e prospettiva,* which owes much to theatre design, returned to Venice for a while and then settled in Rome in about 1745. His major work, *Le antichità Romane,* a series of etchings of Roman buildings, began to appear in 1756. He first emerged as a polemical writer in 1761 with the publication of *Della magnificenza ed architettura de' Romani,* in which he declared his enthusiasm for all forms of Etruscan and Roman – and his profound distaste for Greek – art. This provocative essay drew a solemn reply from Mariette which Piranesi countered in his still more perverse *Osservazioni . . . sopra le lettere da M. Mariette* and the dialogue *Parere sul architettura* of 1765.

Designs for a side-table, clock and urns, engraved for Giovanni Battista Rezzonico, nephew of Pope Clement XIII and published in 1769. The central clock was executed in bronze, but its present whereabouts are unknown.

Design for a sedan chair, 1769.

opposite Designs for a chimney-piece and two side-tables, 1769.

In the meantime he had been taken up by the Venetian cardinal Carlo Rezzonico (elected Pope as Clement XIII in 1756) who knighted him in 1767. It was a nephew of the Pope, Giovanni Battista Rezzonico, who commissioned Piranesi to erect his only building – the church of the Knights of Malta in Rome, S. Maria del Priorato – and to decorate an apartment in the Quirinal Palace. Designs for the furniture in this apartment were included in Piranesi's folio of 1769, *Diverse maniere d'adornare i cammini ed ogni altra parte degli edifici*, which as the title states is mainly concerned with designs for chimney-pieces. Further evidence of Piranesi's ability as a furniture designer may be gleaned from a number of undated drawings in the Pierpont Morgan Library and the Victoria and Albert Museum. These designs reflect not only the ebullience of Piranesi's strange character but also his views on architecture. To be understood they must be seen in this wider context.

When Piranesi first visited Rome in 1740 the city was already the Mecca for the dilettanti of all nations. Grand tourists and young artists went there to inspect with becoming reverence the ruins and statues of antiquity. For at this date Roman Imperial architecture and the antique marbles, which were to be seen in greater profusion in Rome than anywhere else in Europe, were generally regarded as the greatest masterpieces of art. Young architects were still brought up on the precepts of Vitruvius. They were similarly schooled to accept simplicity, symmetry and decorum as the cardinal artistic virtues. But, as their works reveal, they frequently paid no more than lip-service to these notions. Even if they maintained a careful regard for the letter of the law, so far as the sacrosanct orders of architecture were concerned, they seem to have departed from the essential classical rules without a qualm. Piranesi was partly responsible for reversing this attitude. Attacking the precepts of Vitruvius, declaring that Roman architecture was highly ornamented, he called on architects to free themselves from the bonds of academic theory and to seek to recapture the spirit of the ancients. And in his etched views no less than in his polemical diatribes he revealed a new and exciting vision of the unparalleled splendour of Rome.

This vision of Roman magnificence is also expressed in his furniture designs. While French designers were somewhat timidly straightening out curves and curlicues and replacing wind-blown flowers with architectural ornaments to produce furniture that was supposedly *à la grecque*, he piled up antique motifs – monopods, palmettes, bucrania.

Design for a commode, clock and vases, 1769; as in his other designs, the ornaments are all inspired by antique architecture and sculpture.

swags, medallions, volutes and acanthus leaves – with a truly imperial opulence and disregard for 'good taste'. In much the same way he heaped up fragments from ancient marble altars, vases and capitals to create the fantastic candelabrum which he intended to stand over his own tomb.

The richly sculptural side-table he designed for G.B. Rezzonico is an astonishingly successful exercise in the use of antique motifs. That it is so close to the bronze furniture excavated at Pompeii some years after it was made is probably no more than a coincidence. One is reminded of the Latin tags which he used as mottoes for his *Parere* – 'It is reasonable

146

Design for a side-table, clock, urns, sconces and caskets, 1769.

to know yourself, and not to search into what the ancients have made if the moderns can make it', and 'They scorn my novelty, I their timidity'.

It is not known if Piranesi's designs were much imitated in Italy. To the French they probably appeared as 'farouche' as their originator. Yet his more general ideas, his call for imitations of the spirit of antiquity, no less than his bold conception of furniture as a province of architecture, inspired a whole generation. His presence may be sensed in English interiors designed by Robert Adam, in rooms by Cameron at Tsarskoe-Selo and even in some of the later Louis XVI salons of Paris.

John Goddard

(1723–1785)

Among the Pilgrim Fathers who landed at Cape Cod in 1620 there was a cooper, John Alden, who has been claimed as the first American colonial furniture maker. He appears to have prospered, acquired a farm and twice served as assistant governor of the colony. But when he died in 1687 the furniture in his house consisted only of one table, one bench, one cupboard, two chairs, bedsteads, chests and boxes, valued at no more than thirty-three shillings. The colonial settler did not need much in the way of furniture for his small homestead. As in an English village, until recently, and many parts of Europe to this day, the local carpenter supplied all woodwork from cradles to coffins. It was not until living standards improved in the early eighteenth century that a demand arose for specialist furniture makers. Soon after the mid-century certain towns began to emerge as centres for the production of furniture which was shipped to other parts of North America and, sometimes, still further. The records of the British customs reveal that in 1769 Salem imported 14 chairs and one table but exported 448 chairs, 2 bureau desks and 60 tables. In the same year 1,288 chairs, 27 bureau desks and 102 tables were exported from Massachusetts Bay. Further south the trade figures were reversed. New York imported rather more furniture than was exported. And in Maryland 784 chairs, 74 bureau desks and 68 tables were imported: while only 7 chairs and 2 tables were exported.

One of the towns engaged in this export trade was Newport, Rhode Island, where the inter-related Townsend and Goddard families provided the leading cabinet makers. Some of their products were taken as far as the West Indies. The quantities of furniture exported should not, however, lead us to suppose that the industry was highly developed. Business transactions were often of an engagingly primitive nature. In 1755, for instance, Job Townsend charged a client £31 for a maple-wood desk to be paid, not in cash, but in '2 Chani bowls large, 1 ditto small, 1 pr. Glasses, 1 Gal. Genneve, 2 pieces Britannia'. For three tables and a 'Corner Cubbord' he made for a barber he took payment in 'A Year's Shaven, a Cutt Wigg, a foretop to the Wigg and 24 feet of Mahogany'.

It is against this background that we should see one of the outstanding colonial furniture makers, John Goddard, who was born at Dartmouth, Massachusetts, on 20 January 1723. His grandfather seems to have been the first of his family to settle in New England: his father, Daniel, was a 'housewright'. In the 1740s the family moved to Newport where John and his younger brother James were apprenticed to Job Townsend

Mahogany knee-hole dressing-table
made by John Goddard of Newport,
Rhode Island, *c.* 1760–70.

Carved and gilt side-table made to the design of Piranesi for Cardinal G. B. Rezzonico, *c.* 1769.

Mahogany chest-of-drawers probably made by John Goddard, *c.* 1760.

and married two of his daughters, Hannah and Susanna. Job's brother Christopher was also a cabinet maker and they both had sons and grandsons who followed the same trade. They were all Quakers.

John Goddard set up his own workshop soon after his marriage. By the 1760s he had established himself as the leading cabinet maker in Newport, working for such local big-wigs as Governor Hopkins and Jabez Bowen (later to become a member of the Council of War in 1781 and Deputy Governor of Rhode Island). Another of his clients was Moses Brown, the philanthropist and pioneer cotton manufacturer of Providence.

A sudden beam of light is thrown on Goddard's workshop by two letters he wrote to Brown in 1763. 'Friend Brown,' he began, on 30th June, 'I send herewith the Tea Table & common Chairs which thou spoke for with the Bill.' He then goes on to refer to a chest-of-drawers he had been asked to make for Jabez Bowen, saying that he could not do it before the Fall 'as I have but little help' and asking 'whether he means to have them different from what is common, as there is a sort which is called Chest on Chest of Drawers & Sweld front which are Costly as well as ornimental'. But Goddard was slow in delivering further furniture to Brown who, in October, drafted a letter to him with grammar and punctuation distraught by anger. 'This ye was to do, that is, Finish ye Work I Wrote for ye first you did after my Brothers wifes furniture were done but Instead you have made work for Gov. Hopkins's family spoke for in May and delivered it before ours and we have ye greatest Reason to think you once sold part of that made on purpose for us. . . .' Goddard, who had received a similar expostulation from Bowen, sent an answer of the type commonly – if fallaciously – supposed to turn away wrath. He was 'really sorry thou should Immagin such hard thoughts of me . . . for my part I cannot Conceive how it could enter thy Heart to suppose such a thing, Unless thou have been MisInform'd'. Yet he was bound to confess that he had given precedence to the order from the Governor of Rhode Island. 'Thou must have expected I should have Engag'd work to keep my Boys Imployed if it should a little retard thy work for we must do so or we should be out of Imployment.'

The tea-table Goddard made for Brown is now at Winterthur – a handsome piece with delicately shaped top and claw and ball feet. Three desks – two of the bureau-table type, one with a bookcase above – may also be ascribed to him. They all have the gracefully articulated 'sweld front' or 'block front' which, at one time, he was supposed to have invented, though it was in fact developed by the generation of his father-in-law. They also have the shallow shell relief carvings which are a kind of hallmark of Newport cabinet makers (though, like the block front, these are also employed elsewhere).

A handful of bills reveal the range of work executed by Newport furniture makers, and although none is from Goddard his were presumably similar. Prices varied according to the richness of the carving and the quality of the wood (Goddard used both San Domingo mahogany and local cherry wood). Thus we find Christopher Townsend charging in 1744 £3 for a child's coffin and £65 for a desk and book-case. For a mahogany high chest-of-drawers he charged £30, for a mahogany tea-table £8. 10s. but for a maple tea-table only £2. 10s. Some twenty years later he obtained £140 for a mahogany dressing-table. In 1767 Job and Edmund Townsend charged £330 for a mahogany desk. Although these prices seem much higher than those of Chippendale in London it should be remembered that the paper currency in which they are reckoned had sunk to one tenth of its value in sterling.

Stylistically, this furniture derives from England – whence much furniture was imported throughout the eighteenth century. But Goddard and the Townsends were naturally conservative and made only the slightest concessions to the tides of taste which swept over Europe. Very seldom did they make use of the rococo frills and frip-peries indulged by their contemporaries in Philadelphia. Newport furniture seems to typify the earnestness of the mid-eighteenth-century New Englander, who had a greater regard for integrity than fine speech, for sound craftsmanship than fashion, and who contributed so much to the creation of the United States. It is as sensible, well-made and unpretentious as the prose of Benjamin Franklin – similarly based on English models of the earlier part of the century and just as unmistakably American.

Yet the Goddards and Townsends played no part in the Revolution. As Quakers, they were also pacifists. John Goddard was listed as a suspect sympathizer with the English in 1776; and in 1779, when his brother Daniel went off with the English, he was confined to his house for a while. He had begun to settle down to work again by 1782 when a newspaper advertised that he had a warehouse 'on the wharf of Mr Moses Brown' at Providence. But the Revolution had ruined him and when he died in 1785 he left insufficient money to pay his debts. His business was, however, carried on by his sons Stephen and Thomas until Stephen's death in 1804. A card-table which bears their label reveals that they had begun to work in the Hepplewhite style.

Stephen Goddard's son, John II, also worked as a cabinet maker, dying in 1843. He was survived by his uncle Thomas who died at the

Mahogany tea-table made for Jabez Bowen of Newport in 1763.

Pinewood table veneered with mahogany and satinwood, made by Stephen and Thomas Goddard, c. 1785–1804.

age of 93 in 1858, a lonely relic from the Colonial period. 'During almost a century,' wrote his obituarist in the *Newport Mercury*, 'he was known as the kindest of neighbours and the firmest of friends. No man, probably in this or in any other community (whose subsistence depended on the labour of his hands) ever devoted more hours to gratuitous attendance on the sick than Mr Goddard. In rain or shine, in sickness or in health, the call of suffering humanity never failed to strike the answering chord in his bosom, or to be attended with promptitude and alacrity; and had he not outlived in great measure the generations who best knew and most benefited by his self-sacrificing benevolence of spirit, it would be idle to recall them by this publication.'

Jean-Henri Riesener

(1734–1806)

The statutes of the Parisian *Corporation des menuisiers-ébénistes* were very carefully framed to exclude competition from foreigners. There were, however, loopholes which enabled a number of Germans to set up in Paris. These craftsmen were thus able to enjoy the most lavish patronage ever extended to furniture makers while in return members of the French court and Parisian *beau monde* were enabled to purchase some of the finest furniture ever made. The arrangement was mutually beneficial and only native-born craftsmen had reason to complain. As we have already seen, Oeben intruded himself into Paris by securing royal protection. J.-H. Riesener gained acceptance by marrying Oeben's widow.

Jean-Henri Riesener, the son of a tipstaff in the law courts of the Elector of Cologne, was born at Gladbeck near Essen in 1734. As a young man he went to Paris where, soon after 1754, he began to work under Oeben, becoming 'premier garçon' by the time of Oeben's death in 1763. Oeben's widow was left in financial difficulties, decided to carry on her husband's business (a normal practice for widows of all French craftsmen at this period), and put Riesener in charge of it. This infuriated his fellow assistant, Jean-François Leleu, who was five years older than Riesener and thought he had a better right to be promoted. Not content with leaving, establishing himself as a *maître* and setting up his own workshop, he threatened Riesener with physical violence and the police were obliged to intervene. Riesener became a *maître* in 1767 and in the following year married *la veuve* Oeben. (Little is known of the love lives of cabinet makers and any attempt to interpret this succession of events is bound to be speculative.) On the accession of Louis XVI in 1774 he succeeded the very aged Gilles Joubert as *ébéniste ordinaire du Roi*.

When Riesener took over Oeben's *atelier* the great *bureau du Roi*, commissioned in 1760, was still the major work in hand. He completed it, incorporated his signature in the marquetry and delivered it in 1769. He also completed and signed the similar roll-top desk begun by Oeben for Stanislas Lesczynski (now in the Wallace Collection). There were other works which had been begun before Oeben died and which Riesener finished. He also took on new commissions, though, as his wife was still technically the head of the studio, he was obliged to go on using Oeben's *estampille* until he became a *maître* himself. (Since Oeben did not become a *maître* until shortly before his death, most of the pieces of furniture marked with his *estampille* are, in fact, partly if not wholly

Portrait of Riesener by Antoine Vestier, 1786, showing the great Franco-German *ébéniste* seated at one of his own tables with designs for ornamental enrichments.

the work of Riesener.) During the last years of Louis xv's reign he was employed by two high officials of the *Garde-Meuble*. He also made very handsome secrétaires, similar to the *bureau du Roi* but on a smaller scale, for the comte and comtesse de Provence.

The great period of his career begins with his appointment as *ébéniste* to Louis xvi in 1774. Almost immediately he supplied a commode richly decorated with marquetry and gilt bronze mounts for the King's bedroom at Versailles (now in the Wallace Collection), and in the following year replaced it with another still richer (now at Chantilly). He seems to have kept up an almost constant supply of new secrétaires. He also produced some 'mechanical' pieces, notably a table made in collaboration with a German mechanic, Merklein, to stand beside Marie-Antoinette's bed. This masterpiece of ingenuity contains in its remarkably slender form mechanism to adjust its height, for use as a *table à manger*, to transform it into a dressing-table – 'by pushing a simple

Multi-purpose mechanical table made by Riesener, with mechanism by Merklein, in 1778, to stand by Marie-Antoinette's bed.

Marquetry top of a table made
for Marie-Antoinette in 1776 and
mounted on its present base in
the nineteenth century.

Commode completed in 1775 for the
bedroom of Louis XVI at Versailles.
Costing 28,268 livres, this was one of
the most expensive pieces of furniture
made in the eighteenth century. The
central panel of marquetry originally
bore Royal insignia which were
removed during the Revolution.

Work-table decorated with steel, bronze and mother-of-pearl, made for Marie-Antoinette's use, *c.* 1785.

opposite Marquetry secrétaire made for the Comte de Provence, later Louis XVIII, by J.-H. Riesener in 1774.

button which opens different compartments containing all that is necessary for the toilet' as Merklein's account records – or to convert it into a writing-table – 'by means of a button pressed very gently a reading desk emerges and by pushing another little button out comes a small square rod on which a piece of music or a book may be placed'. It cost 4,000 livres – about £170 in the English money of the day – and was among the less exorbitant of his confections. During these years Riesener supplied the Crown with furniture to the value of some 900,000 livres – £37,500.

It is hardly surprising that, as a result of the abortive economy campaign of 1784, Riesener was employed rather less prodigally by the *Garde-Meuble*. The majority of commissions went to *ébénistes* like Beneman and Stöckel who were neither as ruinously expensive nor as expert. But he continued to work for Marie-Antoinette, making furniture for her apartments at Fontainebleau and a superb secrétaire and commode decorated with panels of Japanese lacquer for her apartments at Saint Cloud in 1787. It is significant that these pieces were decorated with plain veneers, lacquer or mother-of-pearl rather than panels of marquetry which were much more costly. He did not, however, rely exclusively on royal commissions. His patrons included several members of the royal family – the comte and comtesse de Provence, the comte d'Artois, the King's aunts, the duc d'Orléans – numerous *grands seigneurs* like the duc de Penthièvre, the duc de la Rochefoucauld, the duc de Biron, and, inevitably, the rich *fermiers généraux*.

Despite his close connection with the Court, Riesener weathered the storms of the Revolution and Terror, and his workmen are said to have been patriotically employed making rifle butts. It is natural to assume that he witnessed the passing of the *ancien régime* with sorrow. But it is equally possible that he shared the views of Antoine Vestier who had painted his portrait and who, though ruined by the Revolution, declared that he found in the new political order 'a joy which consoles me for my losses'. At any rate, he stayed in Paris and in 1794 he was employed by the Directory to remove royal emblems – 'insignia of feudality' – from furniture. He was even called on to obliterate royal symbols on the bureau he and Oeben had made for Louis xv. At the sales of royal furniture he bought back many of his own works – but seems to have had difficulty in selling them again. There was no demand in the Paris of these years for an *ébéniste* of his talents and he found employment mainly as an assessor in the law courts. In 1801 he retired

Table, *c*. 1780, an example of
Riesener's simple style of work.

and spent his last years in a house in the rue Saint-Honoré with a second
wife, much younger than himself, whom he had married in 1783 and
who is said to have aggravated the distresses of his declining years. He
died in 1806.

Vestier's portrait shows Riesener as a bright-eyed, sharp-featured
man, elegantly dressed in velvet jacket and silk brocade waistcoat with
fine lace at his throat and wrists – very much a prosperous businessman
rather than a proletarian craftsman. He is seated at one of his own tables
and in his hand he holds a pencil. This seems to suggest that he wished
to be portrayed in the role of furniture designer. And there can be no
doubt that he was responsible for the design of the furniture made in
his workshop. He may often have done no more than supervise its
execution.

Riesener began in the chastened rococo style of his master Oeben.
Later in his career he produced a number of very fine tables of an
elegant rectilinear simplicity which borders on austerity. But it would
be a mistake to assume that one can trace in his work a steady progress
from the ornately sensuous to the severely cerebral, as in the *oeuvre* of
neo-classical painters and architects. As Mr Watson has remarked, 'he
could on occasion use the style of the late 1760s in 1780 . . . or that of 1775
in 1791'. Financial as well as aesthetic considerations may well have
determined the style of the very simple pieces which are among the most
immediately appealing of his works. The plain veneers of West Indian
mahogany and slender fillets of gilt bronze which he used in the 1780s
were very much less expensive to produce than the delicate panels of
floral marquetry and richly sculptured bronzes with which his earlier
furniture had been adorned. But he naturally responded, like his clients,
to changes in fashion, abandoning the curves and curlicues of the
rococo for lines that were straighter and forms that were more solid.
He seems to have provided just what his patrons wanted – furniture as
delicate and graceful as that of the Louis XV period, faintly tinged by the
new style which had begun to emerge in architecture and the figurative
arts.

It is not so much on the design as on the quality of his furniture that
Riesener's fame rests and must always have rested. Marquetry panels,
whether they represent elaborate allegories, still-lifes, naturalistically
arranged bunches of flowers, or are simple patterns of trellis work, have
a delicacy of detail and precision of line that has rarely been equalled.
Bronze mounts – which were probably made in his own workshop as
he occupied the privileged position of royal *ébéniste* – are often comparable with the best small-scale sculpture of the period (Clodion has,
indeed, been credited with the model for one of them). The bronzes
are affixed so that no unsightly screw-heads appear on the surface. Even
the carcases of his pieces of furniture are treated with greater care than
was usual.

Marquetry secrétaire probably begun
by J.-F. Oeben *c.* 1760 but finished and
signed by Riesener. It was probably
commissioned for Louis xv's
father-in-law, Stanislas Lesczynski,
King of Poland.

Benjamin Frothingham

(1734–1809)

When George Washington visited Charlestown, Massachusetts, in 1789, he made only one private call, to see 'Major Benjamin Frothingham, a cabinet maker he had known in the army, and who was a member of the Cincinnati'. There can be little doubt that Washington's visit was inspired by a spirit of *cameraderie* rather than an interest in furniture. It may also be that Frothingham owes his renown as much to the fact that he became a major in the Revolutionary army as to the high quality of the few pieces of furniture that can be attributed to him. He was not, of course, the only American furniture maker to be caught up in the Revolutionary war. Stephen Badlam of Dorchester, Massachusetts, became a captain in the artillery, though he is not known to have worked as a cabinet maker until after he was forced by ill-health to resign his commission. Jonathan Gostelowe of Philadelphia rose to the rank of major in the Corps of Artillery Artificers. And many others must have had the uneventful tenor of their lives interrupted by events of the 1770s.

Benjamin Frothingham was born in Boston on 6 April 1734. His father, Benjamin Sr, was a cabinet maker with a shop near Milk Street, in which Benjamin Jr was probably trained. He appears to have set up on his own in Charlestown before 1756. But he must have hankered after a more exciting way of life, for he enlisted in Richard Gridley's artillery company in 1759 and took part in the expedition to capture

Mahogany card table made by Benjamin Frothingham of Charlestown, Mass., *c.* 1756–75.

Quebec. In 1775 he was given the rank of first lieutenant. He had, however, continued to work as a cabinet maker when not on military duty. At the outbreak of the Revolution in 1775 he threw in his lot with his fellow Americans – and what anti-British feelings he may have had must have been much aggravated in June of that year when General Gage had Charlestown burnt, destroying Frothingham's house and workshop. For the next seven years he was fully engaged as a soldier, wounded at Bethlehem but continuing to serve until 1782 when he returned to the work of reconstruction and the quieter life of Charlestown.

Eight pieces of furniture have been found with Frothingham's label, elegantly engraved by the Boston silversmith, Nathaniel Hurd. And many others have by analogy been attributed to him. The majority are in the so-called American Chippendale style – rather like those made by John Goddard and the Townsends in Newport, though with even less carved decoration. It seems likely that they were made before the Revolution. The most notable is, perhaps, the sturdy card-table on claw and ball feet now at Winterthur. An inlaid Hepplewhite style sideboard, on the other hand, must surely date from after 1782, when the N.E., for New England, was patriotically removed from his label. Stylistically this piece is, of course, English; for it was not until many years after the Revolution that American craftsmen weaned themselves from the pattern books of the mother country. Ironically enough, American furniture of the Federal period is much closer to English prototypes than that of the late Colonial era.

Frothingham married before 1774 and had six children, of whom the eldest, also called Benjamin, became a cabinet maker. He died in 1809 and Benjamin III in 1832.

Frothingham's label, engraved by Nathaniel Hurd of Boston, attached to the card-table reproduced opposite. Only a few other pieces of furniture signed or labelled by Frothingham are known.

Giuseppe Maggiolini

(1738–1814)

Pieces of late eighteenth-century Italian furniture decorated with finely executed marquetry are almost invariably attributed to Giuseppe Maggiolini. He was not the only skilful Italian *intarsiatore* – or *marqueteur* – of his time; work of very high quality was produced in Turin by Ignazio and Luigi Revelli and in Rome by Rosario Palermo. But Maggiolini was and is the most famous. He was highly regarded by his Milanese contemporaries and eulogized as the 'Gloria della sua patria'. In 1784 a chest-of-drawers he had made for Conte Giacomo Serra of Genoa was described in a periodical in a manner normally reserved for large-scale paintings and works of sculpture. As a result his name has been used rather too freely by students and collectors of Italian furniture and many works have, with slight justification and less justice, been added to the corpus of his productions. Fortunately there are enough of his signed works to support the high claims made for him by contemporaries. And many details of his career are recorded in a booklet by the *Molto Reverendo* G.A. Mezzanzanica, whose word one hesitates to doubt, despite his hagiographical tone, not so much because of his cloth as because he was the son of Cherubino Mezzanzanica, who had entered the Maggiolini workshop at the age of ten and eventually inherited it from Giuseppe's son, Carlo Francesco.

Giuseppe Maggiolini was born in 1738 at Parabiago, a village some fifteen miles outside Milan on the way to Lake Maggiore. He began his career as a *garzone* in the carpenter's shop at the nearby monastery of S. Ambrogio della Vittoria – a house of the Cistercian order which had for centuries encouraged woodwork. In about 1760 he set up his own workshop in the Piazza at Parabiago, making fairly simple household objects, though he is said to have produced an elaborate coin cabinet for a numismatically inclined monk. His first contact with the grander world was in 1765 when he was employed by the painter-architect Giuseppe Levati who was supervising the decoration and furnishing of a villa belonging to the Litta family at Lainate. In 1771 he went to Milan to make some of the decorations for the public *festa* in honour of the marriage between the Austrian Governor General of Milan, the Archduke Ferdinand, and Beatrice d'Este. Although the Milanese furniture makers ganged up against him and forced him to return to Parabiago, he was later employed extensively by the Archduke and appointed his official *intarsiatore*. Maggiolini made furniture for him to give to Stanislas Poniatowski and Elizabeth of Russia. He also made elaborately inlaid floors (now destroyed) for the Palazzo Ducale, Milan,

opposite Marquetry chest-of-drawers by Giuseppe Maggiolini, *c.* 1790.

GIUSEPPE MAGGIOLINI

Mahogany commode inlaid with ebony, palisander and other woods, made in Milan in 1790.

which was being partly rebuilt and wholly redecorated by the leading architect of the day, Giuseppe Piermarini.

Maggiolini was much patronized by the luxury-loving society satirized – one might also say immortalized – in Giuseppe Parini's poem *Il Giorno*. The francophile nobleman, Parini's anti-hero, whose rising, toilet, dressing, prancing and flirting were so devastatingly described, would surely have responded to the elegant opulence of Maggiolini's marquetry commodes and tables. Members of this society were apparently prepared to pay, or at any rate promise, high prices for furniture that was *alla moda* – and Maggiolini received up to 1,400 *zecchini* (£700 in the English money of the day) for a single chest-of-drawers – though this may well have been exceptional. One may therefore question whether he welcomed the French Revolution, the French invasion and the expulsion of the Austrians with quite as much joy as Parini and his friends. Afterwards he was employed by the Napoleonic viceroy, Eugène Beauharnais, and by the Milanese who allied themselves with the new régime. He does not, however, seem to have abandoned his original style for the Empire manner. He died in Parabiago on 18 November 1814.

Essentially a craftsman, rather than a designer, Maggiolini worked to a somewhat closely restricted range of furniture patterns. He is known to have disliked carved work and his furniture reveals an antipathy even for curved outlines. His chests-of-drawers and cupboards are almost box-like in their unbending rectangularity. And they are enlivened only by their marquetry decorations. A list drawn up in 1795 reveals that he was then making use of no fewer than eighty-six different types of wood

Drawing of a decorative device by the Lombard painter Andrea Appiani. Drawings of this type were used by Maggiolini for designs for marquetry.

of varying colours and grains. Unlike such predecessors as Piffetti he spurned the use of bone and ivory and of staining the pieces of wood he fitted into his inlays. He used wood more as the *pietre dure* craftsmen of Florence used semi-precious stones. His pieces are indeed virtuoso performances, the last products of a great tradition founded by the intarsia workers of the fifteenth century.

For the designs of the decorative panels, Maggiolini resorted to painters working in Milan, especially Andrea Appiani and Giuseppe Levati. They provided him with drawings of delicate trophies of musical instruments, cornucopia-like scrolls of acanthus leaves, ruffled ribbons, tendrils of ivy and bunches of flowers, besides more strictly antique architectural ornaments. He may also have availed himself of the engraved designs published in Milan by Giocondo Albertolli in 1782, 1796 and 1805 – though no drawings by him appear in the large collection which was used in Maggiolini's workshop and is now in the Castello Sforzesco, Milan.

Music-table decorated with marquetry in several different woods, *c.* 1790.

Georges Jacob

(1739–1814)

Writing of the Directoire period, M.-E.-J. Delécluze remarked that 'in even the wealthier houses of Paris the furniture was still in the style of Louis xv and Marie Antoinette'. He was therefore all the more surprised to find that the furniture in the studio of Jacques-Louis David was in a style of antique severity which matched his pictures. There were 'movable chairs of dark mahogany upholstered in red wool with black palmettes applied to it' which, he observed, were copied from Greek vases. Instead of the usual *bergères* there were on one side a bronze currule chair with x-shaped supports terminating in the heads and feet of animals, on the other a great armchair of solid mahogany, decorated with gilt bronzes and upholstered in red and black. All this furniture in a style which we should now characterize as 'Empire', had in fact been made some years earlier, in about 1788, by Georges Jacob to designs by David himself and his pupil Moreau. David had also provided designs for similar furniture made by Jacob for the son of Philippe Egalité, the young duc de Chartres (later Louis Philippe) – an inventory of his belongings in the ci-devant Palais Royal lists 'a mahogany bed, decorated with gilt bronzes, in the antique taste, made by Jacob to the design of David'. And such furniture had appeared in two of David's paintings, *Paris and Helen* and *Brutus*, both of which were completed in 1789.

These references are of some importance for they date with precision what are in all probability the first pieces of useful household furniture made in direct imitation of Greek and Roman prototypes. (The Athénienne, a mainly decorative piece of furniture which had come into fashion rather earlier, was of a different character, derived from an antique altar.) Hitherto only decorative objects such as pedestals had been modelled at all closely on antiquities: chairs, tables and beds of the 1770s and 1780s had been but a little simpler and more rectilinear in form than their rococo predecessors, and the only concessions made to the antique cult were in their applied decorations. It is revealing that the leading part in this change of attitude should have been played by a painter and not a furniture maker or designer. (In Denmark also the first full Greek Revival furnishings were made for and to the designs of the painter Nikolai Abildgaard.) And one may wonder whether earlier, if less radical, changes in Jacob's style had been similarly inspired. For these severe antique revival pieces belong only to the last years of his career.

Georges Jacob was born in 1739, of Burgundian peasant stock. He went to Paris when young and is said to have served his apprenticeship

Carved and gilt wood armchair by Georges Jacob, made for the Turkish Room of the Comte d'Artois in 1777.

GEORGES JACOB

The Lictors Bringing Brutus the Bodies of his Sons by Jacques-Louis David, 1789. David, who was a patron of Jacob, was among the first to commission furniture to be made after antique prototypes both for his own use and, as in this picture, to serve as studio properties.

under Louis Delanois, a successful *menuisier* who clung obstinately to the rococo Louis XV style while the rage for the so-called *goût grec* was at its height. Jacob became a *maître menuisier* in 1765. Some of his early works are still predominantly rococo, but he soon adopted the more fashionable Louis XVI style, making chairs with simple outlines and straight legs, and deriving motifs for carved ornaments from antique architecture. By the early 1780s he seems to have established himself as one of the leading chair makers in Paris. He was among the first to use mahogany extensively and seems to have been responsible for lightening and simplifying chair design by planing away the inner angle of the frame beneath the seat. He also made beds. And, unlike other *menuisiers*, he occasionally produced tables, which were normally the province of the *ébéniste*.

In the 1780s Jacob's clients included a number of foreigners as well as members of the Parisian *beau monde*. In 1782, for example, he made a

bed for Carl August, Duke of Zweibrücken-Birkenfeld, which caused quite a stir and was described in some detail in the *Journal de Paris*. It was decorated with a marble group of *Cupid and Psyche* carved by Martin-Claude Monnot who, it is tempting to suggest, may have had some hand in its design. The bed, now in the Residenzmuseum, Munich, is certainly more heavily sculpturesque than most of the period. Another bed by Jacob has posts crowned with plumed Roman helmets and is of a type that was to become very popular in the Empire period. It was bought by George IV and is still in the English royal collection. Jacob also supplied chairs for Carlton House through the *marchand-mercier* Daguerre between 1785 and 1790. They are similar to chairs supplied by Daguerre for Woburn Abbey, and as Henry Holland was in charge of work both here and at Carlton House, he probably approved even if he did not influence their design.

Firescreen, *c.* 1775–85.

Armchair made for the Elector Palatine Karl Theodore in 1782.

Among Jacob's works for the Crown the most interesting is a set of furniture (to the design of Hubert Robert, the painter) for Marie-Antoinette's dairy at Rambouillet which was built on the very eve of the Revolution. Jacob described the chairs in his account as 'of a new pattern in the Etruscan style . . . after the design of . . . . Robert'. The word 'Etruscan' was used at this period to describe the antique vases recently discovered in Italy (though it was known that most of them were of Greek origin). But the chairs made for Rambouillet owed nothing to Greece or Etruria save details of surface decoration. It has been said that they anticipate the furniture of the Directoire period – but it would be more accurate to say that Jacob later repeated the design, as in a set of chairs made during the Consulate for Napoleon's apartment in the Tuileries. Jacob worked for other members of the royal family – for the King's cousin, the duc de Chartres (as we have seen) and for the King's brother who owed him 85,000 livres when he fled before the

Canopied bed of the type called a *lit à la polonaise, c.* 1785.

growing clouds of Revolution in 1789.

Jacob was one of the many fine craftsmen who were almost ruined by the Revolution. But, thanks to David, he survived the Terror and even found employment under it. David introduced him to Percier and Fontaine to whose design he made the furniture for the *Comité du salut publique*. With the fall of Robespierre and the creation of the Directoire, opportunities began to open once again for the furniture maker. In 1796 Jacob retired and handed over his business to his two sons, Georges II and François-Honoré-Georges. But in 1800 he returned to help in the large task of furnishing the Consular apartments in the Tuileries. And on the death of Georges II in 1803 he rejoined his other son with whom he worked under the business name of *Jacob-Desmalter et Cie*. They provided much of the finest furniture for the Napoleonic palaces, often working to the designs of Percier and Fontaine in a style of truly imperial opulence. Now that the guild system had been broken

Mahogany chair from a suite of furniture made by Jacob, to the designs of the painter Hubert Robert, for the Queen's Dairy at Rambouillet. It was delivered in 1787.

by the Revolution, the firm freely produced both *menuiserie* and *ébénisterie*. The workshop grew to an industrial size, but high standards of craftsmanship were still maintained. Georges Jacob finally retired in 1813 and died in the following year. François-Honoré-Georges, known as Jacob-Desmalter, continued to produce furniture in the Empire style until 1825 when he passed the business on to his son, Georges-Alphonse, who kept it going until 1845 when he retired and sold it to Jeanselme. Georges-Alphonse died, appropriately enough, in the last year of the second Empire, 1870.

Despite the very high quality of the furniture made by the elder Georges Jacob under the *ancien régime*, his fame rests mainly on that produced for the Bonapartes. The first piece of importance is a secrétaire made in 1798 for Josephine who had commissioned Percier and Fontaine to decorate the apartments she and Napoleon occupied in the rue de la Victoire. It is a somewhat unwieldy mahogany affair with statuettes inset at the angles and a heavy gilt bronze frieze with chimeras seated amongst luxuriant scrolls of acanthus foliage. There can be little doubt that it was designed by Percier and Fontaine who probably provided designs for most of the other grandiose Jacob pieces. But if the Jacob family can be given little credit for inventing the Empire style – so carefully devised to provide an appropriate setting for the Napoleonic court – they played a part of major importance in its realization. And the capabilities of the workmen they employed may well have determined its development.

It is easy to forget or underrate the importance of the time factor in Empire schemes of interior decoration. Percier and Fontaine were required to create or refurnish state apartments at great speed. Hence the prominence of draperies which could at short notice be swathed over windows and beds and thrones, immediately giving a rich appearance to the simplest rooms. Similarly, one finds in Jacob furniture that time-consuming (and, of course, very expensive) patterns of inlaid work, delicately contrasted veneers and elaborate carved ornaments are eschewed. Shapes are generally simple and decorations limited to applied reliefs or statuettes in cast and gilded bronze. Designs for chairs, tables, chests-of-drawers were standardized and repeated again and again. All that was required of the individual craftsman in the workshop was a mechanical realization of the design. Georges Jacob thus has a claim to be called both the last of the eighteenth-century *menuisiers* and the first of the nineteenth-century furniture manufacturers.

Mahogany chair 'à l'anglaise' made *c.* 1785–90 and supplied through the *marchand-mercier* Daguerre to the Prince of Wales for furnishing Carlton House.

Bed made for the Empress Josephine, probably to the design of Percier and Fontaine, in the workshops of Jacob Desmalter et Cie, 1810.

David Roentgen

(1743–1807)

'David Roentgen and his two hundred cases have arrived safely and at the right moment to satisfy my gluttony', wrote Catherine the Great to Baron Grimm in 1785. Already the darling of the European courts and soon to be called 'the most celebrated *ébéniste* in Europe', Roentgen was certainly the most successful cabinet maker of the eighteenth century. He was also the first to establish a furniture industry on a fully international basis. Some of the most notable French *ébénistes* had occasionally worked for foreign patrons, mainly in Germany and England, and some English furniture makers had done a small export trade, mainly in japanned pieces. But none had successfully exploited the European market for furniture of very high quality. In some ways he anticipated the luxury-trade furniture industrialists of the nineteenth century. Although he has been classed among and competed successfully with Parisian *ébénistes* he has more in common with the cabinet makers and 'upholders' of London, and like them he was less a craftsman than an efficient company director. His father Abraham, who founded the business, had established strong links with England. And David Roentgen significantly styled himself 'Englischer Kabinettmacher'.

The Roentgens were Protestants, and that may be why Abraham, who was born at Mühlheim on the Rhine in 1711, the son of a joiner, went to make his fortune not in France but in Holland and England. After working as a journeyman at The Hague, Rotterdam, and Amsterdam, he settled in London in 1731, and is said to have been employed by several cabinet makers for marquetry work, engraving and what were described as 'the mechanics of cabinet making'. While in London he joined the Moravian Brethren, a Pietist sect recently founded by Count Nikolaus Ludwig Zinzendorf. In 1738 he went back to Germany and joined a Moravian colony near Frankfurt and two years later set off for Carolina as a missionary. But the ship on which he was sailing for America was wrecked off the Irish coast. After working for a while in Galway he returned to Germany. In 1750 he became a member of the Moravian colony which had been permitted to establish itself at Neuwied, near Coblenz, by Count Friedrich Alexander von Wied, 'for the Increase of our Residence at Neuwied, its commerce and the growth thereof' – to which the Roentgens were to contribute greatly. Short of workmen skilful enough to satisfy his demands, he sent one of his assistants to be trained in England under his former employer, Gern, in 1756. Ten years later he paid a brief visit to London himself and

Writing and games table by Abraham Roentgen, the father of David Roentgen, *c.* 1755–60.

opposite Combined secrétaire and medal-cabinet of mahogany with gilt bronze mounts made in Roentgen's Neuwied workshops, *c.* 1785–9.

brought back an English apprentice with him. Shortly afterwards he seems to have allowed his elder son, David (born 1743) to take over the management of the business. Abraham formally retired in 1772 and died in 1793.

Under Abraham's direction the workshop of Neuwied produced attractive furniture in a restrained rococo style which shows the influence of Chippendale. Many pieces were fitted with complex locks, secret drawers and various mechanical devices. Clocks, musical boxes and mechanical toys were also made. But, despite the patronage of local nobility, the firm was often in financial difficulties. David seems to have appreciated that a wider clientèle was needed and that, in order to obtain it, the now out-moded rococo style would have to be abandoned.

The era of prosperity dated from 1769 when David Roentgen organized a very successful sale of furniture by lottery in Hamburg. But the great market at this time was in Paris where the Crown, the Court, various members of the *gratin* and, of course, the rich financiers and *fermiers généraux* were annually spending vast sums on fine furniture. Roentgen was soon to enable them to spend still more. He made his first visit to Paris in 1774, struck up an acquaintance with a German engraver, Johann Georg Wille, and established other contacts. In 1779 he returned with cartloads of the best furniture made at Neuwied and set up a depôt. The success of this venture was spectacular. He sold to Louis XVI for an

right Marquetry bureau inlaid in silver, ivory, ebony, satinwood, etc., with gilt bronze mounts, by Abraham and David Roentgen, Neuwied, c. 1765.
above A detail of the fall-front of the bureau. The Roentgen factory was famed for the high quality of its marquetry.

unprecedented sum – variously given as 80,000 and 96,000 livres (£3,300 to £4,000 in the money of the day) – a secrétaire richly adorned with marquetry and incorporating a clock and musical box which, like most toys, soon went wrong. In the next decade Roentgen's bills for furniture supplied to the Crown totalled nearly a million livres – still more than Riesener's. He was appointed *ébéniste-méchanicien du Roi et de la Reine*, and the jealous Parisian *Corporation des menuisiers-ébénistes*, realizing that it would be impossible to defeat him, forced him to join them and become a *maître*.

Yet still he sought new worlds to conquer. The influential Baron Friedrich Melchior von Grimm – author of the *Correspondance littéraire* which kept the crowned heads of Europe *au fait* with intellectual, artistic and literary events in Paris – recommended him to the Empress of Russia. In 1783 David Roentgen made the first of several visits to St Petersburg where he sent seven large consignments of furniture, including several massive bureaux which are still in the Hermitage. He also travelled to Italy, Holland and, of course, to various German states. But the Revolution deprived him of French patronage, and although he was appointed Court Furnisher (and diplomatic agent of the Lower Rhineland) to Friedrich Wilhelm II of Prussia, he was ruined. His Parisian depôt was confiscated and soon afterwards his workshops at Neuwied were sacked by Republican troops. He saved only those parts of his stock

Writing-table of oak with birchwood veneer and gilt bronze mounts, made in David Roentgen's Neuwied factory, *c*. 1780–90.

DAVID ROENTGEN

opposite Carved and painted wood writing-desk by G. M. Bonzanigo, *c.* 1780.

Low cupboard, one of the simpler pieces of furniture made at the Roentgen factory shortly before the French Revolution.

stored in depôts in Kassel, Gotha and Altenburg. At the time of the French invasion he fled to Berlin and did not return to Neuwied until 1802. He appears to have made an attempt to re-establish his business but died in 1807, while on his travels.

In his heyday, David Roentgen had enjoyed, one might say exploited, the best of several worlds. If Neuwied was far from the main centres of patronage, it was equally far from the sources of interference. He suffered none of the petty tyrannies imposed by the guilds. Nor was he subject to the major tyrannies of royal patrons. He seems, in fact, to have created a seller's market in which crowned heads competed for his productions. And the fact that both Louis XVI and Catherine II were prepared to pay unprecedented sums for his more elaborate pieces of furniture must have lent a certain *chic* to all the works stored in his various depôts.

His most elaborate pieces of furniture were well supplied with gadgets and secret compartments which had for long been a speciality of German craftsmen and have never entirely ceased to delight even the most sophisticated collectors. At the press of a button doors spring open, drawers rise up from unexpected places, a musical box may begin to tinkle a tune. In executing such mechanical devices he had the expert assistance of Peter Kinzing, who also made clocks which are incorporated in some of his furniture. The exteriors were generally decorated with panels of marquetry, bunches of flowers tied with ribbons and sometimes figurative allegorical or chinoiserie scenes made up from numerous minute laminae of different coloured woods. For the more elaborate marquetry he seems to have commissioned a painter, Januarius Zick, to execute drawings for the craftsmen to follow. It would be interesting to know if he employed a staff of draughtsmen either to realize his own ideas or to originate designs. For his many travels can have allowed him little time to do more than supervise production at the Neuwied workshop.

From the 1760s to the 1790s the Roentgen workshop kept abreast of developments in taste. Curves are gradually eliminated, forms are given increasing solidity and massiveness, naturalistic ornaments are replaced by columns and architraves and other architectural devices. Yet Roentgen was also sensitive to the individual preferences of his grander clients. The huge secrétaire he sold to Louis XVI in 1779 seems to have been almost a caricature of the Louis XVI style, with its many marquetry panels and unclassical profusion of antique ornaments. On the other hand, the bureaux he supplied for Catherine the Great are of a ponderous architectural monumentality, well designed to satisfy her 'gluttony' for buildings as well as furniture. His works may lack the subtlety and exquisite refinement of those made by his compatriots Oeben and Riesener and by his one-time apprentice Weisweiler in Paris. But it is easy to see why they enjoyed a huge success.

Giuseppe Maria Bonzanigo

(1745–1820)

It is hardly surprising to find that the decorative arts of Piedmont were strongly influenced by those of France. Here, in the eighteenth century, much greater respect was paid to *finesse* in craftsmanship than in other parts of Italy. Fashionable French designs were often imitated soon after they appeared in Paris. And a few Piedmontese artists and craftsmen, like the sculptor and *ciseleur* Francesco Ladatte, received part of their training in Paris. Yet the furniture of a Piffetti or a Bonzanigo could hardly be mistaken for French products. Although both these fine craftsmen owed something to France, their works are almost defiantly Italian in their exuberant elaboration. Nor do they seem to have been much appreciated by French visitors. General Jourdan, under the Empire, may have thought of buying a work by Bonzanigo to send to Paris. But the remarks of A.L. Millin, who visited Turin in 1811, provide a more accurate reflection of French opinion. He praised the 'délicatesse' of Bonzanigo's carvings but, he remarked, 'in many of his works he shows more dexterity than taste'. To eyes trained on the opulent simplicity of Jacob, the furniture made by Bonzanigo must have seemed painfully lacking in restraint and *mesure*.

Like so many of the most interesting makers of Italian furniture, Giuseppe Maria Bonzanigo was primarily a sculptor – and one suspects that he would not have relished being taken for a *menuisier* or *ébéniste*. He was born in 1745 at Asti, where his father and uncle, who hailed from Bellinzona, were working as woodcarvers, specializing in elaborate cases for church organs. But he was to choose to work on a much smaller, sometimes minuscule, scale. By 1773 he had settled at Turin and begun to work for the court so vividly described in the memoirs of his near contemporary Vittorio Alfieri. The first payment made to him was for some frames for portraits in the royal apartments. During the next twenty years he executed a considerable quantity of furniture for the Royal palaces – chests-of-drawers, screens, cupboards, doors and door cases – all delicately carved with sharply cut festoons of flowers and trophies of musical instruments. In 1787 Vittorio Amadeo III, acknowledging his 'singular mastery', appointed him official woodcarver to the Crown with a salary of 200 lire a year which was increased to 300 in 1792. Some idea of the prices he obtained for his works may be derived from the fact that in 1775 he was paid 1,000 lire (about £50 sterling of the day) for designing and making two large screens and one rather elaborate firescreen – which seem incredibly mean in comparison with the rewards which were promised, if not invariably paid, to royal cabinet makers in France.

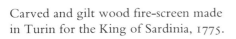

Carved and gilt wood fire-screen made
in Turin for the King of Sardinia, 1775.

Carved, painted and gilt wood
side-table, *c*. 1780.

In point of craftsmanship, Bonzanigo's furniture suffers little from comparison with the best French *menuiserie* of the same period. For though the materials may be less fine, the standard of carving is remarkably high. Flowers nodding on tremulous stalks are rendered with a fragile delicacy one associates with the art of the ivory carver. He also executed objects as small as carved buttons. But only on a relatively few pieces of furniture, like his fire-screens, is such minute delicacy wholly appropriate to the scale. Bonzanigo often veers perilously close to the ostentatious virtuosity of nineteenth-century craftsmanship.

The invasion of Piedmont by the French in 1796 deprived Bonzanigo of further royal commissions, but not of other work. He had for long carved decorative reliefs and portraits as well as furniture, and he was apparently able to keep up a trade in such works – with a difference in subject matter. Millin records that whereas, before the Revolution,

Carved and gilt wood screen with
original woven silk panels, *c.* 1780.

Bonzanigo's studio had been full of portraits of the King of Sardinia and the Bourbons, in 1811 it was well stocked with carvings of Napoleon, Madame Mère, the Empress Marie Louise, the King of Bavaria and the little King of Rome. One of his most elaborate works, the *Monumento Militare* (a cabinet enshrining portraits of all the kings of Europe), he prudently modified so that it could be crowned with a Napoleonic eagle and portrait of Napoleon. Yet this change in iconography was accompanied by no change in style. He still maintained the florid version of the Louis XVI manner in which his earlier works had been executed.

Bonzanigo employed a large studio of assistants. And in 1803 he issued proposals for establishing a gallery and workshop 'to perfect the art of carving in wood and ivory'. But nothing came of this. He seems to have resumed work for the King of Sardinia after the Restoration and lived on until 1820.

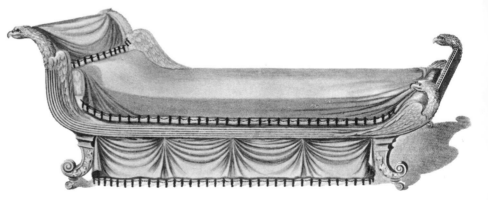

Thomas Sheraton

(1751–1806)

The names of George Hepplewhite and Thomas Sheraton are among the best known in the history of English furniture. But not a single piece of furniture made by either of them has survived. Their fame rests entirely on their publications and their names are – or should be – used not as craftsmen's labels but as stylistic categories to distinguish two styles of late Georgian furniture. Hepplewhite's *The Cabinet-makers' and Upholsterers' Guide* which was published posthumously in 1788 and reprinted in 1789 and 1794, contains nearly three hundred designs which epitomize the taste of the 1780s. Sheraton said that it was already out of fashion by 1791 when he began to issue the instalments of his *The Cabinet-Maker and Upholsterer's Drawing-Book*. 'Notwithstanding the late date of Hepplewhite's book,' he wrote, 'if we compare some of the designs, particularly the chairs, with the newest taste, we shall find that this work has already caught the decline, and perhaps in a little time will die in the disorder.' The fashion-conscious outlook and less than charitable tone of this remark, combined with the elegant and highly sophisticated pieces of furniture illustrated in the book, might lead an innocent reader to suppose that Sheraton was a spry young metropolitan worldling. Nothing could be further from the truth.

Thomas Sheraton was born at Stockton-on-Tees in County Durham in 1751. He appears to have been trained as a cabinet maker though he also had ability as a draughtsman. In 1782 he published in Stockton *A Scriptural Illustration of the Doctrine of Regeneration* which reveals that he was already a member of the Baptist congregation. The preface declares that he was 'a mechanic, and one who never received the advantages of a *collegial* or *academical* education'. Indeed, he harps on this theme with the persistence of a Uriah Heep. The 'mean author' begs his readers to overcome prejudice, 'the corroding worm at the bottom of all', and overlook his humble status. A resolute self-improver, however, he learned enough Greek to expatiate on the derivations of geometrical terms and, one would have thought, to bewilder the reader of the first two parts of his *Drawing-Book,* which he began to publish soon after he settled in London in 1790.

Although he described himself on the title page of the *Drawing-Book* as 'Thomas Sheraton, Cabinet-Maker', it is highly improbable that he had a workshop. On the trade card he had printed in about 1795 he declared that he 'Teaches Perspective, Architecture and Ornaments, makes Designs for Cabinet-Makers and sells all kinds of Drawing Books &c.' This probably gives an accurate account of his trade activities at this date. The *Drawing-Book* was reprinted twice, in 1794

Grecian couch of carved and gilt wood, showing the influence of Sheraton's designs.

Engraved design for a Grecian couch, 1805, which was almost certainly the model for the couch above.

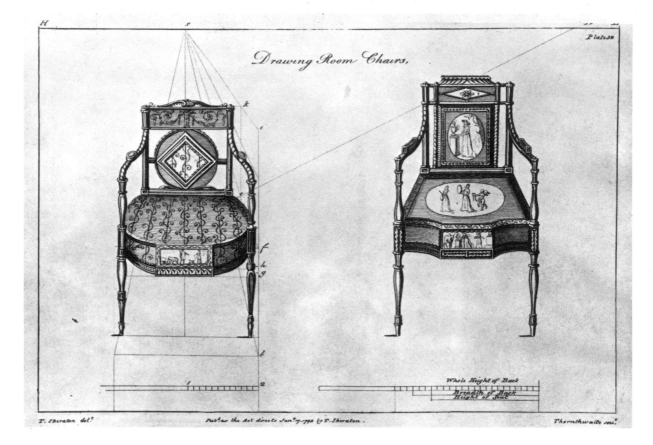

Drawing Room Chairs.

T. Sheraton delt.   Pub⁴ as the Act directs Jan⁷ 17.1792 by T. Sheraton.   Thornthwaite sci.

Whole Height of Back
Breadth of Back
Height of Seat

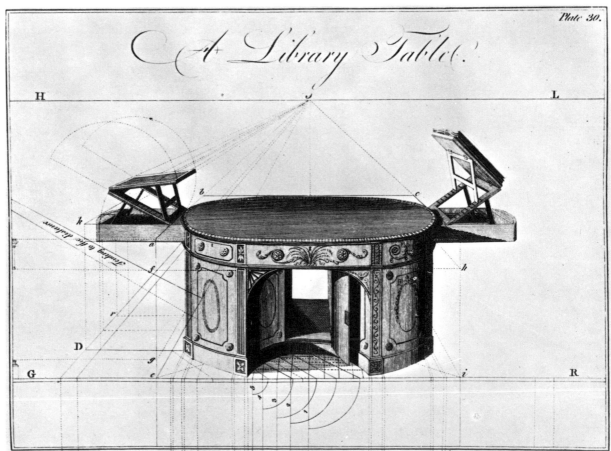

Plate 30.

A Library Table.

and 1802. In the meantime he was more closely engaged in theological problems and published in 1794 a tract entitled *Scriptural Subjection to Civil Government*. After returning to the north of England he was ordained a Baptist minister in 1800. Three years later, while preparing his second book of furniture designs, the *Cabinet Dictionary*, he wrote: 'Though I am thus employed in racking my invention to design fine and pleasing cabinet work, I can be content to sit on a wooden bottom chair myself, provided I can but have common food and raiment where with to pass through life in peace.' But it was not without difficulty that he obtained even these modest necessities.

Adam Black, later to achieve fame as an Edinburgh publisher and politician, has left a pathetic and vivid account of him. 'He lived in an obscure street, his house half shop half dwelling house, and looked himself like a worn-out Methodist minister, with threadbare black coat.' In his diary Black said that Sheraton was 'a man of talents, and, I believe, of genuine piety . . . he is a scholar, writes well; draws, in my opinion, masterly; is an author, bookseller, stationer, and teacher. We may be ready to ask how comes it to pass that a man with such abilities and resources is in such a state? I believe his abilities and resources are his ruin, in this respect, for by attempting to do everything he does nothing.' And in his *Memoirs* he recorded: 'I was with him for about a week, engaged in most wretched work, writing a few articles, and trying to put his shop in order, working among dirt and bugs, for which I was remunerated with half a guinea. Miserable as the pay was, I was half ashamed to take it from the poor man.'

The articles to which Black refers were presumably for *The Cabinet-Maker, Upholsterer, and General Artists' Encyclopaedia* of which only the first thirty folio instalments were completed before Sheraton's mind gave way (it was published as a single volume in 1805). Sheraton also completed another tract, *The Character of God as Love,* similarly published in 1805. He died in the following year and was described in an obituary in the *Gentleman's Magazine* as 'a very honest, well-disposed man; of an acute and enterprising disposition'. In 1812 a selection of plates from his three pattern books appeared as *Designs for Household Furniture, by the late T. Sheraton, cabinet maker.*

The list of more than seven hundred subscribers to Sheraton's *Drawing-Book* makes a curious contrast with that prefaced to Chippendale's *Director*. Here there is no impressive array of titles: the majority of Sheraton's subscribers were cabinet makers and upholsterers, craftsmen and tradesmen, many of them working in the provinces. His book

Designs for two chairs from Sheraton's *Drawing-Book*, published in London in 1792.

Design for a library table with folding book and music rests, 1792.

Lady's work-table made in late
eighteenth-century England and
corresponding closely with the design
by Sheraton illustrated below left.

Engraved design for two
writing-tables, 1792.

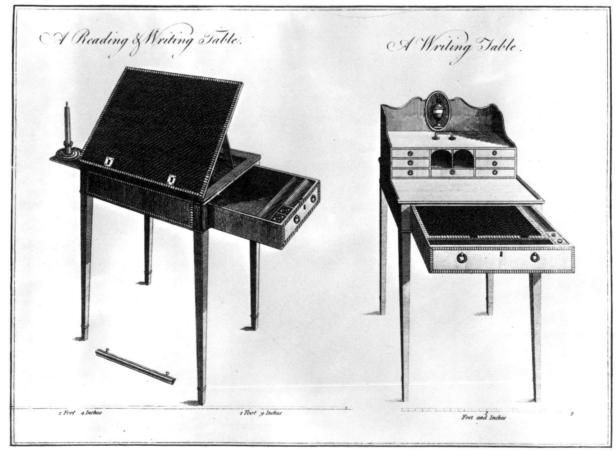

was, indeed, addressed primarily to the trade and its aim was practical – to acquaint cabinet makers with the most up-to-date designs. He remarks that 'in conversing with cabinet makers', he found 'no one individual equally experienced in every job of work. There are certain pieces made in one shop that are not manufactured in another'. He had therefore applied 'to the best workmen in different shops, to obtain their assistance in the explanation of such pieces as they have been most acquainted with'. On several occasions he acknowledged his indebtedness to those who had helped him. He seems to have studied the Louis XVI style furniture which had recently been brought across the Channel by the *émigrés* and, perhaps, some pieces made in London by refugee craftsmen. In the appendix to the third part of his book he also illustrated the Chinese drawing-room designed for Carlton House by Henry Holland and only very recently completed.

If Sheraton did not invent the furniture style named after him, he certainly played a leading role in formulating it. The designs in the

Two English chairs of painted West Indian satinwood made *c.* 1795 and probably influenced by designs in Sheraton's *Drawing-Book*.

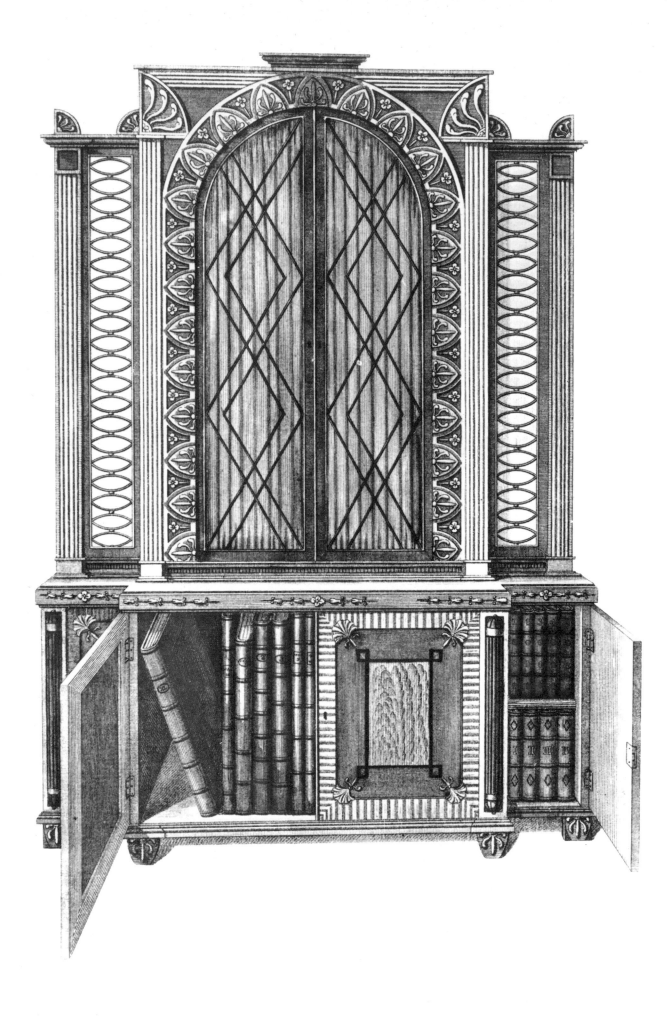

Engraved design for a bookcase from Sheraton's *Encyclopaedia*, published in London in 1805. Like all the pieces illustrated in this work the design is heavier than those in the *Drawing-Book*.

Drawing-Book show a remarkable stylistic unity – a marked preference for simple, sometimes severe, outlines combined with flat (painted or inlaid) decoration of great delicacy and elaboration, sometimes with stringing lines and contrasting veneers in geometrical patterns, sometimes with intricate arabesques or figurative panels. Whereas many earlier designers – especially those working in the rococo style – seem almost to have been ashamed of using wood as their medium, seeking to disguise it as if it were gold or silver or treating it in a manner more suitable for a malleable substance like glass or porcelain, Sheraton's patterns emphasize the essential qualities of wood. The grains of veneers are carefully, one might say lovingly, delineated: the forms are those which come easily to craftsmen working with saws and lathes. He made free play with antique ornaments of the type used by Adam – urns, paterae, vases and swags – yet without so much as a hint of pedantry or *anticomania,* or any of that obsession with bold richness which Adam caught from Piranesi. It is all very elegant, very delicate and perhaps rather feminine.

But fashions were changing fast and most of the designs in Sheraton's *Encyclopaedia* are in quite a different style, one which owes much to the re-establishment of French influence during the brief Peace of Amiens. Draperies which had been discreetly used in the *Drawing-Book* lose their shyness and acquire the lavish panache of Percier and Fontaine. The forms of antique furniture are imitated especially in sabre-legged chairs derived from the Greek *klismos.* The monopod makes its appearance as a support for sideboards and couches; hairy lion-paw feet peep out from the bases of tables; the heads of lions, sphinxes and rams are used as terminals. And many of the pieces could as easily be realized in marble as in wood. Several of the designs are successful, but many remind one of his own remark about racking his invention.

Sheraton's claim that he made 'Designs for Cabinet-makers' is interesting if also perplexing. On one occasion only is he known to have provided a design for a particular piece of furniture – a somewhat preposterous grand piano in a satin-wood case banded with mahogany and encrusted with Wedgwood and Tassie medallions, made in 1796 by John Broadwood for Don Manuel de Godoy who gave it to Queen Maria Louisa of Spain. There are, however, a number of pieces of furniture which correspond closely with the designs in the *Drawing-Book* and the *Encyclopaedia.* And as, in the former work, Sheraton went out of his way to indicate the designs he had taken from other people, it seems reasonable to credit him with the invention of the others.

Adam Weisweiler

(*c.* 1750–*c.* 1810)

The importance of the part played by Germans in furnishing the royal palaces and richer houses in the Paris of Louis XVI can hardly be exaggerated. As we have already seen, the German immigrant Oeben was succeeded by his compatriot Riesener as *ébéniste du Roi,* and a special title was created for Roentgen, though he never had a workshop in Paris. Guillaume Beneman, Martin Carlin, Joseph Gegenbach (who was called Canabas), Bernard Molitor, and Adam Weisweiler were all of German origin. Indeed, Jean-François Leleu and Pierre III Migeon were among the few French-born *ébénistes* to attain distinction in the last two decades of the *ancien régime* (and the former had been trained by Oeben). For long it was supposed that this Teutonic invasion was encouraged by *l'Autrichienne* Marie-Antoinette. But, in fact, German furniture makers had been drawn to Paris earlier in the century and they appear to have arrived in increasing numbers as the fashion for very expensive furniture grew and the city became the most profitable Continental centre for the patronage of outstanding craftsmen. It is, however, difficult to discover why the Germans were better able to satisfy French patrons than native-born craftsmen. Were they technically more highly skilled in the execution of marquetry or the fabrication of mechanical devices? Or were they, perhaps, less bound by tradition, readier to take up new ideas and thus more adept at exploiting the fashionable craving for novelty?

Mr Francis Watson has remarked that Adam Weisweiler represents 'the best side of that teutonic element which was so prevalent in the late Louis XVI period'. He was born in about 1750 and is said to have been trained in Roentgen's workshop at Neuwied – though no trace of Roentgen's influence is evident in his work, except perhaps for a tendency to prefer plain veneers to elaborate marquetry. By 1777, when he married, he had already settled in Paris. Next year he became a *maître* and set up his workshop in the rue du Faubourg Saint Antoine – the main centre for *ébénistes.* During the following decade he produced a considerable quantity of very fine furniture in an individual style, specializing in pieces of light, almost fragile appearance. Lines are clean, legs slenderly tapered, mounts exquisitely chiselled and used with restraint. Sometimes he made use of *pietre dure* panels – originally made in the time of Louis XIV – or of plaques of Sèvres porcelain. But more often he applied panels of glossy black and gold Japanese lacquer, and seems to have had a particular fondness for this opulent yet simple colour scheme, carried out in dark wood with gilt bronze mounts.

opposite Writing-table decorated with ebony veneer and Japanese lacquer by Weisweiler, with bronze mounts attributed to Pierre Gouthière, made for Marie-Antoinette's apartments at Saint Cloud, 1784.

194

Curious interlaced stretchers on tables and feet like spinning tops for cabinets are among the personal peculiarities of his work.

Yet one may question how far he was responsible for creating the style with which his name is associated. He seems to have worked almost exclusively for the *marchard-mercier* Dominique Daguerre, who in 1778 took over the business of Poirier (Bernard II van Risen Burgh's dealer). In 1782 the sale of furniture belonging to the actress Josephine Laguerre included a cabinet made by Weisweiler and supplied to her

One of a pair of ebony cupboards decorated with panels of Japanese lacquer, *c.* 1780–90.

by Daguerre. It was through him that Weisweiler supplied furniture for Marie-Antoinette at Saint Cloud and for the Prince of Wales at Carlton House. Daguerre had a virtual monopoly of Sèvres plaques for furniture which Weisweiler not infrequently used. He also seems to have had some special connection with the *ciseleur-doreur* Gouthière, who was probably responsible for the bronzes on Weisweiler's finest pieces. With a flair for understanding exactly what his richest clients wanted, Daguerre made his shop in the rue Saint-Honoré something

Cabinet, *c.* 1780–90. The *pietre dure* panels are of a type much used on Louis XIV furniture and were probably taken from pieces which had been broken up in the late eighteenth century.

of a social centre. When the Grand Duke Paul of Russia and his wife went there in 1784 they had difficulty in penetrating the fashionable throng examining furniture made for the Duke of Northumberland. Not content with this, he also opened a branch in London – which was to stand him in good stead after the Revolution. And he so insinuated himself into the good graces of Marie-Antoinette that she entrusted many of her possessions to him in the stormy autumn of 1789. If he did not, as seems more than likely, provide Weisweiler with designs, he

Side-table with white marble top and shelf, *c.* 1780–90.

must surely have given him detailed instructions.

Weisweiler survived the Revolution. He may even have profited from it and certainly seized the opportunity to buy real estate in Paris. In the early years of the Empire he secured the patronage of the Bonaparte family – his most notable products of this period being the beautiful jewel boxes made for Queen Hortense in 1806. After the death of his wife in 1809 he retired; the date of his death is unknown. His business was carried on by his son Jean who lived until 1844. ✦

Secrétaire veneered with ebony, purple-wood, holly satinwood, and decorated with panels of Japanese lacquer and gilt bronze mounts, *c.* 1780–90.

Samuel McIntire

(1757–1811)

Upholstered mahogany sofa with carved back-rail attributed to McIntire, c. 1795.

Carved wood and composition chimney piece made for the house of Elias Hasket Derby in Salem, Mass., c. 1795.

In eighteenth-century Europe architects often designed and sculptors occasionally made furniture. Yet Samuel McIntire of Salem, Massachusetts, who was renowned in New England as sculptor, architect and furniture maker, can hardly be ranked with such sophisticated architects as Piranesi and Robert Adam or such sculptors as Brustolon and Cressent. He was, rather, a woodcarver able to turn his hand to the design of a house and the carving of its doorcases and interior trim, to chipping out a bust, or to embellishing the woodwork of a sofa. Indeed, he belongs to a tradition which goes back to the Middle Ages – to a time when no invidious distinctions were drawn between artists and artisans. This is not to suggest that he was no more than a rustic craftsman. He was a man of wide culture who kept himself *à la page* with the stylistic developments of Europe. And there is no reason to believe that the reputation he enjoyed among his contemporaries was exaggerated by the graceful tribute on his tombstone in the Charter Street Burying Ground, Salem: 'He was distinguished for Genius in Architecture Sculpture and Musick; Modest and sweet Manners rendered him pleasing: Industry and Integrity respectable: He professed the Religion of Jesus in his entrance on manly life; and proved its excellence by virtuous Principles and unblemished Conduct.'

He was born in 1757, the son of Joseph McIntire, a joiner, from whom he probably learned his trade. A contemporary recorded that 'he was descended of a family of Carpenters who had no claims on public favour and was educated at a branch of that business'. These carpenters were more probably engaged in shipbuilding – the main industry of Salem – than in household work. And it is often said that Samuel McIntire began his career by carving figure-heads for ships. The writer of his obituary declared, however, that he was 'originally bred to the occupation of a housewright but his vigorous mind soon passed the limits of his profession and aspired to the interesting and admirable science of architecture in which he advanced far beyond most of his countrymen. He made an assiduous study of the great classical masters with whose works notwithstanding their rarity in this country, Mr McIntire had a very intimate acquaintance.' At the time of his death his library included an edition of Palladio, Isaac Ware's *Complete Body of Architecture*, one of Batty Langley's architectural books, James Paine's folio of his own designs, a dictionary of arts and sciences, a 'book of sculptures' and 'two volumes of French architecture'. And there can be no doubt that he had seen copies of other similar books.

Mahogany chest-of-drawers or chest on chest attributed to William Lemon and Samuel McIntire, made at Salem, Mass., in 1796. McIntire is known to have carved decorations for furniture made by other craftsmen.

McIntire began to emerge as an architect, rather than a mere housewright, after the American Revolution, in 1782, when he built the first of a number of plain, square three-storey houses notable mainly for their carved wood decorations. He was soon taking on more exacting commissions, building the Salem Court House and the North and South Meeting Houses. Encouraged by local successes, no doubt, he sent in a design for the Capitol in Washington in 1793 (though without, even on this occasion, going so far afield himself). In 1795 he began what was to prove his most important work, the Derby Mansion built for the principal merchant of Salem, Elias Hasket Derby, and finished in 1799. This 'most superb house', a contemporary records, was 'more like a palace than the dwelling of an American merchant'. Another remarked, when it was pulled down in 1815: 'It was the best finished, most elegant & best constructed House I ever saw', adding in a remark which suggests that ideals of palatial splendour were still rather ingenuous in Salem: 'It was entirely of wood with an excellent façade in the Ionic order.' The general design for this house had been provided by a more sophisticated architect, also an unsuccessful entrant for the Capitol competition, Charles Bullfinch. But McIntire seems to have been responsible for the design of details as for the execution. In 1800, however, Derby entrusted him with the design as well as the construction of a house, Oak Hill at Peabody, built for his daughter Elizabeth. In 1805 he executed wooden arches as gateways to Washington Square which had been made out of the old Salem Common.

A diarist of Salem, the Rev. William Bentley D.D., wrote in 1802: 'As a carver we place Mr Macintire with Skillings of Boston. He cuts smoother than Skillings but he has not his genius. In architecture he excells any person in our country & in his executions as a Carpenter, or Cabinet maker.' But it is now difficult to discover just how much work he did as a cabinet maker. It is certain that he carved not only chimney-pieces and door cases but also furniture for the Derby Mansion. A bill records that he also executed the delicate relief carving on a chest-of-drawers which Mrs Derby had made for her daughter Mrs William Lemon in 1796: he charged three guineas for carving 'Base Mouldings & Brackets' and 'To Carving Freeze Roses &c for the top'. But he evidently took no part in the actual construction of the piece. In 1802 he charged one Jacob Sanderson £1. 7s. 'to carving sofa and top rail' and in the following year the same amount for 'carving & working top rail'. These pieces cannot now be traced, but several sofas have carved decorations, especially baskets of flowers, so close to those on the Lemon chest-of-drawers that they can fairly certainly be attributed to him. Although the tall chest-of-drawers follows a mid-eighteenth-century English pattern, chairs from the Derby Mansion and the various sofas are all much more up-to-date, clearly influenced by Hepple-white's pattern book which was published in 1788. (It should also be remembered that despite American hostility to importations from England before the Revolution, furniture continued to arrive from London during the War and in quantity soon afterwards.) In the design of door cases and chimney-pieces McIntire fell under the influence of Robert Adam. His was not an original talent: his fame derives from his skill as a carver.

McIntire's spare time seems to have been devoted to reading and music. His small library included not only the architectural volumes already mentioned but also books of history and travel, a score of Handel's *Messiah* and other music books. Other possessions included a 'large hand organ with ten barrels, a double bass and a violin'. Bentley says of him: 'In Music he had a good taste & tho' not presuming to be an Original composer, he was among our best judges & most able per-formers. All the instruments we use he could understand & was the best person to be employed in correcting any defects, or repairing them. He had a fine person, a majestic appearance, calm countenance, great self command & amiable temper. He was welcome but never intruded.' It is pleasant to think of him as one of the figures in the Salem where Nathaniel Hawthorne was born in 1804.

At his death in 1811, Samuel McIntire's house and shop were valued at $3,000, his personal property at $1,900 besides $963 in notes. This suggests reasonable prosperity even if it does not compare very favourably with the more than $24,000 left by his contemporary, Stephen Badlam, who also made furniture for E.H. Derby. McIntire's son, Samuel Field McIntire, carried on the business, advertising in the *Salem Gazette* on 30 April 1811: 'The subscriber carries on Carving as usual at the Shop of the deceased in Summer Street where he will be glad to receive orders in that line. He returns thanks for past favours.' Four years later he advertised again, indicating the range of work he undertook: 'Ships Heads, Festoons for Sterns, Tablets and Blockings for Chimney Pieces, Brackets, Draperies – Eagles from 5 inches to 2 feet 6. A variety of Figures, Butter and Cake Stamps, Furniture Carv-ing and Bellows tops.'

Duncan Phyfe

(1768–1854)

opposite Mahogany work-table made *c.* 1810, probably in New York, and attributed to Phyfe.

The American furniture makers previously mentioned in this book – John Goddard, Benjamin Frothingham, Samuel McIntire – were essentially woodcarvers, craftsmen ready to turn their hands to various types of household and other carpentry. They are as distinct from the London furniture manufacturers (Chippendale or Vile and Cobb) as from the highly specialized *menuisiers* and *ébénistes* of Paris. But Duncan Phyfe, who has been called 'the greatest of all American cabinet makers', worked very much according to English precedent, learning his craft as a young man, founding a workshop which grew in size until he was employing some hundred men, and amassing a considerable fortune before he retired. There can be no doubt that he was a highly accomplished businessman with a sharp eye for the needs of the public and a willingness and ability to answer them. He was both a craftsman and a founder of the American industrial tradition.

Duncan Phyfe arrived in America in 1783 or 1784, soon after the independence of the United States had been recognized by the British Government. His father, who spelt his name Fife, had lived at Loch Fannich, 30 miles north west of Inverness, where Duncan was born in 1768. Why the family decided to emigrate from this remote part of the Highlands to America it is impossible to say. The most plausible reason is perhaps to be found in the sorry condition of Scotland in 1782 – 'a year of dearth and distress' according to John Ramsay of Ochtertyre, 'one of those memorable seasons which baffle the skill and labour of the husbandman, and which, happily for mankind, do not occur above twice or thrice in a century'. Up to the outbreak of the American Revolution highlanders distressed by the introduction of new systems of agriculture had been crossing the Atlantic in increasing numbers. To quote Ramsay again, 'a number of respectable people, who till then would not have exchanged their native soil for the best country upon earth, resolved to quit it for ever and betake themselves to the wilds of America, many of them without money, industry or recommendation.' It is hardly surprising that the tide of immigrants should have begun to flow again as soon as opportunity afforded.

On the journey to America two of the Fife children died. Soon after arriving, Duncan's father settled in Albany and began work as a cabinet maker. This was presumably his calling in Scotland, though no very exacting standards of craftsmanship can have been demanded of him on the shores of Loch Fannich. By 1792 Duncan, then described as a

joiner, had gone to New York. Two years later the New York Directory and Register refers to him again, but with his trade changed to that of cabinet maker and his name rendered not as Fife but Phyfe. For this curious change in spelling no reason is recorded. Can he have supposed that Phyfe looked frenchified and would help him to compete with the French émigré craftsmen who had begun to arrive in New York?

New York had not in the colonial period been a centre for the production of furniture comparable with Boston, Newport or Philadelphia. Furniture had been imported in quantity both from England and from other parts of America. Even in 1779 New York imported English upholstery to the value of £820. Immediately the war was over the transatlantic trade was resumed. In 1783 'Cabinet Ware and Upholstery' sent from England to the United States was valued at £4,443 – the biggest importers being in the Carolinas (£1,065) and the next in New York (£817). In 1798 South Carolina imported English furniture worth £1,155 and New York £596. A little earlier, in 1794, an English visitor to Philadelphia had noted that in William Bingham's house 'the chairs of the drawing-room were from Seddon's in London, of the newest taste'. Thus, the American cabinet maker who wished to supply the most fashionable homes – however Republican their owners – had to compete with imported goods. He was presumably helped by the Embargo Act of 1807 which forbade all commerce with Europe, and the War of 1812 which temporarily knocked England out of the market and did much to inflame Anglophobia. But as a result the British immigrant perhaps had to face stronger competition from such immigrant Frenchmen as Charles-Honoré Lannuier and G.J. Lapiere.

To judge from his financial success, Duncan Phyfe was able to benefit from this state of affairs. In 1795 he moved his shop from Broad Street, New York – the main centre for cabinet makers – to the more fashionable Partition Street where he bought the house No. 35. He added to this the house on one side in 1807, that on the other in 1811. And by 1815 his business had increased to such an extent that all three buildings were needed to serve as workshops, warehouse and show-room; and he bought as his residence a house on the other side of the street. The three buildings with the elegant show-room in the centre are depicted in a watercolour painted after 1815.

He began by working in the Sheraton style, never straying far from the designs published in English pattern books. He also imitated the

One of a set of ten mahogany side-chairs made for William Bayard of New York City in 1807 at a price of $15 apiece.

Mahogany sewing table with marble slab on top and brass bands, made at Phyfe's factory and bearing the label: 'D. PHYFE, CABINET MAKER, 33 & 35, PARTITION STREET, New York', c. 1810–16.

DUNCAN PHYFE

French Directoire and, later, Empire styles. From about 1830 he answered the call for what he is said to have scorned as 'butcher furniture' – pieces of a more opulent massiveness. But he appears to have been either too timorous or too prudent to play the role of an innovator. Although his name has been given to the American furniture styles of a long period and he has been credited with individuality, the designs he used seem to have differed little if at all from those employed by other New York cabinet makers of the day. He did not, for instance, make any Empire style furniture comparable either in design or execution with the rare pieces which bear Lannuier's label. But whereas Lannuier's output must have been limited, his work appealing mainly to the ultra-sophisticated, Phyfe's production was considerable and intended for a much wider public.

Phyfe appears to have established himself as the leading cabinet maker in New York by the late 1790s. And as New York began to assume its nineteenth-century place as the richest city in the United States and thus the leader of fashion, he was called on to provide furniture for clients elsewhere, especially in the South. His prices were relatively high. In 1807 he charged $15 each for a set of scroll-back side chairs made for William Bayard of New York and now in the Winterthur Museum. Bills of 1812–13 show him pricing a work table at $52, a pair of foot-stools at $13, a pair of bed-steps at $35, a bedstead at $28, a piano stool at $25 and a set of dining-tables at $80. Some furniture he supplied to Charles N. Bancker of Philadelphia in 1816 included mahogany chairs at $22 each, a sofa at $122, a pair of card-tables at $130 and a 'Piere table' at $265. The surviving pieces that bear his label are of consistently high quality. He used the finest San Domingo mahogany – and West Indian exporters are said to have called the best wood 'Duncan Phyfe logs'. Veneers are neat, carving is well executed, and such pieces of ornamental brass work as claw foot-tips for table legs are well made. His best furniture stands up well to comparison with that produced by the best firms of a similar type in Europe – Gillows in England and Jacob-Desmalter in France – though it would be difficult to claim more for it. After 1830 or thereabouts the quality of production seems to have declined and he began to use rosewood and other cheaper materials.

Phyfe was described by a contemporary as 'a very plain man, always working and always smoking a short pipe'. He is also said to have been a strict Calvinist and a member of the Brick Presbyterian Church. But he played no part either in church or public affairs. He married in 1793 Rachel Lowzade, of Dutch extraction, who bore him four sons and three daughters. In 1837 he took two of his sons, Michael and James, into partnership, changing the name of the firm to Duncan Phyfe and Sons – but on Michael's death in 1840 he had to change it again to Duncan Phyfe and Son. In 1847 he retired and sold his stock by auction. He died in 1854 leaving a fortune estimated at nearly $500,000.

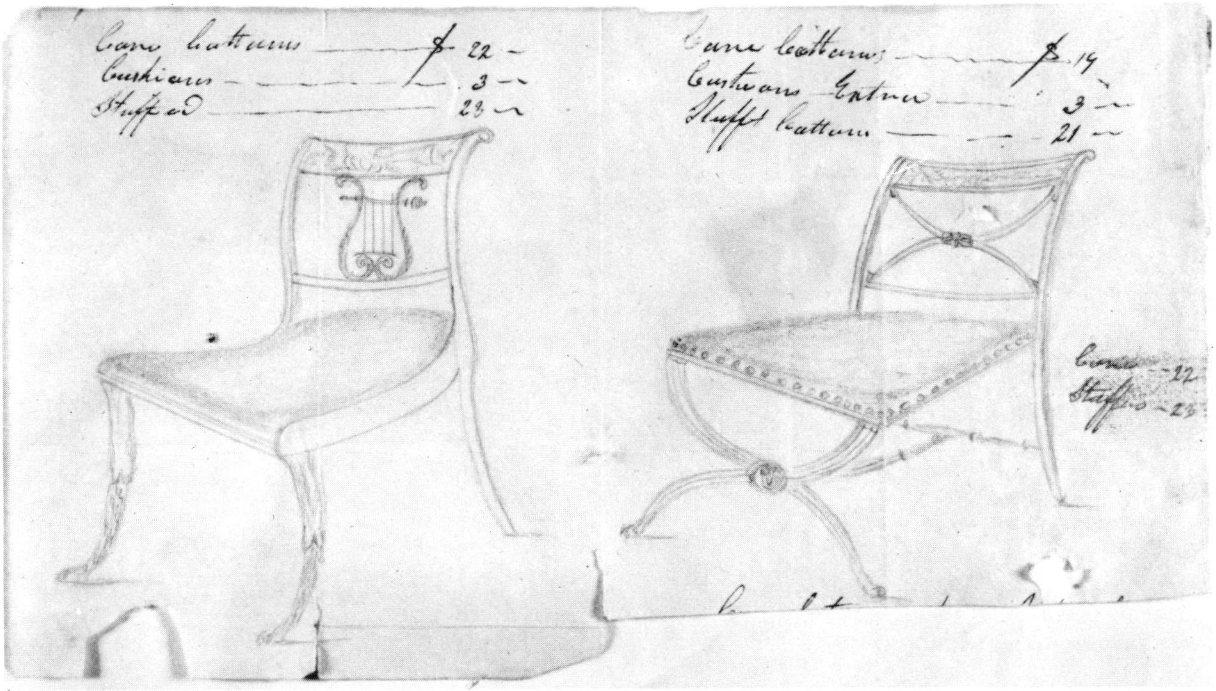
Cane bottoms $ 22 —
Cushions 3 —
Stuffed 23 —
Cane bottoms $ 19
Cushions Extra 3 —
Stuff'd bottom 21 —
Cane 22
Stuff'd 23

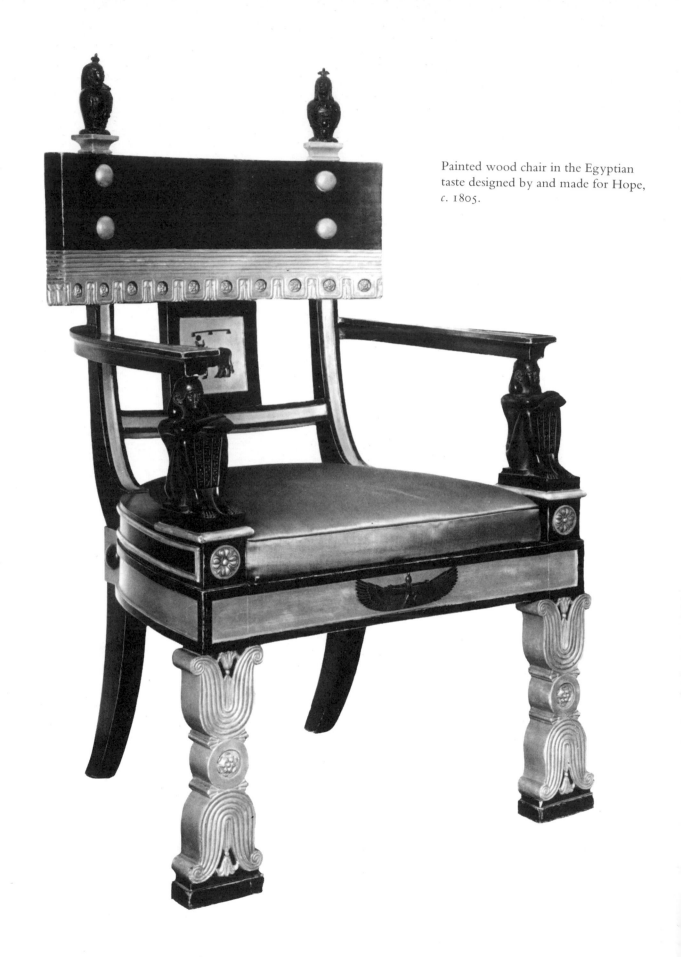

Painted wood chair in the Egyptian taste designed by and made for Hope, c. 1805.

Thomas Hope

(1769–1831)

With Thomas Hope, antique revival furniture design reached its *ne plus ultra* of pedantic correctness and archaeological discomfort. His Grecian couches remind one of Douglas Byng's song about 'naughty 40 BC' when it was 'hard to go wrong on a marble chaise longue'. And the furniture and interiors Hope had executed to his own designs will have little appeal for those in search of the intimate and cosy. Yet for clean lined elegance and graceful poise, Hope's furniture has seldom been surpassed. It has an astringent quality – as refreshing as a glass of very cold and very sour lemonade on a hot summer's night. Significantly enough, it returned to fashion among collectors in the 1920s, just at the moment when others, more forward looking, were beginning to appreciate the different but equally spare beauty of tubular steel furniture.

Unlike the earlier designers mentioned in this book, Hope was a dilettante, a 'gentleman of sofas' as Byron called him. His interest in decorative design seems to have sprung from a desire to provide appropriate furniture for his own houses – presumably because he was dissatisfied with that which could be bought from the cabinet makers of London. This is not the place to record the long, complicated and often obscure history of his life. Suffice it to say that he was born in Amsterdam in 1769, the son of a rich banking family. In his youth he spent eight years travelling in Greece and the Eastern Mediterranean where he acquired a passion for Greek art and architecture. Perhaps as a result of the French invasion of Holland, he settled in London in about 1796. A true cosmopolitan, he travelled extensively in Europe. In 1799 we find him in Athens again, in 1802 in Naples and Rome. But he had already begun to form a collection of antique and modern works of art – his first important commission had been given to Flaxman in 1792 – and seems to have decided that it should be housed in England.

In 1801 Sylvester Douglas wrote that Hope was 'said to be the richest, but undoubtedly far from the most agreeable man in Europe. He is a great traveller and collector at any expense of vertu of all sorts . . . and has furnished his magnificent house . . . with a profusion of those things . . . .'. The house in question must have been that in Duchess Street, London (built by Robert Adam in the 1770s), off Portland Place. It was not until 1807 that he bought the house he was to make famous, Deepdene in Surrey. In the meantime he had entered the fashionable world of antiquaries and men of taste. In 1800 he was elected to the Society of Dilettanti. He first emerged as a pundit in print in 1804, publishing

Engraved design for a Grecian chair, 1807.

Observations on the Plans and Elevations designed by James Wyatt, Architects, for Downing College, Camb. . . . in which he advocated an uncompromising Greek Doric design in place of Wyatt's rather humdrum and, by international standards, old-fashioned, Roman Doric project. In 1807 he published his folio volume: *Household Furniture and Interior Decoration* which firmly established him as *arbiter elegantiarum*. Two volumes on the *Costumes of the Ancients* followed in 1809, and *Designs of Modern Costume* in 1812. In 1819 he surprised the literary world with *Anastasius or Memoirs of a Greek written at the close of the Eighteenth Century,* a three-decker novel which provided a modern parallel to Barthélemy's *Voyage du jeune Anarcharsis* and quickly became a best-seller. He wrote further works, on philosophy as well as architecture, and died in 1831.

opposite top Design for a screen from *Household Furniture and Interior Decoration*, 1807.

opposite bottom Painted wood sofa designed by Hope and made *en suite* with the chair on page 210.

Engraved design for a room in the Egyptian taste, published in *Household Furniture and Interior Decoration*, 1807.

In *Household Furniture* Hope acknowledged his indebtedness to several sources he had used, notably Montfaucon's early eighteenth-century *L'antiquité expliquée*, the works of Piranesi, Vivant Denon's *Voyage dans la basse et la haute Égypte* and Wilhelm Tischbein's four volumes of engravings of Greek vases. Somewhat surprisingly he did not mention (although he had subscribed to) C.H. Tatham's *Etchings Representing the Best Examples of Ancient Ornamental Architecture* of 1799, which illustrated many pieces of ancient furniture. Naturally enough he made no reference to the designs for 'Grecian' furniture that both Sheraton and George Smith had begun to publish in 1804 for it was, precisely, against their easy-going eclecticism that he reacted. He may, perhaps, have been influenced by Percier and Fontaine, whom he seems to have

known personally, though he probably considered their furniture designs archaeologically incorrect. Indeed, as a designer of ruthlessly accurate antique-style furniture he appears to have had only two predecessors, both of them painters – J.-L. David and N. Abildgaard – and both of whom designed furniture mainly for their own use.

Under the impact of the neo-classical movement the design of furniture was greatly purified and simplified in the last decades of the eighteenth century. But, as we have seen, surprisingly few precise copies of antique furniture had been made. It was generally believed that the artist should seek to imitate the spirit rather than copy the letter of antiquity. For Thomas Hope, however, imitations in the style of antiquity were too perfunctory by half. Although relatively few examples of Greek and Roman furniture were, as yet, known, he realized that an accurate impression of its appearance might be obtained from a study of sculpture and vase paintings which revealed the elegant shape and proportions of the Greek couch and the unsurpassed grace of the *klismos*. These sources did not, of course, yield prototypes for all the furnishings deemed necessary for the early nineteenth-century house. Hope was obliged to adapt an ancient sarcophagus to provide himself with a wine-cooler. He had to resort to architecture to find designs for sideboards. And when he or his wife needed a long dressing-glass or a pole-screen to shield their faces from the glow of a coal fire, he was obliged to invent. Even so, he did his best to observe the grammatical rules of antique ornament.

Hope did not confine himself to the furniture of Greece and Rome; his attention was caught also by that of Egypt. It was commonly held that the Greeks had derived the first principles of architecture from Egypt (though opinions differed as to whether they or the Romans had brought it to perfection). And it was appreciated that the same might be true of furniture. But until the publication of Denon's book, precious little was known about Egyptian art. Egyptian motifs had been used in architecture and on furniture spasmodically for many years, though even more frivolously than Greek and Roman ornament. In France Egyptian motifs seem to have been adopted mainly, if not exclusively, as Napoleonic symbols, and Denon's engravings were used rather cavalierly. Biennais made a little coin cabinet modelled on the gigantic pylon at Ghoos and the Sèvres factory a dinner service with sugar bowls fashioned like cinerary urns.

But Hope seized on Denon's *Voyage*, which very conveniently

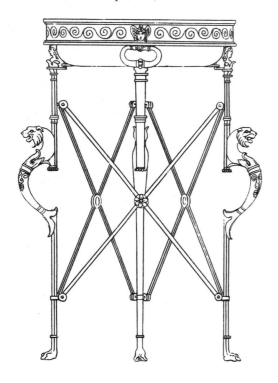

Design for a tripod similar to Roman examples excavated at Pompeii, by Thomas Hope, 1807.

Design for a pole-screen, with an adjustable panel to protect a delicate complexion from the glow of a fire. 1807. Hope was obliged to invent several such pieces of furniture for which there were no precedents in antiquity.

appeared during the Peace of Amiens, and scanned its plates for illustrations of Egyptian furniture. He sought to reproduce the chairs, couches and beds to be descried in the hieroglyphic paintings and carvings. At Deepdene, Maria Edgeworth wrote in 1819, 'There is too much Egyptian ornament, Egyptian hieroglyphical figures, bronze and gilt, but all hideous. In one room . . . there is a bed made exactly after the model of Denon's Egyptian bed, a sofa-bed wide enough for two aldermen, embossed gold hieroglyphic frights all pointing with their hands distorted backwards at an Osiris or a long-armed monster of some sort who sits after their fashion on her hams and heels and has the likeness of a globe of gold on her lapetted, scaly-lapetted head.' Other visitors must have been more favourably impressed, for the taste for Egyptian furniture was soon well established.

Hope had strong feelings not only on decorative design but also on the use of colour in the interior. Many years later Richard Monckton Milnes recorded how he had once sat at dinner next to 'Tommy Hope, Anastasius, he wrote the book upon furniture & decoration & was regarded as the Corypheus of Art & Taste. All our talk was on it, & it was his main injunction to avoid having green. He said it was the color of Nature's freshness & Nature disdain'd imitation. She showed it by having her green turn brown by candle-light. It was the color of all others to have where apartments were in accompanyment with outdoor scenery – as summer houses, & villas on the Thames – these intended only for enjoyment in the day.' (It is interesting to find Mondrian objecting to the use of green in the interior just a century later.)

In order to have his furniture designs realized accurately, Hope relied not on English but on French *émigré* craftsmen and employed two named Decaix and Bogaert. Several surviving pieces testify to their ability. But although this furniture was made for his own houses, he clearly hoped that the publication of his designs would help to improve the taste of his contemporaries. They were, in fact, soon imitated both by the authors of pattern books and furniture makers – but seldom without modification. Generally these imitations lack the nicely adjusted poise and sharp precision of line and detail of the originals. Hope's influence was, however, more far-reaching. He, more than any other single person, established the taste for accurate copies of the furniture style of the past and thus threw open the door to the historical revivalism of the nineteenth century. It is significant that he should have devoted his last years to the study of Gothic architecture.

Giovanni Socchi

(fl. 1805–1815)

opposite The throne room in the Palazzo Reale, Turin, designed by Pelagio Palagi.

Drum-shaped cupboard, one of a series made for Napoleon's sister, Eliza Baciocchi, after she had been created Grand Duchess of Tuscany in 1809.

Wherever the rule of the Bonaparte family extended new palaces were built and old ones re-decorated in the fashionable Empire style. Although time was short an immense amount was achieved in the decade between the formal establishment of the Napoleonic Empire in 1804 and its crash in 1814. When the Bourbons were restored to Naples in 1815 they hurried round to inspect the improvements made to their palaces in their absence. *'Papa mio,'* one of the young princes is said to have remarked to his father after admiring the shining elegance of the villa at Portici – 'if only we had been away for another ten years'. The Bonapartes had, indeed, established a new standard of palatial magnificence and comfort. So far as they could, they obtained furniture, silver, porcelain and even designs for interior decoration direct from Paris. But, either from economy, or from a genuine desire to improve local craftsmanship, they also patronized local craftsmen in each kingdom. Unfortunately little is known of the furniture makers they took up and encouraged to work in a style as close as possible to that of Jacob and other leading *menuisiers* and *ébénistes* in Paris. Giovanni Socchi – or Socci as his name was sometimes spelt – is among the very few who attained a measure of individual distinction. He was employed by Napoleon's sister, Elisa Baciocchi, and several of his works are still to be seen in Palazzo Pitti, Florence.

Elisa Baciocchi, described as 'de seconde en génie de la famille Impériale', was given the principates of Lucca and Piombino in 1805. As soon as she arrived in Lucca she set to work on the redecoration of the Palazzo della Signoria (now Palazzo Provinciale). She also set up a *manufacture royale* under the direction of an *ébéniste* named Youff who was summoned from Paris. Accounts reveal that between 1805 and 1806 she employed a cabinet maker called Luigi Socchi (or Succhi), who may have been a relation of Giovanni Socchi. In 1809 the Grand Duchy of Tuscany was added to Elisa's realm and she promptly complained that 'the Pitti Palace lacks indispensable furnishing'. However, she appears to have made it habitable by moving in a quantity of furniture from Lucca and making a delightful marble bathroom.

Socchi's furniture in the Palazzo Pitti includes a series of very attractive drum-shaped cupboards on pine-cone feet, with gilt wood mounts and white marble tops, made for the Sala dei Tamburi. Though obviously in the Empire style, they are remarkably unlike the furniture that was being made in Paris at this date. A number of tables and chests-of-drawers which are much closer to French models may also be by Socchi, for they are clearly not of French workmanship.

217

Mahogany writing-table made in
Florence, *c.* 1810, and *below* the same
table open, serving as a combined
chair and desk.

But Socchi's fame rests mainly on a series of very ingenious, beautifully made, writing-desks – two in Palazzo Pitti (both signed), one at Malmaison and another (also signed) which recently passed through a London sale room. Each of these pieces looks at first sight like an oval chest-of-drawers on legs. A portion of the front conceals a chair which may be drawn out. If two handles, which are then revealed under the rim of the top, are pulled forwards, the two halves of the top move to either side and a container for pens and papers rises up – converting the whole piece into a writing-table and chair. In the absence of contrary evidence it may be assumed that Socchi was responsible for designing as well as making these pieces of furniture. It is generally said that they were intended to serve as travelling desks, though they are much too bulky. They seem, rather, to reveal a love of ingenuity for its own sake and to be the lineal descendants of the delicately contrived mechanical pieces made by Oeben and Roentgen under the *ancien régime*.

No more is heard of Socchi after the Restoration, but he probably continued to work as a cabinet maker in Florence. And, like most other Italian furniture makers of the time, presumably clung to the Empire style.

Writing-desk signed by Socchi,
c. 1810–15.

Gilt bronze table designed by Palagi
for the Council Chamber of
Palazzo Reale, Turin, and cast in the
Viscari foundry at Milan, 1836.

Pelagio Palagi

(1775–1860)

In the Council Chamber of the Palazzo Reale in Turin, the visitor's attention is drawn to a very splendid gilt bronze table supported on four winged victories. It was on this table on 8 February 1848 that Carlo Alberto signed the 'Statuto' which defined the democratic constitution of his realm – the famous statute which was later to serve for the whole of united Italy and survived as the basic constitutional document until 1948. For all students of Italian history, this table is a relic of more than ordinary interest. But all the furniture in this room – sofa, chairs, stools and candelabra – have also intrinsic merits as fine, probably the finest, examples of mid-nineteenth-century Italian craftsmanship. These pieces are perhaps the last noteworthy manifestations of the Italian liking for sculpturesque furniture. The use of bronze for the table is in itself revealing: for this sculptural medium had been used for furniture in Italy, and especially eighteenth-century Rome, much more frequently than in any other part of Europe. And like so much of the best Italian furniture, this suite was not designed by a cabinet maker: the author was Pelagio Palagi, a painter, sculptor and architect.

Palagi was born in 1775 in Bologna, and trained there as a painter. In 1806 he went to Rome and joined the large team of artists (including Thorvaldsen) employed to transform the Quirinal into a palace fit for Napoleon who was expected to visit the city. After the Restoration he painted frescoes for the room enshrining Canova's group of *Hercules and Lichas* in the vast and opulent palace which the banker Torlonia was building. He also worked in Naples. In 1818 he went to Milan where he opened a private art school in which, according to a contemporary, he exerted 'una certa tirannia' over the students. His authoritarianism was, however, thought to be beneficial and in 1832 he was invited to Turin, put in charge of the direction of the royal palaces and appointed director of the school of ornamental design of the royal Accademia Albertina which the young King Carlo Alberto was seeking to enlarge and improve.

Like so many artists who were trained when neo-classicism was at its height, Palagi developed the Romantic currents which ran through the whole movement. An eclectic historical revivalist, he resorted to the styles of the past not as a means to create ideally beautiful works of art but as ends in themselves. For the royal summer palace, Racconigi, he built a large hunting pavilion in an elegant Gothic style. In the Palazzo Reale he worked in a bold version of the Empire style. This he doubtless considered appropriate as a setting for Carlo Alberto who had been

PELAGIO PALAGI

born during the French occupation of Piedmont, educated in Paris and Geneva, held a commission in Napoleon's army, dallied with the Liberals in his youth and then attempted to play the part of an eighteenth-century enlightened despot in the very different atmosphere of the nineteenth century.

As we have already seen, the Empire style had been introduced into Italy by members of Napoleon's family. After 1815 it survived as the expression of modern palatial magnificence *par excellence*. But Palagi strove to create a still more magnificent and showy style in the furniture he designed for the Turin palace. To the chairs and stools he gave an appearance of solemnity and solidity, by reference back to the Italian furniture of the seventeenth and eighteenth centuries. He had the whole surface of the woodwork thickly gilded and made great play with robustly carved or modelled human and mythological figures. The table is more elegant, closer to the Empire style of Percier and Fontaine, and is overcharged in a symbolical rather than a decorative sense. In retrospect it seems hardly surprising that Carlo Alberto should have approved a style of decoration which wedded the eighteenth century to the Empire. And there is a certain poetic justice in his adoption of this Italianate late Empire table to sign the document which was to play a vital part in the Risorgimento. For to some extent the Napoleonic unification of Italy inspired the movement which culminated in the re-unification under Carlo Alberto's son, Vittorio Emanuele II.

opposite Detail of the base of a bronze candelabrum designed by Palagi and cast in Milan in 1836.

One of a suite of carved and gilt wood stools designed by Palagi for the Palazzo Reale in Turin, 1836–40.

Karl Friedrich Schinkel

(1781–1841)

Since the beginning of the eighteenth century nearly all major (and many minor) architects have exerted considerable influence on the design of furniture. And Karl Friedrich Schinkel, whom one is tempted to call the greatest of all German architects, is no exception. He designed not only the 'architectural' furniture which forms an integral part of the interiors of his buildings but also many movable pieces – chairs, sofas, tables, beds and so on. This furniture has been all but totally eclipsed by the grandeur of Schinkel's buildings, but it is of great interest for its own sake, as a manifestation of his fascinatingly ambiguous artistic personality, and not least as an expression of ideas which seem to foreshadow those current in advanced architectural circles in Germany a century later. For it is by turns derivative and daringly experimental, showy and functional, graciously elegant and almost savagely 'brutal'.

He was born at Neurippin in 1781, the son of an archdeacon and inspector of churches. At the age of thirteen he was sent to the Gymnasium zum Grauen Kloster in Berlin and in 1798 began to study architecture under the brilliant but short-lived Friedrich Gilly. After Gilly's death in 1800 he studied at the Berlin Academy where he made his first designs for furniture and architecture. A drawing of 1802 shows the hall of a private house with 'antiken *Möbel*' – a somewhat absurdly squat large round table, a Pompeiian tripod table and curious armchairs – free essays in Greek and Roman styles untouched by archaeological pedantry. In 1803 he set off on his *Wanderjahre*, travelling through Germany and Austria to Italy and returning by way of Paris in 1805. Back in Berlin he began his career as a painter. But he also designed some furniture, notably, in 1809, a bed for Queen Luise in the Charlottenburg Palace. With very few of the airs and graces of the fashionable Empire style, this delicate, light-coloured piece veneered with pear-wood anticipates the Biedermeier style of the post-Napoleonic period.

His work as an architect began in 1815 when he was made Geheimer Oberbaurat in the Prussian Office of Public Works – of which he was to become director fifteen years later. He designed much for the State, for the Royal Family and occasionally for private patrons. At first he worked in a fairly pure Greek Revival style, with occasional excursions into Gothic. The outstanding buildings are the New Guard House (1816), the Theatre (1818–21), Old Museum (1823–30) and Humboldt's country house Tegel (1822–4), all Grecian, and the Gothic war memorial on the Kreutzberg in cast iron (1818) and the Friedrich-Werdersche

opposite Portrait of Prince August of Prussia by Franz Krüger, *c.* 1820. The Prince is shown standing in a room with furniture designed by Schinkel and in front of F.-P. Gérard's portrait of Mme Récamier.

Beechwood toilet-table designed for Queen Luise to go with the bed illustrated opposite.

Kirche (1824–30). But his most interesting buildings are perhaps the later ones in which he gradually freed himself from the tyranny of historical styles, either partially, in the informal use of Grecian motifs (e.g. the buildings in the park at Potsdam), boldly simplified versions of Gothic (the huge Schloss zu Kamenz) or Romanesque (Nazarethkirche, Berlin), or completely as in the astylar brick-built Bau-Akademie (1832–5). During these years he found time for a second visit to Italy in 1824 and a journey through England and Scotland in 1826. He was also engaged in decorating apartments for Crown Prince Friedrich Wilhelm and Prince August, besides building palaces in the Wilhelmstrasse for Prince Karl and Prince Albrecht.

A true Romantic-Classicist if ever there was one (and Siegfried

Beechwood bed designed for
Queen Luise in 1809.

Giedion invented the term mainly to describe him), he handled both
the Grecian and Gothic styles with equal ability in furniture design as
in architecture. An English writer of the day, Joseph Gwilt, complained
that as a Grecian he was woefully incorrect. And as for his 'designs for
Gothic', they 'would not be tolerated in this country for an instant. So
little are the principles and the peculiarities of the style understood by
him, that there is scarcely an architect's office which could not produce
pupils of two or three years standing far his superiors.' Schinkel was
not, of course, striving after correctness. His designs, whether Grecian
or Gothic, whether for architecture or furniture, differ strikingly from
those of his contemporaries in England. His Grecian furniture has none
of the attenuated elegance of 'Regency' and none of the archaeological

227

Two chairs with upholstered seats and backs from a set designed for the Palace of Prince Friedrich of Prussia, 1817.

discomfort of Thomas Hope. It is solid and simple. And the Gothic pieces differ as markedly from the flimsy fantasies of the elder Pugin as from the seriously medieval works of his son.

Schinkel was clearly striving – once again in furniture as well as architecture – after a contemporary style. Historical motifs are seldom overstressed, though he made use of monopods and flamboyant tracery, just as he made use of columns and pointed windows in his buildings. The chairs he designed for Prince August's palace (1818–21) – charmingly depicted in Krüger's portrait of the Prince – are in a version of the Empire style from which most of the characteristic motifs have been erased. Those he designed for Prince Friedrich are more original, with curious rounded backs, a little heavy, perhaps, but eminently practical.

228

Armchair with book stand.

He also designed very simple and obviously very comfortable sofas to stand in the corners of rooms, of a type that was soon to become very popular in both Germany and Austria. It is interesting and perhaps significant that he also had designs carried out in cast iron – a material of which he made daring use as an architect.

Schinkel's buildings appear to have had some influence on the first German architects of the modern movement, especially Peter Behrens. It would be interesting to know if his furniture designs had a comparable influence on the reformatory movement initiated in Prussia by Muthesius at the beginning of the twentieth century. The severer pieces certainly reveal as much *Sachlichkeit* as the products of the English Arts and Crafts movement which Muthesius praised.

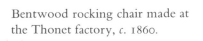
Bentwood rocking chair made at
the Thonet factory, *c.* 1860.

Michael Thonet

(1796–1871)

In the collection of twentieth-century design in the Museum of Modern Art, New York, a place of honour has been given to Michael Thonet's bentwood chairs. They are so logically simple, so unaffectedly elegant and possess such youthful vitality in the spring of their lines, that it is at first difficult to associate them with the mid-nineteenth century. As Le Corbusier said when he chose them for the Pavilion de l'Esprit Nouveau at the great Paris exhibition of 1925, 'these chairs bear titles of nobility'. Had no more than a few of them survived we might well be tempted to see Thonet as a functionalist genius born before his time, struggling heroically against the ornate bad taste of his contemporaries. But nothing could be further from the truth.

Thonet was not, so far as is known, concerned in any way with the high-minded attempts of certain contemporaries to improve design in the industrial arts, still less with theories of functionalism. Nor does he appear to have had much difficulty in establishing the Thonet style – the products of his factory won almost immediate popularity which soon spread throughout Europe and America. By the end of the century the Thonet factories were employing a staff of 6,000 and turning out 4,000 pieces of furniture a day – and no fewer than 50,000,000 examples of one very simple type of café chair have been made since it was first devised in the 1850s. He has a claim to be the most successful of all furniture manufacturers. But, of course, the chairs to which we nowadays accord the highest praise would not, in the nineteenth century, have been regarded as examples of the decorative arts at all. This is not to deny their influence on theorists of the modern movement. In the history of furniture they occupy an important position analagous with that of warehouses and iron and glass railway station roofs in the history of architecture.

Michael Thonet was born in 1796 at Boppard in Prussia, a few miles up the Rhine from Neuwied where David Roentgen had run what was probably the most successful and expensive of *de luxe* eighteenth-century furniture factories. In 1819 he set up his own carpenter's and joiner's workshop, specializing in parquetry. But it was not until 1830 that he began to experiment with new techniques, devising a process of glueing veneers together to make sections of furniture and another for bending beech rods under steam to form the framework of chairs. Apart from their rather curious legs, the chairs he made at this period differ little in design from carved furniture in the Biedermeier style. In 1841 he applied for patents for his bentwood technique in France, England and Belgium. In the same year he exhibited specimens in

MICHAEL THONET

One of the first chairs designed by Thonet, *c.* 1836–40, and made of strips of bent wood.

Coblenz, attracting the notice of Prince Metternich, who invited him to Vienna where he and his family settled in the following year.

At this date one third of Austrian soil was covered with forests; but the wood industry – in contrast to metal mining – was poorly developed. Metternich must have appreciated the value of the new techniques in woodwork which could be put to industrial use – though he can hardly have realized what a potentially valuable economic asset Austria had acquired from the Zollverein, and Thonet in fact began by using imported wood. Involved in financial difficulties almost as soon as he arrived in Vienna, Thonet went into partnership with the firm of Carl Leistler who had established a factory for the production of furniture and inlaid floors. With Leistler, he provided furniture for the Palais Liechtenstein, under the direction of an English architect, P.H. Desvignes. The chairs that Thonet designed show many elements of his mature style – they are light and elegant and one set has backs formed by rods bent into figures of eight. But the majority have upholstered backs and seats, with little triangles of carved decoration between the seat and the legs. All were made of veneers glued together and bent, not of beechwood rods.

Dissolving the partnership with Leistler, Thonet set up on his own in Vienna in 1849, aided by Desvignes who tried to persuade him to settle in London. That year he supplied to the Café Daum the first examples of the chair later to be known as Thonet Nr 4, made of mahogany with bentwood scrolls in the back as the only decorations apart from vestigial capitals at the tops of the legs. Two years later he sent furniture to the Great Exhibition in London. The entry for his exhibits in the official catalogue reads:

> 641 THONET, MICHAEL, *Vienna* – Manufacturer
> *Furniture:* Sofas, Easy chairs. Arm-chairs.
> Stand of rosewood and walnut wood.
> Specimens of inlaid floorings.
> A small round table of rosewood.
> *The above are variously inlaid with metal,*
> *tortoise-shell, and mother-of-pearl.*

As he is mentioned immediately after Anton Staudinger of Vienna, a maker of 'Buhl' furniture, it is perhaps not surprising that more attention should have been paid to the decorations applied to Thonet's furniture than to its structure. The only one of his products to be illustrated in the catalogue was a hideously convoluted and knotted picture-stand. It would be interesting to know if Thonet himself admired this nightmarish object more than his simple bentwood chairs – the chances are that he did.

In 1853 Michael Thonet took his five sons into partnership and renamed the firm: Gebrüder Thonet. Its subsequent history is a straightforward industrial success story. By 1855 exports were going as far

afield as South America. Factories were established in the Moravian beechwoods and in Hungary where local labour was cheap. Gradually the firm adopted mass-production on an increasingly vast scale. At the second Great Exhibition in London, in 1862, Thonet showed no elaborate confections of the kind sent previously but only 'billige Konsumware' – the inexpensive mass-produced pieces with which he was now mainly concerned. By 1871 he had established sale-rooms not only in the various cities of Austria and Germany but also at Brussels, Marseilles, Milan, Rome, Naples, Barcelona, Madrid, St Petersburg, Moscow, Odessa, New York and Chicago. He died on 3 March, 1871.

The Thonet firm continued to grow under the direction of his sons and new factories were opened, at Nowo-Radomsk in Russian Poland, and at Frankenberg in Hesse. Many new designs were introduced, but the fact that none of these had the distinction – or won the popularity – of those first made in the 1850s and 1860s suggests that Michael Thonet had been personally responsible for the design as well as the business side of the firm, even if he employed several draughtsman-designers.

The production of the Thonet factories included tables, beds, cradles, hat-stands and other pieces of furniture but none is as interesting as the upright chairs and rocking chairs. As we have already seen Thonet began by using his laminating and bending process for chairs which differed little in design from those made by traditional carving techniques. Even the chairs for the Café Daum still had parts – the framework of the seats and the tops of the front legs – which had to be carved, if only very simply. It was not until about 1859 when he produced chair Nr 14 that he developed a fully mechanized process and began to make furniture without any decorations at all. This chair consists of no more than six parts – a long beechwood rod bent into a loop to form the back legs and chair back; a smaller loop to fit inside this and give extra support to the back; a hoop to form the framework for a caned seat; a smaller hoop to go below as a stretcher; and two rods gently tapered and bent for the front legs. This chair was not only cheap to make and light to handle but could be transported very economically in parts and assembled with no more than ten screws. It cost about 3s. (75 US cents) in the money of the day. Other designs for chairs – some with more elaborate scrolls in the back, some with arms – are merely variations on this prototype. Settees were also made on the same basic principle.

In evolving the design for chair Nr 14 there can be no doubt that Thonet's prime aim was cheapness. Beechwood was used because it was the most suitable for treatment by the Thonet process – it is resilient, has long fibres and few knots. The trunks were mechanically sawn into strips about 3 cm. (1 inch) square and then turned on a lathe to give them a circular section. They were next placed in autoclaves, in which they were steamed for a short time to render them pliable, and bent round

MICHAEL THONET

opposite Bentwood rocking chair, *c.* 1860. The Thonet factory produced several different types of rocking chair.

Engraving of a bentwood picture-stand made in Thonet's factory, shown in the Great Exhibition in London in 1851 and illustrated in the commemorative catalogue.

opposite Sofa of carved and laminated rosewood made in New York at the factory of J. H. Belter, 1856–61.

metal forms to which they were attached before being placed in a drying kiln. When fully dried they were given their final shaping and finishing on lathes, dyed to darker colours, assembled and polished. No skilled labour was needed except for finishing and weaving the cane for seats and backs.

Thonet's inspiration for his bentwood chairs seems to have derived initially from the cast iron furniture that had become popular earlier in the nineteenth century. The picture stand he showed at the Great Exhibition and some only slightly less tortured tables, which were produced in quantity, are as richly overwrought as most of the metal furniture displayed at the Crystal Palace. And a bed with complicated scrolls filling the head- and foot-board is a direct imitation of iron or brass in bentwood. His wooden furniture was not as durable as that of iron, but it was both lighter and very much cheaper. The majority of the chairs and settees illustrated in Thonet's catalogues are fairly well provided with loops and curlicues of bentwood giving a rich appearance which suited them for the mid- and late-nineteenth century home. Chair Nr 14 is, in fact, exceptional in its simplicity – the phenomenally low price both determined its design and assured its popularity as a purely utilitarian article of furniture.

A rather more difficult problem is posed by the rocking chairs that are the most graceful of Thonet's products. Their origin has been sought in a steel chair made in the United States by Peter Cooper in about 1850 – though there is no reason to suppose that Thonet ever saw it – and in the rococo scroll work on the staircase of Palais Liechtenstein in Vienna. But might they not have derived from carriage designs? Their elegant linearity echoes the curves of the springs of phaetons and pony carriages which were made in all parts of Europe, including Vienna, at this date. The first rocking chair was produced in 1860 and it is perhaps significant that at about the same date the Thonet factories began to make carriage wheels as well as furniture.

Thanks to low prices and an efficient sales organization, Thonet's chairs were secured a wider diffusion than any furniture hitherto made. Examples of them are to be seen in the nursery of Tolstoi's house in Moscow. One spots them in Toulouse-Lautrec's paintings of the *Moulin Rouge*. And tens of thousands are still in daily use throughout the world. They were quite simply the least expensive of all chairs. No one seems to have appreciated their merits as examples of furniture design until the 1920s when Le Corbusier began to use them. He referred to 'the humble Thonet chair of steamed wood, certainly the most common as well as the least costly of chairs . . . whose millions of representatives are used on the Continent and in the two Americas'. Shortly afterwards the Thonet firm began to manufacture tubular steel chairs to the designs of Mart Stam, Marcel Breuer and Mies van der Rohe – but that is another story.

John Henry Belter

(1804–1863)

In his last years Duncan Phyfe, surrendering to public demand, had abandoned the somewhat austere elegance of his earlier furniture for the richer, ampler style demanded by the public. The nineteenth-century trend in taste away from the severe and back to the opulent was no less apparent in America than in Europe. On both sides of the Atlantic furniture was expected to demonstrate its costliness in rich decorations – and to manifest to the eye as well as the body its gently embracing cosiness. Such furniture was the speciality of J. H. Belter, who succeeded Phyfe as the most fashionable manufacturer in what Henry James called 'the small warm dusky homogeneous New York world of the mid-century'.

John Henry – originally Johann Heinrich – Belter was of German origin, born in 1804. He was apprenticed as a woodworker in the little kingdom of Württemberg which embraced the Black Forest whence came so many of the elaborately overwrought carvings, especially clock-cases, beloved in the mid-nineteenth century. The capital of Württemberg, Stuttgart, was also famed for the production of pianofortes in monstrously rich cases of mahogany or rosewood. It may well have been in this branch of the cabinet-making business that Belter began to work. But nothing definite is known of him until 1844 when he settled in New York, at 40½ Chatham Square – the fashionable centre for cabinet makers – and married Louisa Springmeyer, whose brothers he was later to take into partnership. He took a shop on Broadway and in 1858 opened, on Third Avenue, a large factory where he is said to have employed as many as forty apprentices. For the more skilled tasks he relied on immigrant German carvers.

Rosewood, popular with the public in America no less than in Europe, appears to have been Belter's favourite medium. This dark, heavily grained wood, which came mainly from Brazil and the West Indies, lacked sufficient strength for carved work and was difficult to use for veneering on curved surfaces. When carved decorations were wanted on rosewood furniture they were generally applied on top of the veneer. It was Belter's achievement to invent a process by which rosewood could be used for the most voluptuously carved and intricately curved pieces. And in 1856 he applied for a patent, setting out in somewhat complicated terms the method he employed. Laminae of rosewood, with the grain of each layer at right angles to the next, were glued and pressed together. There might be as few as three or as many as sixteen layers – usually there were between six and eight – to make a

One of a pair of sofas of carved and
gilt rosewood upholstered in red silk
damask, made at Belter's factory in
New York, c. 1850.

JOHN HENRY BELTER

Rosewood table with marble top,
probably made in New York at
Belter's factory, *c.* 1860.

panel less than an inch thick. The panel could then be shaped in moulds
by steam heat and later carved. The similarity of this laminating and
steam moulding process to that invented by Michael Thonet at Boppard (rather to the north of Württemberg) in the late 1830s suggests
that Belter may have derived it from him – though he applied it to very
different ends. There is certainly nothing 'functional' about Belter's
furniture, whether made of rosewood by his patent process or carved
from the black walnut which had a similar appearance and was much
less expensive.

Stylistically his furniture belongs to the heavily florid neo-rococo
– the *zweites Rokoko* – which had begun to succeed the Biedermeier in
the Austria and Germany of the 1830s. Contours are rounded, legs bend
into double-scrolled curves, there is much carving both in relief and in
the round of fruit and flowers and juicy leaves with every now and then
a bold asymmetrical cartouche. In Europe this type of furniture undoubtedly owed most of its appeal to a nostalgic yearning for the
elegancies of the *ancien régime*. In an era of upstarts and *nouveaux riches,*

Bed of laminated rosewood, *c.* 1860.

of swiftly changing social patterns and political unrest, it stood as a comforting symbol of the tranquil and stable eighteenth-century world of princely courts that had passed for ever. But in America it can have had few connotations of this kind. And we must suppose that Belter's furniture was admired mainly for its fine quality and air of richness.

Belter died in 1863. He was not, by American standards, prosperous – the furniture in his home was valued at $1,122 and his personal estate at $8,321.80. He probably had difficulty in competing against imported French furniture – which always retained a certain snob value – and the Civil War would also have had a dampening effect on his trade. The Belter firm floundered on for a few years and then, during the slump that followed the War, went bankrupt in 1867. In this very year, however, a new firm of fashionable furniture makers was established in New York – Sypher & Co. who began to produce reproductions of early American furniture which had, naturally enough, a nostalgic appeal far stronger than any works in European styles.

Augustus Welby Northmore Pugin

(1812–1852)

Engraved design for a chest illustrated in Pugin's *Gothic Furniture in the Style of the 15th Century*, 1835.

Illustration of the 'extravagant style of Modern Gothic Furniture and Decoration' in Pugin's *The True Principles of Pointed or Christian Architecture*, 1841, which set about introducing new standards of taste.

'Christian verity compels me to acknowledge that there are hardly any defects which I have pointed out to you in the course of this Lecture which could not with propriety be illustrated by my own productions at some period of my professional career. Truth is only gradually developed in the mind, and is the result of long experience and deep investigation. Having, as I conceive, discovered the true principles of pointed architecture, I am anxious to explain to others the errors and misconceptions into which I have fallen, that they, profiting by my experience, may henceforth strive to revive the glorious works of Christian art in all the ancient and *consistent* principles. Let then the Beautiful and the True be our watchword for future exertions in the overthrow of modern paltry taste and paganism, and the revival of Catholic art and dignity. "Laus Deo".' Thus spake Augustus Welby Northmore Pugin at the close of the second of two lectures on *The True Principles of Pointed or Christian Architecture* delivered at St Marie's, Oscott, and published in 1841. The words could hardly be more characteristic of him. He was then only twenty-nine years old but, as he says, his own work had already undergone a radical transformation. And he had begun a revolution in taste in both architecture and the decorative arts.

He was born in 1812, the son of a French draughtsman, Augustus Charles Pugin (on special occasions 'de Pugin') who settled in London. Like most *émigrés,* he claimed to be a passionate royalist. Indeed, he had a dramatic story of how he fell fighting for the King, was supposed dead and thrown into a mass grave near the Bastille, climbed out, swam the Seine, escaped to Rouen, took ship for England and landed in Wales. But Benjamin Ferrey, one of his pupils, let a sizeable cat out of the bag by blandly remarking: 'He knew David the historical painter intimately, and probably belonged to the same political club' (i.e. the Jacobins) – which may help to explain why he allowed his son to be brought up as a Protestant. At any rate, he was in London in 1792 when he joined the Royal Academy School as a student. He found employment as a draughtsman under John Nash and seems to have assisted him in designing Gothic details for castellated houses. He married a Miss Welby – known as the Belle of Islington, and a remote connection of a baronet – and prospered.

At this moment, partly as a result of the French Revolution which put an end to the Grand Tour, Englishmen were taking greater interest in the antiquities of their own land. And the elder Pugin was much in

AUGUSTUS WELBY NORTHMORE PUGIN

opposite The Green Dining Room, decorated by Morris and Co. in 1866–7. Philip Webb designed the ceiling, frieze and gesso panels on the walls, Edward Burne-Jones the pianoforte and William Morris the carpet.

Chair of painted and gilt wood designed by Pugin for Windsor Castle and made by the firm of Morel and Seddon, 1828–30. Pugin was later to scorn such early essays in a 'false' Gothic style.

demand for his watercolour drawings of castles and abbeys – so much so that he took on a staff of young artists who were both pupils and assistants. He supplied illustrations for numerous works including Ackermann's *Microcosm of London* (1808), E. W. Brayley's *Series of Views in Islington and Pentonville* (1823) and his own *Specimens of Gothic Architecture* (1821–3). For Ackermann's *Repository of Arts* he contributed from 1810 onwards designs for furniture in the Gothic taste, conceived in a style mid-way between the feathery frivolities of Strawberry Hill and the more serious-minded manner of his son. Many are strikingly similar to the *style troubadour* objects made in Restoration France and much popularized by the duchesse de Berry.

The younger Pugin was thus introduced to the delights of Gothic and the Picturesque at an early age. He was an infant prodigy. At the age of fifteen he designed some furniture (made by Morel and Seddon) for Windsor Castle and some silver for the royal goldsmiths, Rundell and Bridge. In 1830 (aged 18) he tried unsuccessfully to establish a workshop to provide architects with panels of Gothic-style carving. Next year he designed the stage sets for a dramatized version of *Kenilworth*. He was converted to the Roman Church in 1834 and two years later published his first book, *Contrasts* – an impassioned appeal for a return to the glories of the Catholic Gothic world in art and life. The remainder of his life has been neatly summarized by Professor Pevsner: 'got married in 1831, lost his wife one year later, got married again in 1833, lost his second wife in 1844, got married once more in 1849, and lost his mind in 1851'. He died in 1852.

The furniture Pugin designed for Windsor Castle in 1827 closely resembles the prints his father had provided for Ackermann. But he was soon speaking of it with disgust, almost in the tone of a reformed drunkard describing the horrors of drink. 'The modern admirers of the pointed style have done much injury to its revival by the erroneous and costly system they have pursued,' he wrote, with references to Wyatville's Windsor and the 'enormities' he had himself perpetrated for it. 'The interiors of their houses are one mass of elaborate work; there is no repose, no solidity, no space left for hangings or simple panels: the whole is covered with trifling details, enormously expensive, and at the same time subversive of good effect. These observations apply equally to furniture; – upholsterers seem to think that nothing can be Gothic unless it is found in some church. Hence your modern man designs a sofa or occasional table from details culled out of Britton's Cathedrals, and all the ordinary articles of furniture, which require to be simple and convenient, are made not only very expensive but very uneasy. We find diminutive flying buttresses about an armchair; everything is crocketted with angular projections, innumerable mitres, sharp ornaments and turretted extremities. A man who remains any length of time in a modern Gothic room, and escapes being wounded by some

of its minutiae, may consider himself extremely fortunate. There are often as many pinnacles and gablets about a pier-glass frame as are to be found in an ordinary church.'

Although he despised the neo-Greek and neo-Roman almost as much, if not more than, such examples of neo-gothic furnishing, his attitude of mind is strikingly close to that of neo-classical theorists in their attacks on the rococo in the 1750s and 1760s. Like them, Pugin called for truth, simplicity and reason. Like them he associated arts and morals and believed that an artistic renaissance must form part of a more general reformation of civilization. And, again like them, he sought not to substitute one frivolous fashion for another but to establish a style based on immutable truths. But whereas they had found their ideal in the art and civilization of classical antiquity, he found it in the pious Middle Ages.

According to Pugin, 'The two great rules for design are these: 1st, that there should be no features about a building which are not necessary for convenience, construction or propriety; 2nd, that all ornament should consist of enrichment of the essential construction of the building.' These sentences have sometimes been read as a precocious enunciation of functionalist theory. But one has only to look at his buildings – enriched with what *Bishop Blougram* was to call 'chalk rosettes, ciphers and stucco twiddlings everywhere' – to see how far his ideas differed from those of twentieth-century functionalists.

Surprisingly enough, the furniture Pugin designed – generally for houses of which he was architect – accorded rather better with his principles than the buildings themselves, and sometimes comes near to satisfying a modern interpretation of his *dicta*. Unlike earlier designers of neo-gothic furniture, he attempted to reproduce the essential qualities and structure, not just the ornament, of medieval chairs and tables, buffets and armoires. He began, he tells us, with a 'tolerably good notion of details in the abstract' but employed them 'with so little judgement or propriety, that, although the parts were correct and exceedingly well executed, collectively they appeared a complete burlesque of pointed design'. But the plates in his *Gothic Furniture in the Style of the 15th Cent.* of 1835 show that he had already acquired enough knowledge to invent in the late Gothic style. His etching of a chest, for example, might easily be mistaken for an illustration of a genuine medieval piece. Tables and chairs are more readily recognized as nineteenth-century works – probably because he had fewer originals from which to derive ideas.

The designs in *Gothic Furniture* are all fairly richly decorated with panels of linen-fold or ogee tracery, crockets and statuettes. So too are the objects he designed (including Gothic umbrella stands) for the Houses of Parliament and for the Great Exhibition of 1851. But the pieces of furniture made for houses he built in the 1840s are sometimes

Chair designed by Pugin and made for Scarisbrick Hall, probably by the firm of J. G. Crace, *c.* 1840.

strikingly simple, comely rather than elegant, with a minimum of decorative enrichments. The basic structure of the carpentry is emphasized with unusual honesty, and often the only specifically Gothic elements are the large wrought iron hinges of a cupboard or the bold supports of a table. Such pieces now seem his best and most significant, but it would be rash to ascribe much influence to them. None were included among the many published engravings of Pugin's furniture and the furniture itself was soon hidden away in remote country mansions.

It would be easy to exaggerate Pugin's importance, both as a designer and as a theorist. He was not the only person to despise the earlier neogothic furniture and call for a return to the true principles of medieval art. In France, Viollet Le Duc was carrying on a similar campaign (though without the appeal to Catholicism), calling for 'a return to healthy ideas'. The plea for constructional honesty, which he, Pugin and others took over from the neo-classical theorists, was destined to survive the Gothic Revival.

Oak cabinet designed by Pugin for Abney Hall, Cheshire, c. 1847.

Philip Webb

(1831–1915)

In 1857 William Morris and Edward Burne-Jones – the ebullient Topsy and the languid Ned – both recently down from Oxford, took a house in Red Lion Square, London. Here they set themselves up as painters under the tutelage of Dante Gabriel Rossetti. They had made friends as undergraduates, young high-churchmen intending to become clergymen. But after taking his degree Morris decided that he wanted to be an architect and joined the office of G. E. Street where he first met Philip Webb. When Street moved from Oxford to London, Morris changed his mind again and thus began his long partnership with Burne-Jones. Dissatisfied with the furniture commercially available, Morris designed for the Red Lion Square house some rough chairs, tables, a settle and a wardrobe which were made by a local carpenter and which he and Burne-Jones painted with scenes from Dante, Malory and Chaucer. It was all rather hard and unyielding in an earnest high-minded way (Burne-Jones said that 'in an age of sofas and cushions', John Henry Newman had taught him 'to be indifferent of comfort'). The walls they hung with brass rubbings. Webb, who formed the third member of the triumvirate, took some part in the work.

Next year Morris, who had just become engaged to Jane Burden, commissioned Webb to build him a house at Bexley Heath in Kent. The house was finished in 1860 and the painted settle and wardrobe from Red Lion Square were installed. Other furniture was specially made, but this time to the more expert designs of Webb. The success of the collaboration led to the establishment of the firm of Morris, Marshall, Faulkner and Company – with Morris, Burne-Jones, Webb, Faulkner (another Oxford friend who became a mathematics don), Rossetti, Ford Madox Brown and Marshall (a surveyor and friend of Brown) as partners. Morris, who had a private income of £900 a year, was able to help the firm through its initial financial difficulties and soon it had ample commissions for stained glass, painted decorations, furniture and embroideries for churches and private houses.

Webb was one of the chief designers in these early years, responsible for all the furniture and much else besides. Born in Oxford in 1831, the son of a doctor, he was apprenticed first to an architect in Reading and then, in 1852, employed as a clerk by G. E. Street, who had just become architect to the Diocese of Oxford, with much to do in the way of church building and restoration. Street moved to London in 1856 and Webb, like Morris, went with him. But he had set up his own practice by 1858. Even before the establishment of the Morris

The 'St George' cabinet, of mahogany
and pinewood on an oak stand,
designed by Webb in 1861 for
William Morris, who painted it.

firm, he was designing furniture as well as houses. In about 1860, for example, he designed tables, wardrobes, wash-stands, towel-horses, billiard-room benches and a pianoforte for a Major Gillum.

Morris, Webb and their friends saw themselves as revolutionaries in matters of household taste. 'All the minor arts were in a state of complete degradation,' Morris later wrote, 'and accordingly in 1861 with the conceited courage of a young man I set myself to reforming all that and started a sort of firm for producing decorative articles.' But one is bound to ask whether they did effect a revolution and, if so, whether it was as sudden and startling as their disciples have led us to suppose. Were they late Romantics, or pioneers of modern design?

They were not, of course, the first artists to be contemptuous of the furniture commercially available and to design what they wanted for themselves. J.-L. David, Abildgaard and Pugin had all done the same. They were not the first group of artists to apply their talents to household and decorative objects: Sir Henry Cole had founded 'Summerly's Art Manufactures' in 1847 to improve industrial standards by employing painters and sculptors to design a variety of useful articles in porcelain, glass and metal. As recent writers have shown, the famous Red House that Webb designed for Morris was not very different from parsonages built some years earlier to the designs of Street and Butterfield. Nor was the furniture he designed for it very different from Pugin's simpler pieces of the 1840s. So far as theory went, the doctrine of truth to materials and function had a long history. And Webb's belief that 'all art . . . meant folk expression embodied and expanding in the several mediums of different materials' is merely an application of a commonplace of Romantic aesthetics to the decorative arts.

And yet, the products of the Morris firm – Webb's furniture or Morris's own wallpapers and textiles – are distinct in more than quality from the majority of similar products of the same period. And the difference derives as much from attitudes of mind as from artistic personality. A comparison with Pugin is revealing. Like him they looked back nostalgically to the Middle Ages – not as to an age of faith but (like Viollet Le Duc in France) to one of social harmony. Like him they rejected post-Renaissance art, but not because they found it anti-Catholic. Webb saw the introduction of the Renaissance style into England as: 'a "taste" imposed on the top as part of a subtle scheme for dividing off gentility from servility . . . an Architecture of Aristocracy provided by trained middlemen of "taste", who now wedged them-

Oak table designed by Webb, 1865–7.

selves in between the work and the workers, who were consequently beaten down to the status of mere executioners of patterns provided by an hierarchy of architectural priests.' Webb sought 'a customary art growing up from the bottom and out of the hearts of the people'. And this he found not only in medieval art but also in the simple country furniture – as in 'vernacular' architecture – which had been produced ever since the Middle Ages independently of men of taste in London. (These ideas were, of course, to survive marginally in the theory of the modern movement.)

As a result, Morris and Webb veered away from, without rejecting, historical revivalism. They had never intended (as had Pugin) to revive the form of medieval furniture: rather they tried to create a new astylar style, to make, as Lethaby wrote, 'the buildings of our own day pleasant without pretences of style'. They steered a middle course between the opulence of lavish upholstery, richly carved mouldings and intricately wrought metalwork applied to furniture, on the one hand, and, on the other, an austerity which would have seemed just as

opposite Canopied sideboard of mahogany with brass fittings, designed by Webb and made by Morris & Co., *c.* 1880.

pretentious in another way. Lack of pretentiousness may seem no more than a negative virtue – but it is a quality rarely to be found in the decorative arts.

Webb's furniture is almost ruthlessly honest – massively solid (the veneer was anathema to him) with the joinery unconcealed and often emphasized. Generally it was of plain oak, usually stained green or black but sometimes decorated on the surface by painting, gesso work or lacquered leather. Save in the very earliest pieces, there are no traces of ostensibly Gothic ornaments – no crockets, pinnacles or panels of tracery. Often it looks rather gaunt – and this was a quality he much admired, writing of Mantes 'with its great gaunt church. I do love a gaunt church'. Yet he was capable of rich effects when he thought they were justified, as in the design of pianofortes decorated with silvered and lacquered gesso relief work. He was also prepared to use materials other than wood – the bed he designed for himself was of wrought iron. It is characteristic of him that when electric light came into general use he immediately set about devising suitable fittings. His assistant George Jack wrote: 'He insisted on slightness – fairy-like treatment – using silken cords with amber and other large beads for decoration; never a large cluster of lights in one fitting, nor a powerful light in one bulb.'

George Jack wrote of Webb that 'a very inventive imagination was at all times struggling with an austere restraint which feared unmeaning expression' – and this remark seems to provide the key to the personality behind his furniture and architecture. As a man he was much less severe than his work might give one to suppose. Looking back at the long period of work under him Jack commented: 'It is strange how little I can recall of the old life. It is like trying to remember past sunshine – it pleases and it passes, but it also makes things to grow, and herein Webb was like the sunshine, and as little recognized and thanked.'

Webb resigned his partnership with the Morris firm when it was reorganized in 1875; but he continued to provide designs for furniture. By then, however, he was more fully occupied in his own architectural practice which, on his retirement in 1901, he handed over to George Jack. His last years, until his death in 1915, were spent very appropriately in a cottage in Sussex, dreaming perhaps of the brave days in Red Lion Square with Topsy and Ned. 'The best of those times was that there was no covetousness,' he told Lethaby, 'all went into the common stock – and then, we were such boys.'

Edward William Godwin

(1833–1886)

'Beauty had existed long before 1880,' wrote Max Beerbohm, looking back from 1894. 'It was Mr Oscar Wilde who managed her *début*. To study the period is to admit that to him was due no small part of the social vogue that Beauty was to enjoy. Fired by his fervid words, men and women hurled their mahogany into the streets and ransacked the curio-shops for furniture of Annish days. Dados arose upon every wall, sunflowers and the feathers of peacocks curved in every corner, tea grew quite cold while the guests were praising the Willow Pattern of its cup.' But behind Wilde stood his architect, E. W. Godwin – 'the greatest aesthete of them all' – now remembered mainly, if at all, as the father of Gordon Craig but famous in his day as architect, furniture designer, theatrical designer, and advocate of dress reform. He was largely responsible for two innovations of greater consequence than their names imply – the so-called Queen Anne style of interior decoration and 'Anglo-Japanese' furniture. And his artistic development provides a microcosmic picture of the more general trend in European design from historical revivalism to *art nouveau* aestheticism.

Born in Bristol in 1833, Edward William Godwin was trained as an architect. At the age of twenty-five he won an open competition for Northampton town hall with a twelfth-century Gothic design which was erected between 1861 and 1864. He soon had a flourishing practice and was busily engaged on other civic buildings, churches, private houses and some of the most notable warehouses of the day. In 1862, together with his friend William Burges – a greater architect and a more exuberant Gothic revivalist – he came under the influence of Japanese works of art displayed in quantity for the first time in England at the second Great Exhibition. Burges saw in contemporary Japanese art an almost miraculous survival of medieval standards of craftsmanship, love of rich decoration, and indulgence in grotesquerie. But Godwin responded in a totally different way, savouring the bold asymmetrical compositions, clarity of line and colour, lightness and airiness of Japanese prints. So smitten was he that he redecorated his own house in Bristol in what he thought to be a Japanese style – with bare floors sparsely covered with rugs, white walls hung with Japanese prints, and a few pieces of simple early eighteenth-century (Queen Anne) furniture. And lest his wife should strike a discordant note, he dressed her in a kimono. The general effect must have been quite startlingly fresh and clean in contrast to the dark, over-furnished, heavily draped and padded, antimacassared interiors of the day. It is hardly surprising that it should have been widely imitated.

opposite Ebonized wood sideboard designed by Godwin and made by William Wall, *c.* 1867.

EDWARD WILLIAM GODWIN

In 1868, after the death of his first wife, Godwin left Bristol and settled in Hertfordshire with the twenty-year old actress Ellen Terry – the victim of an unhappy child marriage with the elderly painter G.F. Watts. From this time onwards he was less active as an architect than as a designer of furniture and of theatrical sets and costumes. He had already been commissioned by the Earl of Limerick to build and design all the furnishings and decorations for Dromore Castle; and he was much employed designing furniture for William Watt of Grafton Street, and also wallpapers, carpets and textiles for various other manufacturers. Ellen Terry returned to the stage in 1874 and in the following year Godwin designed costumes and scenery for the Bancrofts' production of *The Merchant of Venice* in which she played Portia. But in 1875 he left her for Beatrix Philip, the schoolgirl daughter of a sculptor.

By about 1870 Godwin had become one of the leading figures in the 'Aesthetic' movement. And it was only natural that Whistler, whom he had known since 1863, should have chosen him as architect for the celebrated White House in Tite Street, Chelsea, designed in 1877 and completed in the following year. The interior followed the pattern of Godwin's Bristol house. But the boldly asymmetrical white-painted brick façade was strikingly novel – 'original, challenging, witty, if architecture can be witty, and certainly highly capricious in its fenestration', as Professor Pevsner remarks. He later built studio houses for other

opposite Walnut cabinet with Japanese box-wood plaques and ivory handles designed by Godwin *c.* 1876 and made by the firm of William Watt or Collinson and Lock.

Godwin's wash drawing for the cabinet illustrated opposite.

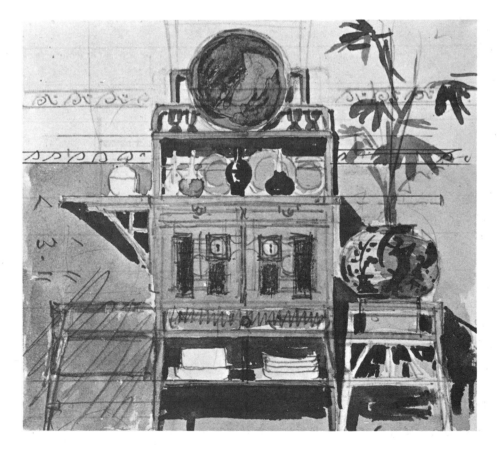

Ebonized oak chair designed by Godwin. The legs are derived from chairs represented on ancient Greek vases.

artists in Tite Street. With Whistler he designed the 'Butterfly suite' of furniture for the Paris exhibition of 1878 – a symphony in yellow with primrose walls, ochre carpet, furniture of the lightest grained mahogany upholstered in citron (aesthetes inclined to yallery as much as greenery). The following year Whistler went bankrupt as a result of his libel action against Ruskin, though there were other factors including expenditure on the White House and such minor items as a bill of £600 for out-of-season fruit to a greengrocer (who was paid off with a couple of *Nocturnes*). Before leaving the White House, Whistler wrote above the front door: 'Except the Lord build the house, they labour in vain that build it. E. W. Godwin, F.S.A. built this one'.

Oscar Wilde commissioned Godwin in 1884 to transform the interior of his house, No. 16 Tite Street, into a model of aesthetic décor. Each room was based on a different colour scheme, the most daring being the dining room in 'shades' of white with an occasional touch of.yellow, as on the curtains. Wilde was delighted with Godwin's designs, telling him of one set: 'Each chair is a sonnet in ivory and the table is a masterpiece in pearl.' Unfortunately, however, these ethereal splendours could not be realized without difficulty, and a law suit against a contractor. This was Godwin's swan-song: he died in 1886. His widow married Whistler two years later.

Godwin's position as Oscar Wilde's architect and as interior designer to the Aesthetes has tended to overshadow his significance as a furniture designer. Like so many of the most important furniture designers – Thomas Hope and Morris before him, Mackintosh and van de Velde afterwards – he began by designing for his own house simply because he knew of no designer whose work he liked. His Anglo-Japanese furniture differs markedly from the robust settles and tables made to Webb's design for Morris. It is light to the point of flimsiness and thus makes a still greater contrast with the solid, carved or padded pieces generally popular in the Victorian home. Though based on an intensive study of past styles – his notebooks include sketches ranging from Egyptian furniture and Greek vase painting to medieval architectural details – Godwin's designs make a more decisive break with historical revivalism than anything Webb had produced at this date. 'The day of architectural revivals may be setting,' he wrote in 1875, 'I for one sincerely hope it is.' His furniture was Anglo-Japanese in name only and though he may have been inspired by Ukiyo-e and some pieces were very discreetly decorated with Japanese motifs, they were wholly unlike anything made in Japan. As early as 1867 he wrote: 'such effect as I wanted I endeavoured to gain as in economical building by the mere grouping of solid and void and by more or less broken outline' – a remark which helps to link his furniture with his remarkable warehouse buildings in Bristol.

Godwin showed little or no interest in the revival of craftsmanship,

EDWARD WILLIAM GODWIN

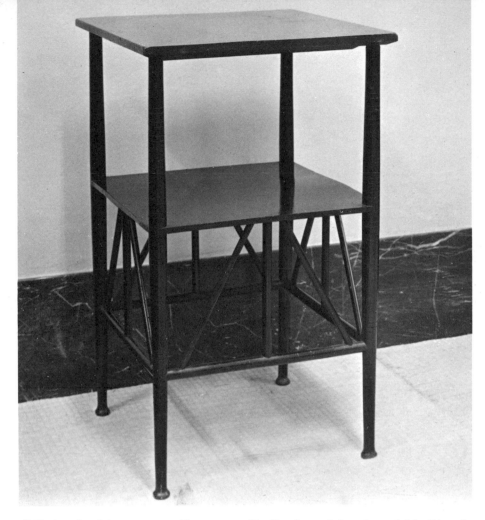

Ebonized wood coffee-table designed by Godwin. Tables of this type were made in the factories of both William Watt and Collinson & Lock from about 1880.

differing in this respect still more radically from Morris and his friends. He cherished no vision of happy medieval guildsmen and was clearly less concerned with the process by which furniture was made than with the final product. His favourite material was ebonized wood, often in square section lathes of machine-made regularity. His designs were thus excellently adapted for factory production – and widespread imitation. By 1877 he was complaining of how his coffee-table had been plagiarized; he met it almost everywhere he went 'in private houses, in showrooms, in pictures and in books'. Few of his imitators were, however, able to resist the temptation to embellish his designs and make them look more obviously Japanese by the addition of bits of bamboo or simulated bamboo and a profusion of japonaiserie motifs.

The chief merits of Godwin's furniture are its simplicity, its well adjusted proportions and the subtlety of contrast between solids and voids. A piece of furniture, he wrote, 'cannot be artistic by any happy-go-lucky process. Little things of this kind to be artistic, imperatively demand no inconsiderable amount of thought and much careful full-sized drawing'. At a time when furniture was admired mainly for the richness, the ingenuity or (by Morris & Co.) the integrity of its workmanship, he reasserted the importance of the designer over the craftsman and, perhaps unwittingly, pointed the way forward to the mass-production furniture of the twentieth century.

Page from a trade catalogue issued
by Majorelle, *c.* 1910,
'Chambre à moulurations ornées';
the whole suite cost 2,850 francs.

Louis Majorelle

(1859–1926)

Differences between English and French *art nouveau* furniture are to be explained not only by national aesthetic preferences but also by the economic and industrial systems of the two countries. In England *art nouveau* emerged from and was strongly influenced by the Arts and Crafts movement. But in France the industrial revolution, which moved at a laggard pace in the nineteenth century, had hardly touched the furniture industry – and thus there was no cause for a counter-revolution of the type sponsored by William Morris and Philip Webb. France was, indeed, economically under-developed. The small workshop run by a *maître* with a handful of *compagnons* was still the norm in every branch of industry (of 65,000 industrial concerns in Paris in 1848 only 7,000 employed more than ten workmen, and even at the beginning of the present century the overwhelming majority of French workshops had less than five employees). Although much ordinary furniture was made by machinery, the craftsmen who specialized in luxury furniture were not so much engaged in fighting a rearguard action against mechanization as keeping alive the great traditions of *ébénisterie* handed down from master to pupil since the eighteenth century. They continued to practice with skill, and sometimes refinement, the difficult arts of veneering, parquetry and marquetry, and the casting, chiselling and gilding of bronze mounts. And they seem to have found a ready market, both at home and abroad, for imitations and sometimes direct copies of eighteenth-century furniture: for there were many who looked back nostalgically to the world before *le déluge*.

It was in this tradition that Louis Majorelle began his career. He was born at Toul in 1859, the son of a cabinet maker Auguste Majorelle who, in the following year, moved with his family to Nancy and set up a modest workshop in the faubourg Saint-Pierre. The business prospered and he soon acquired better premises in the rue Girardet. Auguste specialized in making reproductions of eighteenth-century ceramics and furniture – and at the Paris exhibition of 1878 he won a prize for his *vernis Martin*. Meanwhile Louis had been trained as a painter in Nancy and was sent in 1877 to the École des Beaux Arts in Paris where he became a pupil of Millet. But on his father's death in 1879 he gave up painting (save as a spare-time occupation) and settled down to run the workshop in Nancy.

Louis Majorelle abandoned the production of ceramics to concentrate on furniture, and he seems to have continued to work in eighteenth-century styles until the last decade of the century. In the 1880s, however, another Nancy factory owner, Émile Gallé – famed mainly as a glass-maker but also a furniture designer – had begun to develop the new style, later to be known as *art nouveau* in England (after Bing's shop in Paris), *Liberty* in Italy (after the shop in London), *Jugendstil* in Germany (after a periodical), and by various, mainly opprobrious names in France. This style which began to emerge more or less simultaneously – and largely independently – in various parts of Europe expressed a self-conscious reaction against the historical revivals of the nineteenth century. But it was far more dependent on the past than most of its protagonists cared to think. The furniture designed by Gallé in the later 1880s owes a debt to the more extravagant rococo pieces of the Louis XV period. And, what is perhaps more important, though often

Mahogany and gilt bronze occasional table or *guéridon*, made at Majorelle's factory in Nancy in 1902.

overlooked, Gallé's cabinets with the bombé fronts and marquetry flowers straying languidly over their surfaces could have been executed only by *ébénistes* who had inherited the eighteenth-century tradition of craftsmanship.

According to Paul Juyot, 'the signal for the modern Renaissance was given in Lorraine' in about 1888, and by 1890 Majorelle had begun to form 'a new concept of the decorative arts'. In fact he saw the potentialities of the new style not only for luxury furniture but also for industrially produced pieces which might have very nearly as rich an appearance and would appeal to a much larger middle-class market. By 1900, when he exhibited with triumphant success at the Exposition Universelle in Paris, he had become the main producer of *art nouveau* furniture in France and, perhaps, all Europe.

Maintaining a belief in the mystique of craftsmanship, Majorelle wrote, in words that would have won whole-hearted approval from English Arts and Craftsmen: 'Whoever loves his craft believes that it is the most beatiful; for a blacksmith iron is the most beautiful substance and for him there is no more enchanting sound than the ring of the hammer on the anvil; wood provides agreeable sensations for an *ébéniste*: like a flower it allures by its scent, charms by its colour, ravishes the eye by the pattern of its rich arabesques . . .' and so on. But this did not prevent him from mechanizing his workshops. According to a writer of 1901 his factory was 'organized in the manner of a big industrial concern', with *ateliers* for the 'mechanical working of the wood, for cabinet making, for sculpture, for marquetry, for work in bronze etc.'. As a result he was able to produce luxury furniture at a price 'not merely accessible but often advantageous'. Hence his success.

Majorelle's factory produced nothing that could not have been made as well, if not better, by the techniques of hand craftsmanship. Machinery was used merely as a means of increasing output and decreasing prices. In point of design, the furniture was novel enough to be fashionably up-to-date while making no violent departure from the traditions of the past. With its bold lines, relief decorations and fine finish, it had an opulence hard to equal in other machine-made furniture of the day.

Trade catalogues issued between 1900 and 1914 reveal the range of the Majorelle factory. The furniture was designed in suites for *salons*, bedrooms, dining-rooms and studies. Some – like the *Salle à manger 'Paul'* and the *Chambre 'Etoile Bleue'* – is fairly simple. One set described as *Louis XVI* consists not, as one might expect, of 'reproduction' pieces but of rather simple *art nouveau* furniture decorated with motifs inspired by late eighteenth-century ornamental designs. Other suites are more whole-heartedly in the new spirit – the *Salon Fougères* in which every chair and table is decorated with a limp frond of fern; the *Salle à manger 'Chicorée'* with sideboards and tables embellished with spikier foliage; and the *Chambre à Moulurations ornées*, with swirling abstract decorations

opposite
top Writing-desk designed by Henry van de Velde and made in his factory at Ixelles, 1899.

bottom The 'Nénuphar' writing-table, of mahogany with gilt bronze mounts, designed by and made in the factory of Louis Majorelle, Nancy, 1900.

like dank touselled hair on the bed, bedside tables and dressing-tables. The three main pieces in the *'Chicorée'* dining-room cost 1,300 francs, the chairs 60 francs with cane seats and 90 francs if upholstered in leather. A suite consisting of a bed, wardrobe, bedside table and dressing-table, in walnut or mahogany, cost 2,850 francs. (At this date the franc was worth about 9½d. or $0.20, so this suite would have cost £114 or $570.) These are not low prices for mass-produced furniture – a Thonet chair Nr 14 cost only 3s. – but they were appreciably lower than those demanded for hand-made furniture of similar quality and were well within the range of the middle classes who formed the bulk of Majorelle's clientèle. The factory also made rather more elaborate pieces decorated with pictorial marquetry panels, some of which were exhibited in Paris. They doubtless won the firm further renown but must always have been rather exceptional in its production.

As a designer Majorelle was a more than competent popularizer, not an innovator. But it would be a mistake to dismiss him for that reason. Though his furniture may lack the overpowering – one might say narcotically nightmarish – fantasy of that produced by Gallé, it had notable qualities besides its cheapness. Forms are well devised and the decorations seem naturally to grow out of them; some pieces, indeed, like the water-lily table, have a graceful elegance hard to parallel outside French rococo furniture. His worst sin was to provide the basis for a sub-*art nouveau* style which was to be taken up by thousands of furniture factories throughout the world (it is his style that one sees plagiarized in the cheapest bedroom and dining-room suites of glossy wood or even metal painted to simulate wood).

The Majorelle factory was among the casualties of the 1914–18 war. He tried to keep it going, even after the German invasion of Lorraine, but eventually shut it up and fled to Paris. In 1916 the greater part of the factory was burnt down. But in 1918 he returned to Nancy and began the work of reconstruction. *Art nouveau* furniture was now as dead as the dado and Majorelle, like his contemporaries, began to grope his way towards the style which was to emerge fully formed at the Paris 1925 exhibition, on whose jury he served. Decorative ornament was severely limited, waving lines and irregular forms were replaced by straight lines, circles and squares. Despite this vogue for formal severity, he still contrived to give his products an air of opulence which, once again, made them acceptable to a middle-class clientèle – much more so than the obviously machine-made pieces in tubular steel which were beginning to come on to the market. In 1926 he died and the atelier was taken over by his pupil and former works manager Alfred Lévy who, according to a writer in *Mobilier et Décoration* in 1933, 'continues with talent to pursue this process of evolution towards greater simplicity, without however sinking into a nudity and rigidity of form which allows for no expression of sensibility.'

Henry van de Velde
(1863–1957)

Among the practitioners of *art nouveau* there were two parties which now seem more clearly distinct from one another than they did in the 1890s. There were those who, like Gallé and Majorelle, developed traditional methods of craftsmanship, revelled sensuously in fluid lines and naturalistic ornament and worked mainly for the luxury trade. Others, of whom van de Velde is perhaps the most important, had a more cerebral approach to problems of design and went in for much theorizing: they generally preferred angular to curving lines, eschewed ornament and showed concern for the needs of a large public. Though both attempted to create a new non-revivalist style, they were both dependent on the past. As we have already seen, Majorelle's style derived from and was to a large extent conditioned by the long-established practice of making reproduction furniture. Similarly, van de Velde's writings include remarks which may be traced back through the gothic revivalists of the mid-nineteenth century to the neo-classicists of the eighteenth who had also demanded logical construction, truth to materials and the abolition of ornament. He is generally regarded as one of the father figures of modern industrial design but he might equally well be seen as the last of the traditionalists. In the history of modern design his position is more ambivalent than is generally appreciated – and he made it no clearer by disparaging the *art nouveau* style in which he executed nearly all his best work as a designer. A few weeks before his death in 1957, just when the more florid forms of *art nouveau* were beginning to enjoy a revival, he remarked rather crossly in an interview: '*Art nouveau* doesn't exist any more. There are other things more interesting.'

Henry van de Velde, the son of a prosperous music-loving chemist, was born in Antwerp in 1863. He began his career as a painter studying first in his native city and then, from 1884–5, in Paris where he worked in the studio of Carolus Duran and made many personal contacts with the circle of Impressionists and Symbolists – Monet, Signac, Whistler, Pissaro, Debussy, Mallarmé and Verlaine. As a painter he was quick to assimilate the styles of his contemporaries, notably the neo-Impressionists and Van Gogh – but displayed little originality.

Shortly after the death of his mother in 1889 he had a nervous breakdown. Unable to paint, he read extensively in the works of Ruskin, Morris and Nietzsche, and did not fully recover until 1893 when he began to devote himself to the decorative arts. In that year he exhibited an embroidered appliqué panel, conceived as a painting in the style of

Armchair designed by van de Velde,
1898–9.

Chair designed by van de Velde,
c. 1896.

opposite Chair and desk designed by
van de Velde, 1903.

Gauguin, in a show organized by 'Les Vingt' – a group of twenty young artists in Brussels who exhibited not only their own works but also paintings by Seurat, Gauguin, Cézanne, Van Gogh, and the Englishmen Walter Crane and Selwyn Image. At this moment English art was enjoying unprecedented success on the Continent. There was a shop in Brussels, the *Compagnie Japonaise*, which showed modern English metal-work and wallpapers. The latter seem particularly to have charmed van de Velde who later remarked that on first seeing Annesley Voysey's wallpapers, 'it was as if Spring had come all of a sudden'. He must also have seen specimens of English Arts and Crafts furniture illustrated from 1893 onwards in *The Studio*. As he declared in 1901: 'the seeds that fertilized our spirit, evoked our activities, and originated the complete renewal of ornamentation and form in the decorative arts, were un-doubtedly the work and influence of John Ruskin and William Morris.' But his aim was to translate the English style into something Belgian.

In 1894 he married Maria Sèthe and began to build his own house, Bloemenwerf, at Uccle just outside Brussels. He not only designed the house but also the furniture, decorative fixtures and even – like E. W. Godwin before him – appropriate clothes for his wife to wear in it. The interior was distinctly chaste with clean-lined undecorated chairs and tables and cabinets which reveal the influence of Voysey and English craftsmen like Ernest Gimson, but are rather more elegant and echo more distantly the English rustic furniture of the eighteenth century. Bloemenwerf had hardly been completed before it was visited by the German art critic Julius Meier-Graefe and the entrepreneur Samuel Bing, also a German, who had recently opened in Paris a shop called *L'Art Nouveau*, soon to become the main centre for the sale of the finest work in the new style to which it gave its name.

Bing commissioned van de Velde to design four rooms for his shop, and these secured him immediate European renown – besides a fair amount of abuse. In *Le Figaro* he was characterized by Octave Mirabeau as 'le Belge roublard' – the crafty Belgian – and pilloried together with 'the vicious Englishman' and the 'morphinomaniac Jew'. In 1897 these rooms were shown at an exhibition of decorative arts in Dresden where they won unqualified praise and attracted numerous clients. Next year he founded the *Société van de Velde S.A.* with workshops for the pro-duction of furniture and metalwork at Ixelles near Brussels. His designs of this period are less strongly influenced by England, rather more elaborate with boldly springing curves complementing the straight

lines, a sparing use of abstract ornamental motifs and, for chairs, brightly coloured batik upholstery. They demonstrate his desire to revive 'that lost sense of vivid, strong, clear colours, vigorous and strong forms and reasonable construction'.

In 1901 he was called to Weimar to advise the Grand Duke and rebuild the art school and the school for *Industrie und Kunstgewerbe* of which he became director in 1904. From now onwards his time was devoted mainly to architecture and theory. But he continued to design furniture, simpler than before and with no more than the gentlest hint of *art nouveau*, as in the elongated proportions of a writing desk or the lines of a curiously bow-legged chair. As a foreigner he lost his job at Weimar in 1914, went to Switzerland and, after the war, to Holland where in 1921 he started work on his most notable building – the museum commissioned by the art-collector Kröller-Müller at Otterlo (though the actual building was not begun until 1937). In 1925 he returned to Belgium and was appointed principal of the *Institut supérieur des arts décoratifs* in Brussels and professor of architecture at the University of Ghent. His few furniture designs of this period are severe and angular, rather in the Paris 1925 style. He eventually retired to Switzerland in 1947 and died there ten years later.

As early as 1894 van de Velde had written: 'Art must conquer the machine. In the future the role of the artist will be glorious. He will entrust his ideas to thousands of steel hands, led and refined by his immaterial and superior spirit.' He later commended the English Arts and Crafts movement for its systematic discarding of ornament but criticized it as anachronistic – producing sensitively designed objects for a few equally sensitive souls. These and other pronouncements – and his more severe pieces of furniture – undoubtedly had their influence on industrial designers. But he remained an Arts and Craftsman at heart. 'I still prefer the handwoven table cloth to the machine-made product, hand-made silver to machine-stamped cutlery,' he wrote in 1907. And in 1914 at a meeting of the Deutscher Werkbund he entered a discussion on the use of machinery to plead for individuality against standardization. 'As long as there are artists in the Werkbund,' he declared, 'they will protest against any proposed canon and any standardization. The artist is essentially and intimately a passionate individualist, a spontaneous creator. Never will he, of his own free will, submit to a discipline forcing upon him a norm, a canon.' This old-fashioned, romantic conception of the artist is the soft centre of all his theorizing on the decorative arts. For although he moved beyond Ruskin's and Morris's almost Luddite hostility to mechanization and recognized the potential beauty of machine products, he was unable to conceive the relationship between the artist and the machine in terms other than those of conflict.

opposite Armchair designed by van de Velde, 1898–9.

Charles Rennie Mackintosh

(1868–1928)

Just after the outbreak of war in 1914, a couple who had recently settled in lodgings at Walberswick, Suffolk, attracted a great deal of local suspicion. He, a dark-skinned man with a limp, and she, a middle-aged woman who affected self-consciously artistic clothes, spoke to each other with a Scottish accent which seemed 'foreign' to East Anglians. They claimed to be artists. To the meanest intelligence in Walberswick it was quite obvious that they were German spies. While they were enjoying a twilight walk one evening their rooms were searched and numerous letters written in German were found among their papers. It was only with difficulty that the suspects were able to prove that they were in fact Mr and Mrs Charles Rennie Mackintosh, recently of Glasgow.

This trivial incident is not without a certain symbolic significance. For Mackintosh, one of the best architects and designers of the day – he could be called the last great British furniture designer – had by then achieved all his most important work but was still very little appreciated in his native Glasgow and was practically unknown elsewhere in either Scotland or England. But in Germany and Austria his name was already a household word in advanced architectural circles. He is among the very few British artists whose reputation has always stood higher abroad than at home. His work seemed 'foreign' – with all the most unwholesome connotations that the word carried in Edwardian England.

Nevertheless, Mackintosh was the product of a recognizable British tradition and does not appear to have felt much continental influence until after his own very personal style had begun to form. He clearly owed a great deal to both Philip Webb and E. W. Godwin. And like so many other pioneer furniture designers, he began by designing pieces for his own use before receiving any commissions.

Charles Rennie Mackintosh was born in Glasgow on 7 June, 1868. He was thus a generation younger than W. Y. MacGregor and the other landscape painters of the Glasgow school who established themselves as a group in the early 1880s. Glasgow, with its lively circle of painters and collectors of French Impressionist paintings, was at this moment perhaps the most advanced British city so far as the figurative arts were concerned (as Edinburgh had been philosophically a century before). In 1884, after a good Scottish high school education, Mackintosh was articled to an architect, John Hutchison, and began to attend night classes at the Glasgow School of Art. An able draughtsman, he was soon

opposite Stained oak dining-chair designed by Mackintosh, *c.* 1897.

Painted wood cheval glass designed by Mackintosh for his own bedroor in his Mains Street apartment in Glasgow, *c.* 1900–1.

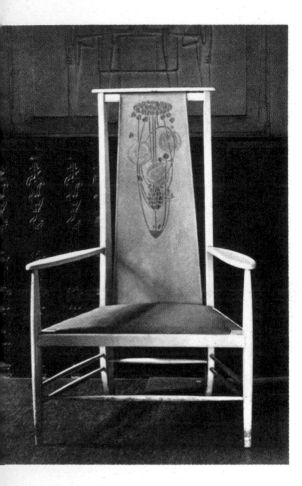

Armchair of wood painted white
with stencilled canvas back, designed by
Mackintosh for his own apartment,
1901–2.

winning prizes for his architectural drawings – competent essays in the academic tradition. On completing his articles in 1889 he joined the firm of John Honeyman and Keppie. He continued to win prizes for his drawings and in 1890 gained a scholarship which enabled him to travel to Italy. In the architects' office he found a congenial friend in Herbert MacNair with whom he was to be closely associated in suceeding years.

Mackintosh began to design furniture in about 1890 – the earliest piece being a very simple painted cabinet bookcase, with asymmetrically arranged doors and shelves in the lower part, recorded in a photograph of his own studio bedroom. Beside it there were chairs, apparently of mid-eighteenth-century date, and over the chimney-piece Japanese prints. The room is reminiscent of E.W. Godwin, apart from a frieze painted with stylized cats and abstract forms which is already in the Mackintosh idiom. His development in the next ten years is so astonishingly swift that it is hard to trace. In about 1895 he was designing for the Glasgow firm of furniture makers, Guthrie and Wells, and in 1897 he began both the first of his series of tea-room interiors and the building that was to be his masterpiece – the Glasgow School of Art. That he should have been selected as architect for the latter was highly appropriate, for the School under the inspired direction of Francis H. Newbery had played a dominant role in Mackintosh's development.

In the 1890s the Glasgow School of Art attracted a number of outstandingly talented pupils including, besides Mackintosh and MacNair, the sisters Margaret and Frances Macdonald, Jessie R. Rowat (who married Newbery in 1899) and George Walton. This little group of friends, sharing artistic aims, seems to have developed the 'Glasgow style' in a spirit of friendly competition. From the date of its first appearance in 1893 *The Studio* was a source of inspiration to them, illustrating the work of contemporaries both in London and on the Continent. But perhaps their greatest debt was to Newbery who, in sharp distinction from most art school principals of the period, encouraged innovation and experiment. As the secretary of *L'Oeuvre artistique* of Liège remarked when he wrote asking Newbery to send examples of his students' work to an exhibition in 1895: 'Our schools of art are far, very far indeed, from being so advanced as yours and what has above all astonished us in your work is the great liberty left to pupils to follow their own individuality which is so different from the ideas current in our schools of art that it is difficult for us to comprehend this freedom although we

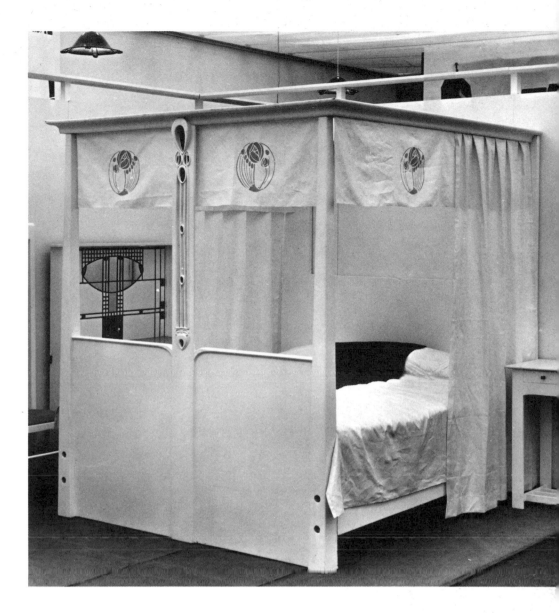

Bed of oak painted white with pink glass panels designed by Mackintosh for his apartment in Mains Street, Glasgow, *c.* 1900.

admire it very much. I think the exhibition of the works of your students cannot but cause serious thought and reflection to those here who direct art instruction.'

This individuality was less appreciated in England. A chorus of derision and censure greeted the objects sent from Glasgow to the exhibition of the London Arts and Crafts Society in 1896. These included a tall settle by Mackintosh, metalwork by the Macdonald sisters and posters. Only the editor of *The Studio*, Gleeson White, seems to have been impressed. He promptly went to Glasgow to meet the artists, half expected to find a pair of languid aesthetes and 'middle-aged sisters, flat-footed, with projecting teeth and long past the hope (which had always been forlorn) of matrimony, gaunt ugly females'. But in the event he was no less taken with the 'laughing comely girls scarce out of their teens' and the genial young Scottish architects than with their work. In the following years he gave them publicity in *The*

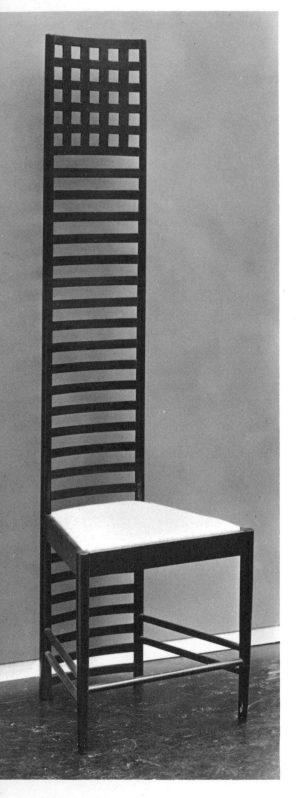

Ebonized wood chair designed
by Mackintosh for the Hill House,
Helensburgh, c. 1902.

Studio and thus introduced them to the whole of Europe. In 1899 they exhibited at the Venetian Biennale (where painters of the older Glasgow school had already begun to show). This exhibition included graphic work but no furniture by Mackintosh. Some of his furniture was, however, shown and much admired at the Vienna Secession exhibition next year and at the Turin Esposizione Internazionale of 1902.

Of the many press comments – both favourable and hostile – on the work of the Glasgow group in these exhibitions those of Roger Marx in the *Gazette des Beaux Arts* of 1902 are of particular interest – and not only because the French are generally supposed to have remained immune to the vogue for Mackintosh and his friends. After describing other exhibits at Turin he remarks: 'the arrangement was exquisite, worthy of the subtle taste of a Whistler and well adapted to display these creations, born under a sky of mist and dreams, to the best advantage. I deny none of the objections raised against the furniture of Charles Mackintosh and Herbert MacNair, if it is isolated and considered strictly from the point of view of practical need and comfort; it matters only that it fits in with its surroundings; each ensemble realizes a harmony, attains a perfect unity; each one is an invitation to the quiet life, to calmness, to dreaming . . .'.

The reference to Whistler is particularly perceptive – and one may wonder if Mackintosh has not learned valuable lessons from his use of colour and his compositional devices (it will be remembered that the City of Glasgow had bought Whistler's portrait of Carlyle in 1891). So far as furniture is concerned, he certainly owed as much to Whistler's architect, Godwin, as to Voysey and the Arts and Crafts tradition that stems from Morris. In many ways, indeed, he reacted against the Arts and Crafts – showing little interest in the details of craftsmanship and less in the natural beauty of wood. His furniture tends to be roughly made and its surface is often painted. As Roger Marx suggested, his aim was not to design individual pieces of furniture but to create whole rooms in which furnishings played a part of vital importance in the moulding of architectural space. Each of his rooms had its distinctive atmosphere to which every detail contributed – including the flowers in the strange containers he devised for them. And it is on record that for several weeks after the opening of Miss Cranston's China Tea-Room he arranged the flowers himself.

Apart from the earliest pieces – the cabinet in his own bedroom and cupboards and chests-of-drawers for Guthrie and Wells – Mackintosh

Interior of the 'Room de luxe' in Miss Cranston's Willow Tea-rooms, Glasgow, designed by Mackintosh, 1904.

designed furniture only for interiors which he had himself created. Sometimes he was responsible for the buildings as well, notably the School of Art and two houses near Glasgow, Windyhill and Hill House. Of the interiors he remodelled and furnished the most important were those of the flat in Mains Street, Glasgow, into which he moved on marrying Margaret Macdonald in 1900, the tea-rooms owned by Miss Cranston in various parts of Glasgow and the Wärndorfer music salon in Vienna.

Miss Cranston's tea-rooms on which he worked from 1897 to 1910 displayed – for, alas, none survives intact – the wide range of his talents both as an architect and as a designer. In each of them there were several rooms which could be treated individually, and he contrived not only decorative but spatial effects which were as daring as they were successful. Furniture was subordinated to these effects. He made great play with either very low or excessively high backs for chairs, contrasts or harmonies with painted or stained wood. The more elegant chairs were ill

opposite One of a pair of painted oak cabinets inlaid with coloured glass, designed by Mackintosh in 1902.

suited for the rough and tumble of public use – but this seems to have worried neither Mackintosh nor Miss Cranston who shared a desire to create the most remarkable series of public interiors in Europe. The Glasgow School of Art furniture was rather less idiosyncratic (chairs in the library are based on the traditional Windsor type) but equally well adjusted to the rooms.

There is much greater subtlety and delicacy in the furniture he designed for private houses. Here again he showed his liking for painted woodwork, usually white with a somewhat shy use of decorative motifs picked out in jewel-like colours – his favourite being a rose which looks as if it had been grown in Japan and then entwined by a Celtic manuscript illuminator. Chairs generally have tall attenuated backs and rather low seats, cupboards are crowned with projecting cornices, the supports of tables are slender to the point of emaciation. And in all pieces the long straight lines which predominate are complemented by very gentle, very subtle curves. These pieces make a striking contrast not only with run-of-the-mill Victorian and Edwardian furniture, but with the extrovert robustness of Arts and Crafts work and the voluptuous opulence of French *art nouveau*. Mackintosh created what Meier-Graefe called 'chambres garnies pour belles âmes'.

As an architect Mackintosh occupies an important place in the modern movement. But as a furniture designer he stands rather outside it. He showed no interest either in functionalism or in mass-production. As a designer of interiors he sought above all to create a poetic atmosphere. And it is significant that his furniture has begun to return to favour only recently, with the general revolt against Bauhaus ideas and ideals.

Mackintosh quarrelled with his architectural partner, John Keppie (Honeyman had retired) in 1914, went off to Suffolk and then on to London. Although he altered and furnished (in a not very satisfactory imitation of Josef Hoffmann) a house in Northampton in 1916 and built a studio in Chelsea for Harold Squire in 1920, his career was at an end. His last years, complicated by financial difficulties and ill health, were devoted mainly to painting. He died on 10 December 1928, almost forgotten in Scotland, hardly known in England. But a few months later a group of Austrian architects was trying to find his address in order to invite him to Vienna. A memorial exhibition held in Glasgow in 1933 stimulated some interest in him. And in 1936 Nikolaus Pevsner's *Pioneers of the Modern Movement* gave him the full recognition he merited.

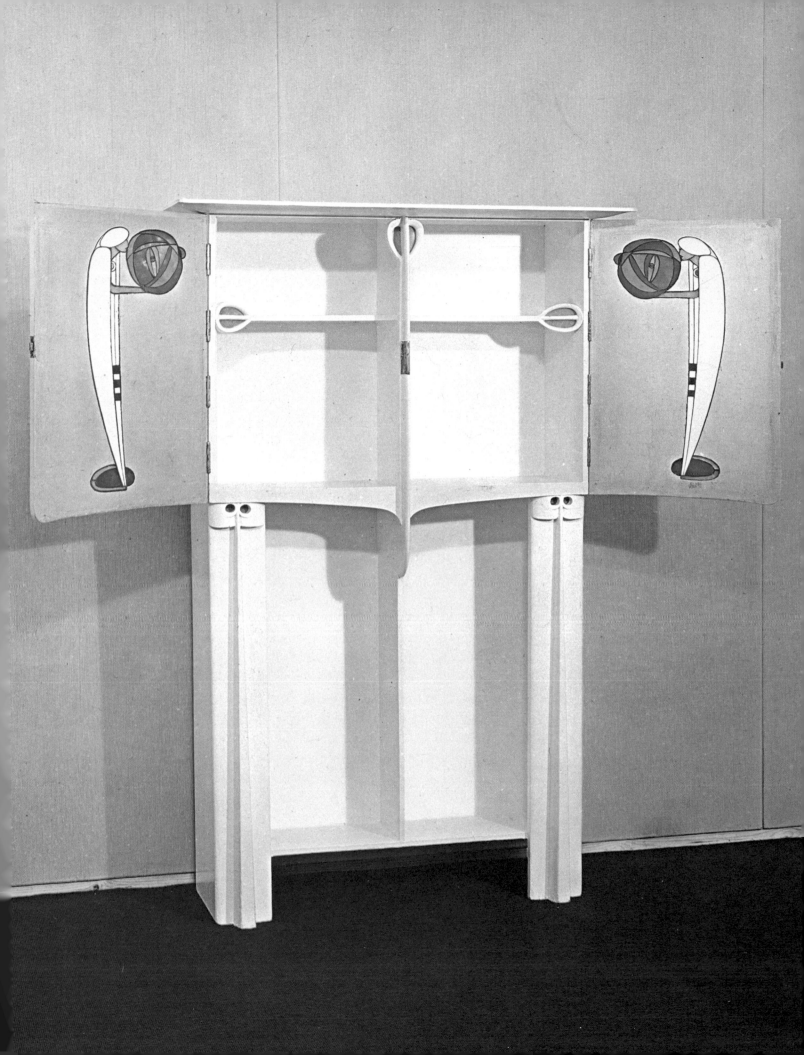

Jacques-Emile Ruhlmann
(1879–1933)

Palisander wood table for the display of prints, which Ruhlmann called the 'Cla-Cla', 1926.

Paris 1925 – the year of the first Surrealist Exhibition, André Gide's *Faux Monnayeurs*, Josephine Baker's début in *La revue nègre*, Eisenstein's *Battleship Potemkin* and Charlie Chaplin's *The Gold Rush*. The melody of Gershwin's *Rhapsody in Blue*, first performed in the previous year, still hangs in the air, clouded with smoke puffed from long cigarette holders. Hair is bobbed, skirts are short, trousers are excessively wide. In a Paris that has once more become the centre of the fashionable and intellectual world, van Dongen is the chosen portrait painter, Poiret the leading *couturier*, and Jacques-Emile Ruhlmann the first furniture designer and interior decorator. At the *Exposition internationale des arts décoratifs* Ruhlmann's *Hôtel du collectionneur* delighted the mondaine. It exerted, wrote a contemporary, 'une seduction spéciale', the general public rubbed shoulders with the sophisticated there.

The history of the 1925 exhibition is revealing. It was first mooted in 1907 just at the moment when the last languid sighs were ebbing from the body of *art nouveau*. In 1913 formal plans were laid to hold the exhibition three years later, but on account of the war it had to be postponed first to 1922 and then to 1925. It was thus conceived very much along the lines of the great nineteenth-century international exhibitions as a display of virtuoso pieces. Opening in an atmosphere of newly recovered prosperity and self-conscious modernism it also expressed a desire to return to the world before the war. Exhibits were 'modern' only because designers had resolutely set their faces against *art nouveau* and all forms of historical revivalism (reproduction furniture was banned). The vast majority were conceived and executed traditionally. And, indeed, most of the exhibitors had already begun to establish their reputations and develop their styles in the pre-war world.

Ruhlmann made his first furniture designs in 1901. He was born in Paris in 1879, the son of a prosperous Protestant family from Alsace, and began his career as a painter. On his marriage in 1907 he designed the furniture for his own house. And in 1910 he began to exhibit furniture regularly at the *salons d'automne*. After the war he took over his father's firm of household painters and went into partnership with a M. Laurent (the new enterprise was named *Établissements Ruhlmann et Laurent*). He expanded the firm by adding a *maison de décoration* which had become by 1925 the most important in Paris, with workshops for *ébénisterie, menuiserie,* upholstery, japanning and *miroiterie*. In a world where nothing succeeded like financial success he soon became a social figure. He must also have had a flair for self-advertisement – and his Delage with

Wardrobe designed by Ruhlmann, 1924, veneered with amboyna wood and decorated with ivory.

black and white coachwork executed to his own design is said to have been almost as famous as Mistinguett's legs and Maurice Chevalier's boater. He died in 1933.

The author of a book on 'French furniture of the present day' of 1926 asked: 'Who, among the artists of this generation knows how to create luxury furniture for the present day, who would be employed by a royal princess or an arch-duchess, if such titles still indicated culture and wealth?' His answer was pat: 'Undoubtedly the *ébéniste* Jacques Ruhlmann would be chosen by them'. His workshop produced what was probably the best made and certainly the most expensive furniture of the time. In 1924 he charged 46,800 francs for a *coiffeuse*, 59,000 for a commode and 79,000 for an amboyna wood bed. The pound was then worth about 24 francs, so quite a large house would have cost less than Ruhlmann's bed. A professional man's annual income was seldom as much as the price of his *coiffeuse*. In the same year a very important commode by Riesener was sold for rather less than that by Ruhlmann. It is hardly surprising that he was called 'the Riesener of the twentieth century'.

JACQUES-EMILE RUHLMANN

Dining-room chair designed by Ruhlmann for his *Hôtel du collectionneur*, shown at the 1925 Paris exhibition.

opposite Lady's writing-desk veneered with macassar ebony and inlaid with ivory, designed by Ruhlmann and made in his factory. It was exhibited in the *Hôtel du collectionneur*.

Although he employed a staff of sixteen draughtsmen Ruhlmann was himself responsible for the design of furniture made in his *ateliers*. His practice was to make very rough sketches which were enlarged and finished in the drawing office, modified and reworked, often several times, until they met with his approval and could be passed to the workshops. He seems also to have made sure that the individual craftsmen maintained the highest standards. From the beginning he showed a preference for the simplest forms and the most expensive materials – amboyna wood, macassar ebony and inlays of ivory. His favoured colour schemes, said to be 'Whistlériennes', were grey and silver or, more usually, black and gold like Russian cigarettes. Bureaux, sideboards and dressing-tables are lightly constructed with delicately curved and tapering legs ending in little metal – often silver – shoes which give them the look of ballet dancers on points. Sometimes these pieces seem to have been inspired by late eighteenth-century designs. His chairs and sofas owe a more obvious debt to the first Empire. In fact his furniture is more closely associated with the eighteenth-century tradition, in both craftsmanship and design, than any of the 'reproductions' made at the same time. Christian Zervos accurately summed up Ruhlmann's approach when he wrote: 'Ruhlmann contends that a new style is no more than the superimposition of new elements on the forms of the past and that the notion of an aerodynamic style ought to be abandoned. But, instead of recreating the last French style Ruhlmann allows his lively imagination to wander through all periods and all styles.' It is perhaps significant that he reverted to the eighteenth-century practice of marking his products with an *estampille*.

Ruhlmann was a magnificent anachronism, an epigone. But although he played no part in the main evolution of twentieth-century furniture design he anticipated a number of modern developments, not only in his occasional use of metal supports but also in his preoccupation with comfort, both physical and visual. His works are functional in the best sense of the word, yet quite untouched by any theories of functionalism. And the day may well come when they are seen to have more than period charm.

Unfortunately, his direct influence was anything but happy. Numerous imitators seized on his designs, jazzed them up by the addition of meaningless decorations and flooded Europe and America with gimcrack furniture made of poor materials in what was later to be called the Odeon style. Though the epigone is little regarded by historians of the arts, it is perhaps more charitable to regard Ruhlmann as the last representative of a great tradition rather than as an innovator. He was the last furniture maker able to compete on equal terms with the best *ébénistes* of the eighteenth century. And the type of clients for whom he worked now fill their houses and penthouses with eighteenth-century furniture.

Le Corbusier

(1887–1965)

The Paris 1925 exhibition included no furniture in what we should now call the modern style. It was dominated by the work of Ruhlmann and such designers as Pierre Chareau, Paul Follot, Pierre Legrain, Robert Mallet-Stevens, Louis Süe and André Mare who merely applied a glossy veneer of modernism to furniture of traditional patterns made by essentially traditional methods. They must share the blame for the development of the jazz modern style of the twenties and thirties. The same figures have pride of place in Pierre Olmer's book on the French furniture *d'aujourd'hui* of 1926 which never so much as alludes to the revolution in furniture design initiated in Holland and Germany by Rietveld, Stam, Mies and Breuer. In France furniture was still conceived in terms of *ébénisterie* and *menuiserie*. A truly new spirit was to be seen only on the periphery of the 1925 exhibition, in Le Corbusier's *Pavillon de l'Esprit Nouveau*, which he had furnished with Thonet bentwood chairs designed half a century earlier. It was not very popular: one of the few reviewers who deigned to mention it dismissed it as 'a temple of nudism'.

Charles-Edouard Jeanneret, who styled himself Le Corbusier, had already emerged as the *enfant terrible* of architecture – a role he continued to play until his death at the age of 78 in 1965. Born in Switzer-

Interior of the *Pavillon de l'Esprit Nouveau*, designed by Le Corbusier for the Paris exhibition in 1925. The chairs were made at the Thonet factory to a design originated more than half a century earlier.

land, he had worked in the Parisian office of Auguste Perret, the pioneer of reinforced concrete, and for a short time in Germany under the brilliant industrial architect, Peter Behrens. In Germany he seems also to have picked up through the Anglophile Muthesius nineteenth-century English theories of architecture and design. At the time of the outbreak of war he had begun to concern himself with the problems and possibilities of mass-produced housing. His first important buildings, the Citrohan House of 1921 and the villa at Vaucresson of 1922, revealed his originality and prodigious talent. In 1920 he founded with the painter and art critic Ozenfant the magazine *L'Esprit Nouveau* and in 1923 he published *Vers une architecture* (later translated into English as *Towards a New Architecture*).

With his belief that the house is a *machine d'habiter* – words that became a catch-phrase of the modern movement – Le Corbusier had little time for 'artistic' furniture of the type shown in 1925. 'Nous ne croyons pas à l'art décoratif,' he said. Indeed, he seems to have reacted to this exhibition in much the same way that more thoughtful people concerned with the decorative arts had reacted to the Great Exhibition of 1851. In 1926 he began to design furniture – or *équipement* as he preferred to call it – in collaboration with his brother, Pierre Jeanneret, and an assistant Charlotte Perriand. In the next two or three years a number of notable designs issued from his office, for chairs made of tubular steel, armchairs, a revolving desk-chair and, perhaps the most interesting, a chaise-longue known as the 'cowboy chair'.

Like Picasso – with whom he had so many similarities – Le Corbusier was both a revolutionary and a traditionalist. This is as clearly evident in his furniture designs as in his theoretical writings and his buildings. But he was a traditionalist of a type far removed from Ruhlmann. His *siège grand confort,* a square-shaped tubular steel chair with bulky rectangular cushions, derives from the English leather-covered club armchair. But the prototype was reduced to its essential components – rigid framework and soft cushions – re-composed and designed for factory production in large quantities. The chaise-longue owes a similar debt to Thonet's rocking chairs but reveals a like process of extracting and then rendering back. Le Corbusier clearly learned much from Thonet's bentwood furniture and, significantly enough, it was the Thonet factories that were to manufacture his own. He must also have been inspired, especially in the use of tubular steel, by Mart Stam and Breuer but the results were much more human and showed a greater concern for comfort. His chaise-longue is still, after forty years, the most successful of reclining chairs, carefully adapted to the comfort of the human body in a variety of positions, and of great elegance in the interplay of gentle curves and straight lines.

This furniture was designed in collaboration with Charlotte Perriand, to whom Le Corbusier gave most of the credit for it. It is now difficult

LE CORBUSIER

left Revolving armchair of chromium-plated steel tubing and red leather, designed by Le Corbusier, 1927.

right Armchair, called the *siège grand confort*, 1926, made of chromium-plated steel tubing with leather-covered cushions. This design has recently been revived and is still in production.

Chaise-longue, called the cow-boy chair, 1927. It is made of chromium-plated steel tubing, oval steel tubes and sheets painted green and black, grey jersey and black leather, and was manufactured by Thonet Industries.

to determine to what extent she was responsible for the designs. In any successful collaboration the individuals sink their identity in the joint work and may even be unaware of how much or how little they contributed. But there can be little doubt that in this case it was Le Corbusier alone who was responsible for the originating ideas, however large a part Mlle Perriand may have played in realizing them. More than thirty years after the event she recalled: 'As early as 1925 at the international exhibition in Paris Le Corbusier and P. Jeanneret defined the interior equipment of a dwelling as cases, seats and tables'. This analytical breakdown of the multifarious types of furniture into cases for storage, seats and tables for work and leisure, which is now taken for granted, seemed rather more striking when first proposed. It was with Le Corbusier that case furniture began to be swept off the floor-space and returned to its medieval position, in the wall, or sometimes to form the wall. Cases were used in this way in the Pavillon de l'Esprit Nouveau and the villa at Ville-d'Avray in 1929. Also in 1929 Le Corbusier, Jeanneret and Charlotte Perriand designed the 'équipement d'une habitation' with an almost ruthlessly standardized system of large pigeon-hole shelves – there is no precise equivalent in English for the word *casier* – to be used in the kitchen, bedroom, bathroom or living room. The *salon des décorateurs* refused to show it, and so it was exhibited in the *Salon d'automne*.

Le Corbusier was activated, according to Charlotte Perriand, by a desire to 'standardize and industrialize equipment and make it available to the general public' – an aim to which most of his predecessors had paid no more than lip-service. He was among the first to appreciate that mass-produced objects could have merits not equal but superior to those of hand-made ones, in beauty as well as utility. Hence the attraction exerted on him by Thonet's bentwood chairs. Charlotte Perriand took up his ideas and developed them brilliantly. But she remained essentially a traditionalist, as becomes evident in the designs she later executed on her own account. Indeed, she soon abandoned the use of steel and glass altogether. Ingenuity and virtuosity led her increasingly astray – as in a horrifying water closet convertible into a bidet. And whereas Le Corbusier had been inspired mainly by factory-made products – such as laboratory jars and simple café glassware – she was attracted by rustic crafts. 'Charlotte loves vernacular architecture and peasant furnishings because she loves the people', declared José Luis Sert, in a remark which betrays the townsman's inability to understand the peasant (whose taste generally favours the garishly urban, not the rough and rustic). And there is more than a touch of arty-craftiness about the tables with thick irregularly shaped wooden tops which she designed in the later 1930s. In view of her subsequent development it is hard to believe that she played a dominant role in the creation of the Le Corbusier furniture. Yet one is bound to add that Le Corbusier produced no furniture designs of importance after she had left his office.

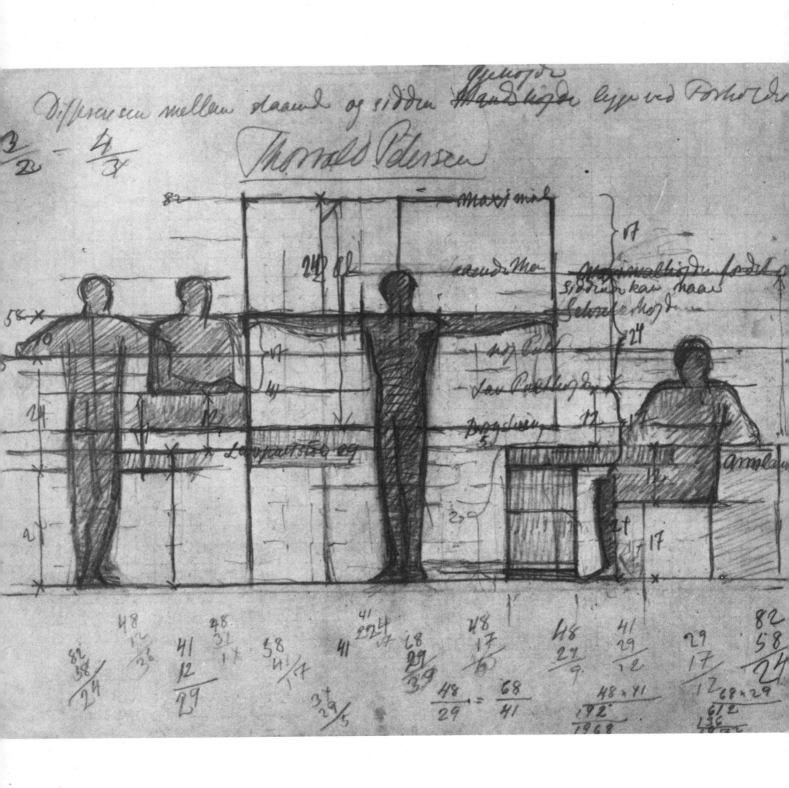

Kaare Klint

(1888–1954)

Ladderback chair designed by Klint and manufactured by Fritz Hansen, Denmark. An example of Klint's use of traditional patterns.

opposite Design by Kaare Klint, showing his concern with the adaptation of furniture to the needs of the human body.

Between the two extremes of inter-war furniture design – the *haute ébénisterie* of Ruhlmann and the antiseptic modernism of Le Corbusier and the Bauhaus designers – there was room for a middle way. It was struck most successfully by Kaare Klint, the originator of the modern Scandinavian style of furnishing which began to emerge in the later 1920s, became popular in the 1930s and still more so after 1945 when it gradually spread over all Europe and North America – to the dismay of the more retrograde traditionalists no less than the high-minded theorists of modern design.

Kaare Klint was born in 1888, the son of P. V. Jensen Klint who became the leading Danish architect of the early twentieth century. He too began his career as an architect, working under Carl Petersen, but soon turned his attention to furniture design. His first work of note was the furniture for a small art gallery at Faaborg, built by Petersen between 1912 and 1915. By 1916 Klint was interesting himself in the design of storage furniture. In 1924 he founded and was appointed first professor of the furniture department of the Danish Academy of Art. And until his death in 1954 he exerted a major influence on furniture design in Denmark and to some extent Sweden, both through his teaching and his own work. Although he occupied an academic post he was no arid dogmatist. Eminently level-headed, he was always more concerned with the function of furniture than theories about it. His designs may now seem to be more than a little unadventurous in comparison with those of his leading contemporaries in France and Germany. Yet the latter already have an unmistakable if pleasantly astringent 'period' flavour, whereas Klint's are unselfconscious almost to the point of anonymity – and that is, perhaps, their outstanding merit.

It is doubtful whether Klint could have developed his style in any country other than his own. Denmark had hardly been touched by the industrial revolution. So he neither had to fight a losing battle for craftsmanship against machinery nor to think in terms of industrial production for a vast and constantly expanding market. Wood was plentiful and there appears to have been no shortage of craftsmen to work it, with or without the aid of machinery. He was therefore largely immune to the complexes that afflicted his contemporaries elsewhere, and was able to design in a perfectly straightforward manner. Though he took over from English theorists their almost mystical belief in honesty to materials and construction and shared their abhorrence of applied decoration, he never sought, like the practitioners of Arts and Crafts, to give an insistently adzed and self-consciously 'hand-made' look to furniture.

Ladderback chair designed by Klint and manufactured by Fritz Hansen.

opposite top Teak deck chair designed by Klint, 1933.

opposite bottom Sideboard designed by Klint and manufactured by Rudolf Rasmussens, Copenhagen. The interior is designed to accommodate standard size table wares.

With no desire to be modern for the sake of modernity, Klint studied and encouraged his students to study the furniture of the past. For he believed that 'the ancients were more modern than we'. His approach was analytical and he sought beneath the decorations of old furniture its essential characteristics of form and construction. He was drawn to and inspired by the furniture designs of ancient Egypt and Greece, eighteenth-century England – especially the simpler works of Chippendale – the wonderfully simple and elegant chairs and tables made by the Shakers in America and, probably, the very neat and practical chests-of-drawers made for ships throughout the nineteenth century. But he was also open to contemporary influence. His teak chair of 1933 clearly derives from Le Corbusier's cowboy chaise-longue of 1929.

Klint was particularly concerned with the study of what we now call ergonomics. Sheets of drawings reveal a painstaking investigation of the needs of the human body, seated either in relaxation or while working at a table. Before designing a sideboard, possibly his most distinguished production, he worked out the average dimensions of the crockery and cutlery used in a Danish home and created a case that would contain in the smallest possible space the maximum amount needed by a single household. He was equally aware of the decorative function of furniture and the need to respect some at least of the prejudices of the middle-class public. He also appreciated how much appearance contributed to comfort – how, for example, most people demand that a chair should look, as well as be, capable of supporting the human body.

The clean beauty of Klint's furniture depends to a large extent on the texture of the waxed and polished but unvarnished wood and the excellence of the construction (his designs were realized by the firm of Rudolf Rasmussens Snedkerier of Copenhagen). It cannot be produced inexpensively and its market has thus been limited to the middle classes. But his classically simple designs did, of course, lend themselves to cheap imitations in inferior materials – with disastrous results. In Italy, for example, vast quantities of spindly chairs and shoddy cupboards of yellow-varnished wood are turned out by factories which specialize in 'Scandinavian furniture', just as others produce 'antique' furniture. On the other hand, the leading Danish designers and makers – notably Hans J. Wegner and Finn Juhl – have tended to elaborate Klint's style, making much greater use of complex curves and sometimes indulging in virtuoso performances of intricate joinery.

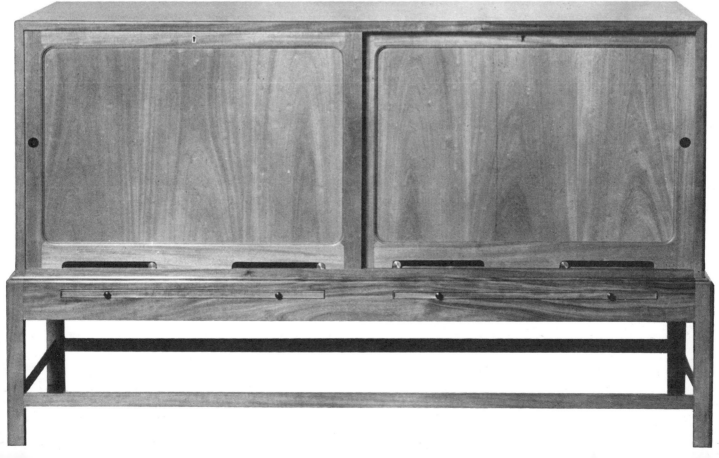

Gerrit Thomas Rietveld

(1888–1964)

In the history of furniture design it would be hard to find two personalities further removed from one another than Kaare Klint and Gerrit Thomas Rietveld, both of whom were born in 1888. One seems to typify traditionalism, the other avant-garde experiment. If no biographical facts were known about them it might well be assumed that Klint was a craftsman who had served his apprenticeship in a cabinet maker's shop while Rietveld studied the theory of design in strictly academic surroundings. Yet, in fact, the reverse was true.

Rietveld was born in Utrecht, the son of a joiner under whom he served his apprenticeship. He began by working in a conventional manner and does not appear to have had any contact with the modern movement until 1916. In that year the architect Robert van t'Hoff commissioned him to make the furniture for his pioneer concrete built house, 'Huis ter Heide'. Like the house itself, the furniture was inspired by Frank Lloyd Wright. And Wright's wooden chairs of 1904 composed of flat boards set in a framework of lathes provided the point of departure for Rietveld's own experiments.

In about 1917 Rietveld designed the first of his chairs. It consists of an elaborate framework of lathes placed at right angles to one another, supporting a board for the seat, a longer board for the back and two smaller ones for the arm rests. The traditional methods of joinery are abandoned – there are no dove-tailed joints or smoothed corners. Every member is made distinct from the others – the lathes of the framework are screwed together in such a way that they seem to adhere by magnetism, and they are painted black with the ends white or yellow, as if they had only just been sawn. The seat is painted bright blue and the back pillar-box red. The effect is akin to that of a painting by Mondrian – though it is important to remember that Mondrian was at this time executing his so-called 'plus and minus' drawings and did not begin to compose pictures of straight lines and rectangles of primary colour until several years later.

Rietveld was from 1917 closely associated with Mondrian and the other Dutch artists and architects – Oud, van Doesburg and van der Leck – involved in the periodical *de Stijl* first published in October 1917. 'The object of this magazine,' the introductory manifesto ran, 'will be to contribute to the development of a new concept of beauty. It aims to make modern man receptive to the new in creative art. It will oppose archaistic confusion – "Modern Baroque" – with the logical principles of a maturing style based on purer relationships with the

Armchair of painted wood designed by Rietveld, 1917.

spirit of our times and our means of expression.' And the first article, by Mondrian, began with the words: 'The life of contemporary man is turning gradually away from nature; it becomes more and more an a–b–s–t–r–a–c–t life.' It was for this abstract life that Rietveld's furniture was designed. 'Our chairs, tables, cupboards,' he wrote in *de Stijl* in 1919, 'will become the abstract-real artifacts of future interiors.'

In this atmosphere of new ideas, Rietveld set about the design of a chair as if, in Giedion's words, 'no chair had ever before been built'. On the initial design he produced a number of variations – one with the seat and back at right angles though still further dissociated, another with the seat and back slightly bent. He also designed tables, a sideboard, a curious small table composed of flat rectangular boards resting on a circular board, even a wheel-barrow based on a combination of triangle and circle. In 1920 he designed furniture and a light fitting for the study of Dr Hartog's house at Maarssen – a remarkable realization of *de Stijl*

Chair designed by Rietveld, 1934.

opposite Collection of furniture designed by Rietveld from 1917 onwards.

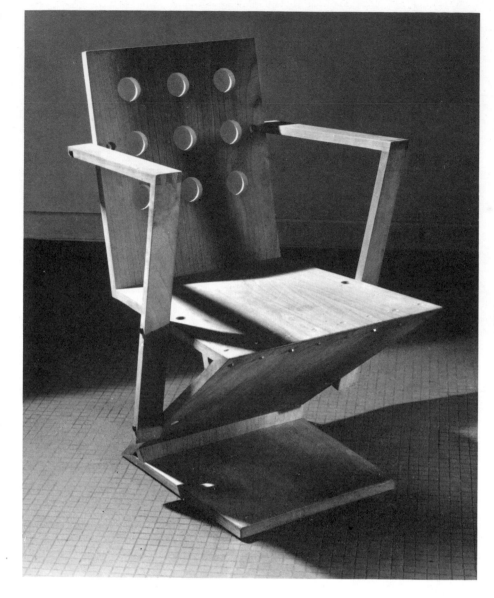

aims – now known only from a photograph. His next important piece of furniture – an assymetrical chair with a flat arm-rest on one side and an upright board on the other (1923) was made for a room which he and the painter V. Huszar designed for an exhibition in Berlin. He had already been responsible for some interiors and shop-fronts before 1924 when he designed his most famous building, the Schröder House in Utrecht. Thereafter he worked mainly as an architect but continued to design furniture, producing in 1927 some moulded plywood chairs which may well have influenced Alvar Aalto, an odd cantilever chair of four square boards joined in a zig-zag in 1934, and an armchair with circular holes in the seat, back and sides in 1942. He lived to see a great revival of interest in his work before he died in 1964.

'These Rietveldian pieces are manifestoes,' wrote Siegfried Giedion. 'They guide the direction of an entire development.' And they do indeed challenge all the assumptions on which the theory of design had hitherto

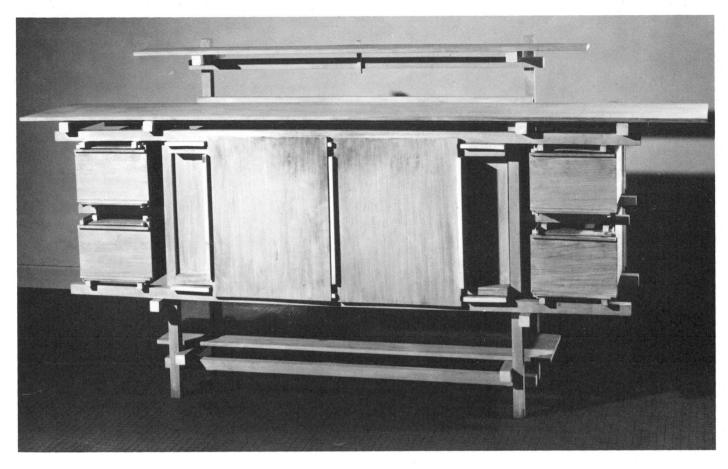

Sideboard designed by
Rietveld, 1919.

opposite Armchair designed by
Rietveld, 1942.

been based – belief in the value of simplicity, logical construction and
truth to materials, to say nothing of fitness for purpose. In his chairs and
sideboard the elaborate play of lines and planes is anything but simple.
Practically any chair with four legs and an upright back is more logically
built. The material – wood – is painted and its texture masked. The
chairs are not comfortable, the sideboard is not even particularly
capacious and both have numerous little inconvenient corners and ledges
which gather dust. Nothing could be further from the ideals of the
Arts and Craftsmen who had dominated the theory of design.

Rietveld reasserted the role of furniture as sculpture – but as abstract
sculpture. Indeed, his chairs can now be seen to have been among the
most exciting three dimensional works of art created at the time. His
chairs do not solve the controversy about craftsmanship and machinery
that had bedevilled the modern movement – they make it irrelevant. He
appears to have shared with van Doesburg and other members of the
de Stijl group the belief that by separating man from nature, the machine
contributes to the spiritualization of life. Art, for them, appeared in
terms of, rather than in opposition to, machinery – an idea distinct from
the age-old 'utilitarian' theory of beauty. His furniture may thus be
said to resemble machinery in an aesthetic rather than a practical sense.
And it is not wholly surprising that its merits have been widely appreciated only since the rejection of functionalism in the 1950s.

Convertible sofa-bed with support of
chromium-plated steel tubing and
upholstery of wool, designed by Aalto,
1930, and manufactured by
Wohnbedarf A.G., Switzerland.

Alvar Aalto

(b. 1899)

In the history of modern furniture design the most significant single event is the invention of the tubular steel cantilever chair by Mart Stam in 1924. Though greeted with horror in all but avant-garde circles, this chair was destined to have an immediate and far-reaching influence. For it not only demonstrated how new materials could be used for furniture, but forced designers to reconsider all traditionally accepted forms. It inspired both the metal furniture of Marcel Breuer and the wooden furniture of Alvar Aalto.

Hugo Alvar Henrik Aalto, perhaps the most distinguished architect working in Europe today, was born in 1899 in Kuortane, Finland – then a province of the Russian Empire. He was trained at the Teknillen Korkeakulu in Helsinki and before graduating in 1921 built his first house, for his parents (his father was an engineer). After the Russian Revolution, Finland had emerged as an independent Republic and Aalto thus began his career in a general atmosphere of optimistic nationalism. His first works were in a modernized version of the classical architecture of early and mid-nineteenth century Finland. But by 1927 when he began the library at Viipuri he had already adopted the international modern style which he gradually developed, with reference to local conditions, into a distinctively Finnish variant. A similar development from an impersonal international style to one that was as obviously Finnish as the sauna bath marks his furniture designs.

He began to concern himself with furniture when building a convalescent home at Paimo between 1929 and 1933. His first design of importance was a convertible sofa-bed, with a thickly upholstered seat and back mounted on a very simple chromium-plated tubular steel frame. He also used tubular steel in conjunction with laminated plywood for a chair designed in 1932. Next year he founded the Artek firm in Helsinki to manufacture and market fabrics, light fittings and furniture made to his designs. He refers to such things as 'architectural accessories' – a term which suggests their decorative as well as practical function (Le Corbusier's word *équipement* emphasizes the difference in attitude of the two architects to household fittings).

As nearly three quarters of the soil of Finland is covered with forests, wood is the staple product of the country. Aalto soon came to appreciate that from a psychological as well as an economic point of view, wood was a far more appropriate medium than metal for the construction of Finnish furniture. In birchwood, which though plentiful, had hitherto been used only for making skis, he found his ideal material. It has a

ALVAR AALTO

Plywood cantilever chair designed by
Aalto and manufactured by Finmar, 1935.

beautiful grain, a golden colour and may be polished to a silky texture. This organic beauty makes it more easily acceptable than cold steel. When laminated as plywood it is no less resilient than steel. And it is much cheaper, easier to manufacture and lighter in weight.

Inspired to some degree by Thonet's bent beechwood chairs, by the tubular steel chairs of Mart Stam and Breuer and, in a practical way, by the process of manufacturing skis, Aalto developed a number of laminated birchwood chairs in the 1930s. In one, a long curving panel of laminated wood is suspended in a framework of thicker laminated strips. Here the framework is solid and only the panel resilient. He achieved greater springiness by adopting the cantilever principle and suspending a scrolled panel, which forms both seat and back, between two U-shaped loops of thicker laminated strips. For non-resilient furniture – three-legged stools and tables – he devised a leg composed of several pieces of laminated wood which fan out to support the top, making a joint that is as elegant as it is strong and durable. The tables are thus composed not so much of four legs as of upturned 'U's which can support a slab of either wood or glass. The stools of the 1930s had circular plywood tops treated as separate members but in 1947 he devised another type in which the tops of the legs fan out to form the seat.

Although he adopted wood as his medium, Aalto abandoned not only carved ornament but all the traditional techniques of joinery. His

298

Laminated plywood furniture designed by Aalto. The stool in the background is of birch plywood, *c.* 1933, the coffee-table of birch plywood with a glass top designed in 1947, the stool in the foreground of ash plywood with a leather top designed in 1954.

designs are perfectly adapted to mechanized production and could hardly be realized by any other means. For unlike the majority of architect-designers, he has been as much concerned with mass production for the largest possible market as with the problem of furnishing his own buildings. For individual clients he has designed only slightly more elaborate and luxurious versions of his mass-produced pieces. He has also concerned himself with special problems in furniture design – small and durable furniture for kindergartens, seats that may easily be stacked for storage (the three-legged stool is particularly well adapted for stacking in large numbers), and tall low-backed bar-stools for which there must have been a sudden demand in Finland after prohibition was abandoned in 1932.

Aalto's furniture, like his architecture, reveals a level-headed regard for simple practical needs, a highly developed sensitivity for linear elegance and an innate feeling for natural forms and textures. In a world that has proved to be less enthusiastic about machine aesthetics than Rietveld and his friends had expected, it satisfies a natural craving for organic materials and shapes. This is perhaps the reason why it has enjoyed an unfaltering popularity comparable only with that of Thonet's bentwood. Inevitably it has been almost as widely imitated as used. Its one defect is that it can be made only where birchwood is cheap and plentiful. But Aalto's use of scrolled plywood provided a point of departure for one of the most notable innovations of recent years – the use of moulded plastic.

Marcel Breuer

(b. 1902)

'Architects, sculptors and painters, we must all return to the crafts. For art is not a profession. There is no essential difference between the artist and the craftsman.' So ran the manifesto issued at the opening of the Weimar Bauhaus in 1919. 'Let us create a new guild of craftsmen, without those class distinctions which raise an arrogant barrier between craftsmen and artists,' it continued. 'Together let us conceive and create the new building of the future which will embrace architecture, sculpture and painting and one day will rise to the skies, from the hands of millions of workers, as the crystal symbol of a new coming faith.' These words by Walter Gropius remind one that for all its apparent modernity, the Bauhaus was built on a solid foundation of generally accepted ideas. The majestic shadow of Goethe still hovered over Weimar – 'I cannot praise the man who fits out the rooms in which he lives with strange, old-fashioned objects. It is a sort of masquerade, which can, in the long run, do no good in any respect, but must, on the contrary, have an unfavourable influence on the man who adopts it,' he had told Eckermann in 1827. And the theorists of the English Arts and Crafts movement are not far away.

In many ways, indeed, the Bauhaus was conceived on lines which were already old-fashioned. There were, as in a museum of decorative arts, departments for metalwork, woodwork, textiles and pottery. While the idea of resolving the conflict between artists and craftsmen was nearly as old as the conflict itself and had little relevance to the burning issue of the day – the relationship between the designer and the technician. As Wagenfeld was later to remark, Bauhaus designs were 'in reality craft products, which through the use of geometrically clear basic shapes gave the appearance of industrial production'. Fortunately, the leading members of the Bauhaus were destined to overturn the assumptions on which it had been raised.

In the field of furniture design, Marcel Lajos Breuer is the most notable of Bauhaus designers. He was born at Pécs in Hungary in 1902 and went to the Bauhaus as a student in 1920. Almost immediately he began to make interesting designs for furniture inspired by Rietveld – a circular tea-table supported on five square legs which project above the top, a stocky side-chair with gaily coloured wool straps (devised by Gunta Stölzl) on the seat and back and, still more strongly Rietveldian, a complex armchair with a canvas seat and two canvas straps across the back instead of the flat boards of the prototype. After he had finished his course in 1925 Breuer was put in charge of the cabinet making workshop.

Pear-wood tea-table designed and made by Breuer at the Weimar Bauhaus, 1921–2.

opposite Cantilever side-chair of chromium-plated steel tubing, wood and cane, designed by Breuer, 1928.

opposite Laminated plywood coffee-tables and chair designed by Breuer while he was in England, 1935–7, for the Isokon Furniture Company.

Armchair of oak with hand-woven wool seat and back straps, designed at the Weimar Bauhaus, 1924.

Although he was styled master of carpentry, Breuer now began to use metal instead of wood for furniture. His first design of importance was a very elegant armchair which is basically a reworking of the Rietveld chair in chromium plated steel tubing with canvas stretched across the seat and back as on a deck-chair. The chair rests on two edges of the steel frame, but the four-legged principle is maintained, and the steel tubing is used in a static non-resilient manner. In 1924, however, the Dutch architect and designer, Mart Stam, had produced a revolutionary prototype – the first cantilever chair, composed of an unbroken line of steel tubes with a back and seat of rubber straps stretched across from one side to the other. As Stam did not have access to the necessary pipe-bending techniques he was obliged to use straight tubes joined by elbow pieces – as in household plumbing – so his chair is resilient only in the seat and back, not in the frame. Stam informed Ludwig Mies van der Rohe of his invention and in 1926 both designers produced cantilever chairs which could be made out of single lengths of tubing (that by Mies is the more elegant, though perhaps too resilient for comfort). Two years later Breuer produced his version composed of a single un-joined loop of tube onto which panels of wood or caning are attached to form the seat and back. He also designed stools and tables with frames of tubular steel and, in 1933, some small tables made of aluminium rods.

The tubular steel chair, at first made by craftsmen but from 1934 at the Thonet factories, soon became popular, especially for office furnishing. And it was widely imitated both in Europe and America. No earlier design for a chair had been so perfectly adapted for industrial production on a very large scale. It was cheap both to make and transport and eminently practical. But these were not the only reasons for its success. It also had the aesthetic merits of a simple piece of machinery; it was unmistakably, almost defiantly, a product of the twentieth century. 'The cantilever chair is rooted in a specific demand of the time,' wrote Giedion. 'A chair was sought that would seem to hover above the ground like cantilever concrete slabs or houses on stilts, houses surrounded by air. One was drawn to things that seemed to defeat gravitation. This emotional need is as innate to our own time as the buttress to the Gothic and the undulating wall to the Baroque.' And Breuer himself remarked of his chairs, 'they do not encumber space with their mass'. They have been criticized as being inhuman, but in fact they tend to stress the importance of Man as the dominant element in the space created by the architect.

When Gropius was succeeded as director of the Bauhaus by Mies

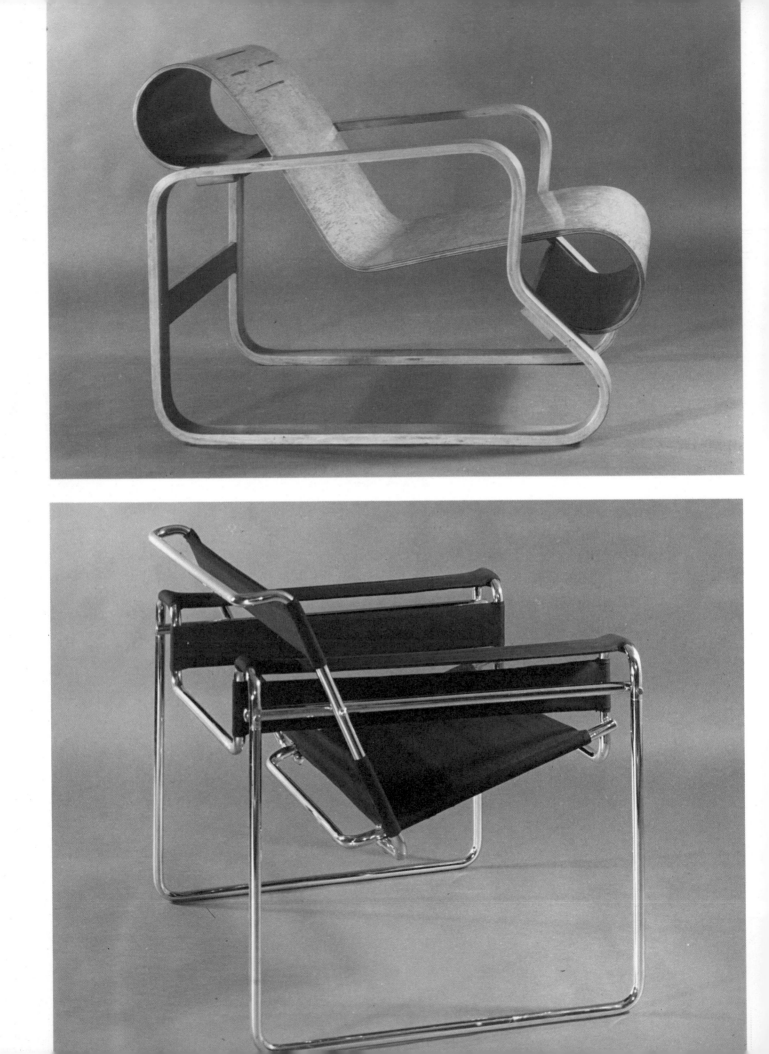

Lounge chair of moulded and bent birch plywood designed by Alvar Aalto *c.* 1934 and manufactured by Artek OY, Finland.

Armchair of chromium plated steel tubing and canvas designed by Marcel Breuer, 1925, and manufactured by Gebrüder Thonet A.G.

van der Rohe in 1930, Breuer left and set up a private practice as an architect in Berlin. This was the time of the emergence of the Nazi party. He stayed on in Germany until 1935 when he settled in England and went into partnership with the English architect F.R.S. Yorke with whom he designed the Royal Show pavilion at Bristol in 1936. While in England he designed for the Isokon Furniture Company a chair and low table made of laminated bent birch plywood. The chair is very obviously inspired by Aalto, though with the structural members given a still more ski-like appearance and provided with a long upholstered pad which makes it rather more comfortable. The table, made of a single moulded panel of plywood, is more ingenious and original – probably the first to be made from a single piece of material.

In 1937 Gropius, who had also spent two years in England, settled in America and invited Breuer to join him as architectural partner and instructor at the Harvard Graduate School of Design. The partnership lasted for only four years but Breuer continued to teach at Harvard until 1946 when he moved to New York. He now works as an architect and industrial designer – in 1955 he designed a rail diesel car for the Budd Company. Most of his post-war furniture designs have been experimental.

It would be easy to dismiss Breuer as a plagiarist, taking up the ideas first of Mart Stam and Mies, then of Aalto – easy, but very unjust. For he realized better than Stam the full aesthetic and practical potentialities of steel tubing. And he was more seriously concerned with mass production than Mies, whose best pieces of furniture (the Barcelona chair, for instance) are *de luxe* products and, ironically enough, require manual work to give them their appearance of machine-made finish. It is due mainly to Breuer that cantilever steel tube chairs are familiar articles of furniture in thousands of private and, more especially, public buildings throughout the world.

But the importance of the cantilever principle in chair design and steel tubing as a medium should not be overrated. Neither the principle nor the material is amenable to much further development. Making the most violent of all breaks in the history of furniture, this chair did, however, demonstrate that chairs need not necessarily be supported on three or more legs and thus it opened the door to experiment in form as well as media. It may also have changed our entire culture in a subtle way, raising an issue on which all are bound to take sides, with little room for compromise – acceptance or rejection of fully mechanized production and the aesthetics of the machine age.

CONVERSATION

FABRIC

PLYWOOD

ALUMINUM

FABRIC

RUBBER

PLYWOOD

RUBBER SEAL

ALUMINUM

THICKNESS OF PLYWOOD VARIES
WITH STRUCTURAL DEMANDS

ONE QUARTER FULL SIZE

Charles Eames

(b. 1907)

In 1940 the Museum of Modern Art, New York, established a department of industrial design which was destined to exert a great and widespread influence not only on the design of household objects, which was its aim, but also on painting and sculpture. Unlike earlier institutions which had been devoted to the improvement of industrial art – the Victoria and Albert Museum, for instance – it welcomed mass-production. Its aims were manifested in the competition held in the year of its opening – 'Organic Design in Home Furnishing' – when the prize for seating was won by two young architects, Charles Eames and Eero Saarinen, who were to become the leading furniture designers of the post-war period. Their 1940 prize-winning drawing was for a chair constructed of moulded plywood and set on four slender aluminium rod legs. It marked a decisive break with the geometrical prepossessions of Bauhaus designers. Though influenced by Aalto (to whom an exhibition had been devoted at the Museum two years before) it reveals a still greater regard for the comfort and psychological needs of the ordinary man than did Aalto's furniture.

Charles Eames is the first American furniture designer of international significance. He was born in 1907 and trained as an architect at Washington University, St Louis, and Cranbrook Academy of Art, Bloomfield Hills, Michigan. In 1939 he began to work in the office of Eliel Saarinen (born in Finland but working in America since 1922) with whose son he composed the prize-winning design for the Museum of Modern Art competition. Wartime shortages and difficulties prevented the execution of the chair according to the design – the legs had to be made of wood and the form of the shell modified. It was not until after the war that Eames was able to embark on his career as a furniture designer.

The war had encouraged considerable technological development in the production of plastics and the shaping of metal sheets. Eames was prompt to take advantage of them for furniture making. In 1946 he began to design his series of shell chairs, based on the principle of the 1940 model but making use of new materials. He first used sheets of steel stamped out to form the seat, back and arms and coated with neoprene, but soon turned to polyester reinforced with fibreglass – a substance that is virtually indestructible, stain resistant and, unlike steel, a good conductor of heat, quickly absorbing the temperature of the room. By 1948 he had devised his classic model, mounted on a delicate metal rod support which provides a visual contrast to the solidity of the moulded shell. In 1946 he also designed what is generally known as the 'Eames chair' – a dining chair with seat and back made of panels of body-

Drawing for an armchair by Eero Saarinen and Charles Eames, one of the winning designs submitted for the exhibition 'Organic Design in Home Furnishing' held at the Museum of Modern Art in New York, 1941.

opposite Lounge chair and footstool by Eames, of laminated rosewood and anodyzed aluminium with down- and foam-filled cushions, 1957, manufactured by the Herman Miller Furniture Company, New York.

Dining-chair of moulded walnut plywood and metal rods, designed by Eames, 1946, and manufactured by the Herman Miller Furniture Company.

opposite Folding screen of moulded ash plywood, chairs and coffee-table designed by Eames, 1946, and manufactured by Evans Products Company.

curved plywood attached to a metal rod frame by little rubber cushions which, in addition to providing resilience, give support to the body in slightly different postures. The design allows for a wide range of variations in the treatment of the seat and back which can be of plain wood or covered with foam-rubber or leather. It was and is still made by the Herman Miller Furniture Company with which Eames has been closely associated. For them he also designed, in 1954, a handsome sofa composed of three long cushion-like members mounted on a discreet chromium-plated steel frame, and in 1957 the much admired and widely plagiarized armchair and footstool. The latter, with feather-stuffed Naugahyde cushions on a framework of anodized aluminium is probably the most luxurious piece of modern furniture – and certainly among the most expensive.

Eames has not confined his attention to chairs. He has designed fine collapsible tables on slender metal rod supports, a remarkably elegant screen composed of undulating panels of ash plywood, radio cabinets and so on. With Eero Saarinen in 1940 he made designs for standardized storage units, based on an eighteen-inch module and so devised that the shelved cabinets stand on bench-like supports which may alternatively be used as seats or tables. Following this up in 1950 he devised a series of storage units in which the wood of drawers and shelves is contrasted with the polished aluminium of the frame. All the components of these units were taken from readily available industrial products – continuous angle-pieces, with rods as tracers, for the frame, and regularly shaped plywood panels for the woodwork.

Eames's former collaborator, Eero Saarinen, from the end of the war until his early death at the age of 50 in 1960, was fully occupied as an architect – and responsible for some of the best buildings of the period. But he also developed the shell chair. And in 1948 he designed a lounge chair of moulded plastic covered with foam rubber and mounted on a simple metal rod support, which soon came to be known as the 'womb chair'. In 1957 he designed what is probably the most elegant set of modern furniture – the 'Tulip' chairs and tables. The chairs are shells of plastic reinforced with fibreglass, the table top a disc of white plastic laminate (though other materials like marble are sometimes substituted) and both are mounted on slender pedestals of white lacquered cast aluminium. He had hoped to make both chairs and tables entirely of plastic, but this proved impossible. It is significant that he should have designed only chairs and tables for, as an architect, he wished to dispense with all other forms of movable furniture – a portent for the future.

Chair of plastic reinforced with
fibreglass, on a white painted support,
designed by Eero Saarinen as part of his
Tulip Suite, 1957, and manufactured
by Knoll Associates Inc.

Bibliography

This bibliography is not comprehensive.
I have listed only the works that I found
most useful whilst writing this book,
and a few others which appeared after
I had completed my text, and of which
I was therefore unable to make full use.

JACQUES ANDROUET DU CERCEAU

E. Bonaffé
Le meuble en France au XVIe siècle
Paris, 1887

H. de Geymuller, *Les Du Cerceau*
Paris, 1887

L. Buffet-Challié in *World Furniture*
editor H. Hayward, London, 1965
pp. 76–86

HUGUES SAMBIN

E. Bonaffé
Le meuble en France au XVIe siècle
Paris, 1887, pp. 80–6

A. Castan, *L'Architecteur Hugues Sambin*
Besançon/Dijon, 1891

E. Prost in *Gazette des Beaux Arts*, 1892,
I, pp. 123–35

H. David, *De Sluter à Sambin*, Paris,
1933, II, pp. 402–35

HANS VREDEMAN DE VRIES

P. Jessen, *Der Ornamentstich*, Berlin,
1920, pp. 88–94

H. Gerson and E. H. Ter Kuile
Art and Architecture in Belgium 1600–1800
Harmondsworth, 1960, p. 14

P. Poirier
Un siècle de gravure anversoise in
Mémoires de l'Académie Royale de
Belgique, XII, I, 1967, pp. 103–15

DOMENICO CUCCI

P. Verlet, *French Royal Furniture*
London, 1963, pp. 3–7

R. A. Weigart and C. Hernmarch
*Les relations artistiques entre la France et la
Suède 1693–1718*, Stockholm, 1964
pp. 15, 16, 39, 41

ANDRÉ-CHARLES BOULLE

P. A. Orlandi, *Abecedario Pittorico*
Florence, 1719, p.

Archives de l'art français, 1855–6, VII
pp. 321–50

F. J. B. Watson
*Wallace Collection Catalogues:
Furniture*, London, 1956, pp. 10–12

For a full bibliography see J. Viaux
Bibliographie du meuble, Paris, 1966

GERREIT JENSEN

R. W. Symonds in *The Connoisseur*
May, 1935

R. Edwards and M. Jourdain
Georgian Cabinet Makers, London, 1955
pp. 35–8

R. Edwards in *The Connoisseur*,
January 1963, p. 33

Th. H. Lunsingh Scheurleer in
Walpole Society, XXXVIII, 1962
pp. 15–18; *The Orange and the Rose*
(exhibition catalogue, Victoria and
Albert Museum, 1964), pp. 27, 67

GERHARD DAGLY

Hans Huth in *The Connoisseur*, 1935
pp. 14–18, and in *World Furniture*
editor H. Hayward, London, 1965
pp. 101–02

W. Holzhausen, *Lackkunst in Europa*
Brunswick, 1959, pp. 177, 189

ANDREA BRUSTOLON

O. Kutschera-Woborsjy in
Kunst und Kunsthandwerk, 1919
pp. 152–76

G. Biasuz and E. Lacchin
Andrea Brustolon, Venice, 1928

A. Coleridge in *Apollo*, March, 1963
pp. 209–12

G. Mariacher in
Bollettino dei Musei Civici Veneziani
1965, pp. 25–43

DANIEL MAROT

M. D. Ozinga, *Daniel Marot*
Amsterdam, 1938

Th. H. Lusingh Scheurleer in
World Furniture, editor H. Hayward
London, 1965, p. 75

JOHN GUMLEY AND JAMES MOORE

R. Edwards and M. Jourdain
Georgian Cabinet Makers, London, 1955
pp. 40–4

CHARLES CRESSENT

M.-J. Ballot in
Archives de l'art francais, 1919, x
pp. 1–368

F.J.B. Watson
*Wallace Collection Catalogues:
Furniture*, London, 1956, pp. 44–5 and
The Wrightsman Collection: Furniture
New York, 1966, pp. 357–8, 368–9,
539–41

F. de Salverte
Les ébénesites du xviii siècle,
revised ed. 1962

T. Dell in *Burlington Magazine*, April
1967, pp. 210–17

JOHANN JAKOB SCHÜBLER

Thieme-Becker, *Künstler-Lexikon,*
vol. xxx, p. 309

S. Giedion
Mechanization Takes Command, New
York, 1957, pp. 286–7, 407, 469–70

PIETRO PIFFETTI

V. Viale in
Mostra del Barocco Piemontese, Turin,
1963, III, pp. 12–24 (with full
bibliography to date)

BERNARD II VAN RISEN BURGH

J.-P. Baroli in
Connaissance des Arts, March, 1957
pp. 56–63

F.J.B. Watson
The Wrightsman Collection: Furniture
New York, 1967

WILLIAM VILE AND JOHN COBB

J.T. Smith, *Nollekens and His Times*
London, 1829, II, pp. 242–4

R. Edwards, 'Attributions to William
Vile' in *Country Life*, 7 October 1954

R. Edwards and M. Jourdain
Georgian Cabinet Makers, London, 1955
pp. 51–6 and 117–18

A. Oswald in *Country Life*
27 February, 1953, pp. 572–4

A. Coleridge, *Chippendale Furniture*
London, 1968

JOHANN MICHAEL HOPPENHAUPT

Thieme-Becker, *Künstler-Lexikon,*
vol. XVII, pp. 487–8

E. Hempel
*Baroque Art and Architecture in Central
Europe,* Harmondsworth, 1965
pp. 268–75

THOMAS JOHNSON

H. Hayward
Thomas Johnson and the English Rococo
London, 1964

THOMAS CHIPPENDALE

R. Edwards and M. Jourdain
Georgian Cabinet Makers, London, 1955
pp. 26–30, 62–72, 88–90

C. Hussey in *Country Life*
23 February, 1956, pp. 337–9

A. Coleridge in *The Connoisseur*
December 1960, pp. 252–6; in *Apollo*
April, 1963, pp. 295–302, and July, 1964
pp. 4–11; *Chippendale Furniture,*
London, 1968

E. Harris
The Furniture of Robert Adam
London, 1963, pp. 27–30

D. Fitz-Gerald in
*The Journal of the Furniture History
Society,* IV, 1968, pp. 1–9

JEAN-FRANÇOIS OEBEN

Documents published in
Archives de l'art français, 1878
pp. 319–38; 1889, pp. 298–367

F.J.B. Watson
*Wallace Collection Catalogues:
Furniture*, London, 1956, pp. 69–75 and
in *The Connoisseur*, August, 1957,
pp. 22–5

GIOVANNI BATTISTA PIRANESI

R.O. Parks, editor, *Piranesi*, catalogue
of exhibition held at Smith College
Museum of Art, Northampton, Mass.,
1961, with good bibliography

F.J.B. Watson in
The Minneapolis Institute of Arts Bulletin
LIV, 1965, pp. 19–31

JOHN GODDARD

T.H. Ormsbee
Early American Furniture Makers
New York, 1930, pp. 51–3

M.M. Swan in *Antiques*, April 1946
pp. 228–31: April 1949, pp. 278–80

J. Downs in *Antiques*, December 1947
pp. 427–31, and *American Furniture
Queen Anne and Chippendale Periods in
the Henry Francis Du Pont
Winterthur Museum*, New York, 1952

E.H. Bjerkoe
The Cabinet Makers of America, New
York, 1957, pp. 105–14 and 213–19

JEAN-HENRI RIESENER

P. Verlet, *Möbel von H. Riesener*
Darmstadt, 1955, and
French Royal Furniture, London, 1963
pp. 18–19, 117–60

F.J.B. Watson
The Wrightsman Collection: Furniture
New York, 1966, II, pp. 555–7

A. Gonzalez-Palacios
Gli ebanisti del Luigi XVI, Milan, 1966
pp. 84–116

BENJAMIN FROTHINGHAM

T. H. Ormsbee
Early American Furniture Makers
New York, 1930, pp. 53–5

J. Downs
American Furniture Queen Anne and Chippendale Periods in the Henry Francis Du Pont Winterthur Museum
New York, 1952

M. M. Swan in *Antiques,*
November 1952, pp. 392–5

E. H. Bjerkoe
The Cabinet Makers of America
New York, 1957, pp. 96–8

GIUSEPPE MAGGIOLINI

G. A. Mezzanzanica
Genio e Laovoro, Biografia o breve storia delle principali opere dei celebri intarsiatori Giuseppe e Carlo Francesco Maggiolini, Milan, 1878

G. Morazzoni
Giuseppe Maggiolini, Milan, 1953

GEORGES JACOB

H. Lefuel, *Georges Jacob,* Paris, 1923 and *François-Honoré Georges Jacob-Desmalter,* Paris, 1925

F. J. B. Watson
Louis XVI Furniture, London, 1960

D. Ledoux-Lebard in *Apollo*
September, 1964, pp. 199–205

DAVID ROENTGEN

H. Huth
Abraham und David Roentgen
Berlin, 1928

P. Verlet in *The Connoisseur,*
October 1961, pp. 130–5

F. Windisch-Graetz in
The Connoisseur, November 1963,
pp. 161–5

GIUSEPPE MARIA BONZANIGO

A. Baudi di Vesme, *Schede Vesme,* I
Turin, 1963, pp. 160 ff.

V. Viale
Mostra del Barocco Piemontese
Turin, 1963, III, pp. 25–6

THOMAS SHERATON

J. Harris
Regency Furniture Designs
London, 1961

E. Fastnedge, *Sheraton Furniture*
London, 1962

ADAM WEISWEILER

F. J. B. Watson, Louis XVI Furniture
London, 1960
The Wrightsman Collection: Furniture
New York, 1966, II, pp. 561–2

P. Verlet, *French Royal Furniture*
London, 1963, p. 21

SAMUEL McINTIRE

W. A. Dyer, *Early American Craftsmen,*
New York, 1915, pp. 16–40

J. Downs in
The Metropolitan Museum of Art Bulletin
October, 1947, pp. 73–80

E. H. Bjerkoe, *The Cabinet Makers of America,* New York, 1957, pp. 152–7

C. F. Montgomery
American Furniture of the Federal Period in the Henry Francis du Pont Winterthur Museum, London, 1967

DUNCAN PHYFE

T. H. Ormsbee
Early American Furniture Makers
New York, 1930, pp. 63–81

C. O. Cornelius
Furniture Masterpieces of Duncan Phyfe
New York, 1922

E. V. Blum in *Antiques,* August, 1948
p. 109

E. H. Bjerkoe
The Cabinet Makers of America
New York, 1957, pp. 170–5

C. F. Montgomery
American Furniture of the Federal Period in the Henry Francis Du Pont Winterthur Museum, London, 1967

THOMAS HOPE

S. Baumgarten
Le crépuscule néo-classique: Thomas Hope
Paris, 1958

H. M. Colvin
A Biographical Dictionary of English Architects
London, 1954, pp. 297–9

J. Harris, *Regency Furniture Designs*
London, 1961

D. Watkin, *Thomas Hope and the Neo-Classical Idea,* London, 1968

GIOVANNI SOCCHI

J. Fleming in *The Connoisseur*
November, 1961, pp. 216–21

PELAGIO PALAGI

A. Griseri in *The Connoisseur*
November, 1957, p. 150

M. Bernardi
Il Palazzo Reale di Torino
Turin, 1959, pp. 114–20

KARL FRIEDRICH SCHINKEL

J. Sievers
Karl Friedrich Schinkel Lebenswerk: Die Möbel, Berlin, 1950

MICHAEL THONET

S. Giedion, *Mechanization Takes Command,* New York, 1948, pp. 490–2; *Bugholzmöbel – Das Werk Michael Thonets,* exhibition catalogue, Vienna, 1965

G. Santoro, *Il caso Thonet,* Rome, 1966

JOHN HENRY BELTER

J. Downs in *Antiques,* September, 1948
pp. 166–8

E. H. Bjerkoe
The Cabinet Makers of America
New York, 1957, pp. 40–1

AUGUSTUS WELBY NORTHMORE PUGIN

B. Ferrey
Recollections of A. N. Welby Pugin
London, 1861

M. Trappes Lomax
Pugin, a Mediaeval Victorian
London, 1933

PHILIP WEBB

W. R. Lethaby
Philip Webb and his Work
London, 1935

*Exhibition of Victorian and Edwardian
Decorative Arts*, Victoria and Albert
Museum, London, 1952, pp. 39–52

P. Thompson
The Work of William Morris
London, 1967

EDWARD WILLIAM GODWIN

D. Habron, *The Conscious Stone*
London, 1949

N. Pevsner
Pioneers of Modern Design, revised
edition, Harmondsworth, 1960
pp. 63–4

Alf Bøe
From Gothic Revival to Functional Form
Oslo and Oxford, 1957, pp. 128–31

E. Aslin
Nineteenth Century English Furniture
London, 1962, pp. 60–4, and in *Apollo*
December, 1962, pp. 779–84

LOUIS MAJORELLE

O. Gerdeil in *L'Art décoratif*, October
1901, pp. 16–25

F. Jourdain in *L'Art décoratif*
August, 1902, pp. 202–08

P. Juyot, *Louis Majorelle, Artiste
décorateur maître ébéniste*, Nancy, 1927

Y. Rambosson in
Mobilier et décoration, July, 1933
pp. 284–93

HENRY VAN DE VELDE

N. Pevsner
Pioneers of Modern Design, revised
edition, Harmondsworth, 1960

P. Selz and M. Constantine, editors
Art Nouveau, Museum of Modern Art
New York, 1960

Henry van de Velde zum 100 Geburtstag
(exhibition catalogue), Stuttgart, 1963

E. Schrijver in *Apollo*, February, 1965
pp. 110–15

CHARLES RENNIE
MACKINTOSH

R. Marx in
Gazette des Beaux Arts, 1902, II, p. 508

N. Pevsner
Pioneers of the Modern Movement, 1936
(new edition as
Pioneers of Modern Design, 1960)

T. Howarth
*Charles Rennie Mackintosh and the
Modern Movement*, London, 1952
(with extensive bibliography)

JACQUES-EMILE
RUHLMANN

C. Zervos in *La revue de l'art*, 1925
XLVII, pp. 68–73

P. Olmer
*Le mobilier français d'aujourd'hui
(1910–1925)*, Paris and Brussels, 1926

Connaissance des arts, February, 1960
pp. 45–55

Les années '25' (exhibition catalogue
Musée des Arts Décoratifs), Paris, 1966

LE CORBUSIER

S. Giedion, *Mechanization Takes
Command*, New York, 1948

Articles by J. L. Sert and C. Perriand in
Aujourd'hui, March, 1956

Les années '25' (exhibition catalogue,
Musée des Arts Décoratifs), Paris, 1966

KAARE KLINT

Ulf Hard af Segerstad
Modern Scandinavian Furniture
London, 1964

GERRIT THOMAS RIETVELD

S. Giedion
Mechanization Takes Command
New York, 1948, pp. 485–90

T. M. Brown, *The Work of
G. Rietveld Architect,* Utrecht, 1958

A. Drexler and G. Daniel
Introduction to Twentieth Century Design
New York, 1959, pp. 30–3

R. Banham
*Theory and Design in the First Machine
Age*, London, 1960

ALVAR AALTO

G. Labò, *Alvar Aalto*, Milan, 1948

S. Giedion
Mechanization Takes Command
New York, 1948, pp. 505–6

M. Labò in
Encyclopedia of World Art, New York
1959, I, pp. 1–5 with extensive
bibliography

MARCEL BREUER

P. Blake, *Marcel Breuer*, 1949

S. Giedion
Mechanization Takes Command
New York, 1948, pp. 489–95

R. Banham
*Theory and Design in the First Machine
Age*, London, 1960, pp. 198–9

A. Drexler and G. Daniel
Introduction to Twentieth Century Design
New York, 1959

W. Schedig
Crafts of the Weimar Bauhaus
London, 1967

CHARLES EAMES

A. Drexler and E. Daniel
Introduction to Twentieth Century Design
New York, 1959, pp. 52–65

H. Schaefer in *World Furniture*
editor H. Hayward, London, 1965
pp. 298–303

Index

Numbers in italics refer to illustrations